T0366190

Tinman Tre

✦

A Life Explored

David Cope

iUniverse LLC
Bloomington

TINMAN TRE
A Life Explored

iUniverse books may be ordered through booksellers or by contacting:

iUniverse LLC
1663 Liberty Drive
Bloomington, IN 47403
www.iuniverse.com
1-800-Authors (1-800-288-4677)

ISBN: 978-1-4917-1651-9 (sc)
ISBN: 978-1-4917-1652-6 (e)

Printed in the United States of America.

iUniverse rev. date: 12/03/2013

Contents

(1941-1956)

(1955-1963)

(1960-1969)

(1970-1977)

(1999-2013)

Preface

"Don't you just feel awful?" Dorothy said.

"Why?" replied the Wizard.

"For not being able to give the Tinman a heart."

"But I don't need to. He already has one."

"No I don't," said the Tinman.

"He's right," added Dorothy to the Wizard. "When I knock on his chest it's empty in there."

"He's doesn't mean he wants that kind of heart," said the Wizard.

"I don't?" asked the Tinman.

"No. You mean the kind of heart that makes you feel something sad or make you love people. That kind of heart."

"Then I want that kind of heart."

"As I say, you already have one of those kinds of hearts."

"I do?"

"Yes. Don't you love Dorothy here?"

"I suppose I do."

"Didn't you come here longing for a heart?"

"Of course I did."

"Well that proves it then. You already have one. For else you would not have felt those feelings."

"Goodness. Do you suppose I do have a heart, Dorothy?"

"It's possible," she answered.

"Of course it is," said the Wizard. "These are called emotions, and you have plenty of them."

"Just like you and Dorothy?" asked the Tinman.

"Absolutely," said the Wizard.

"Absolutely," said Dorothy.

"Absolutely," said the Tinman.

"I'm so happy," said Dorothy. "But you didn't give him the heart. He already had it when we came here. It doesn't prove you have magic."

"But he didn't know it," said the Wizard. "I told him so, and made it true. Don't you see, that's why they call me the Wonderful Wizard of Oz?"

When I wrote *Tinman*, the first book of this series of reminiscences, I gathered together almost five hundred memories I thought might be of interest to readers. These recollections represent what I consider interesting in my life. I limited *Tinman* to one hundred and fifty of these recollections, chosen mostly because they followed a consistent thread that made sense to me. That left three hundred and fifty unpublished, something I rectified by publishing one hundred and fifty more in *Tinman Too*. I thought then that I had finished. However, here now is *Tinman Tre*, one hundred and fifty more recollections, leaving but fifty remaining. I doubt there will be a *Tinman Quatro*, but who knows? Life, hopefully, goes on.

Each of these books follows a general chronological order, beginning with my earliest recollections and ending beyond my latest birthday at the time of writing. I realize that this makes reading the three books somewhat difficult. As if they were about three different people. Unfortunately, I cannot help this, and I hope you find the three books compatible.

Again I occasionally use "Nameless" for individuals in this book, a nomer I hope will protect the identities of those I'm describing. Even though this is probably obvious, I also need to clarify that by using this as a *nom de guerre*, it represents more than one character, depending on the story in which it appears.

Since publication of the original *Tinman*, many have asked if the apparently simple recollections told there represent metaphors or some other form of symbolism. My answer has remained the same—up to you. However, it could be useful, at least to those of you who've asked, to indicate one kind of process that might be applied in attempting to understand my approach. In Chapter 25 of *Tinman*, I recount my participation in an inter-squad football game, where, instead of following the coach's orders, I stole the ball from the opposing team and ran for a touchdown, only to be dismissed from the team for doing so. One might ask, since no further analysis takes place, why would a coach throw someone who'd just scored a touchdown for his team off that very team? Just for not following instructions? Seems quite shortsighted. However, one might consider that if I'd been wrong, and the game had been for real, the opponents might be passing instead of reversing, and the very person I'd been told to block could then catch the pass and run for a touchdown. In other words, though I don't say so in the story, my not following instructions would have worked out very differently. In fact, once understood by an opponent, my actions could easily produce touchdown after touchdown by my team's opponent, simply as a result of my not covering the player I'd been ordered to. Understanding this, might, if readers so choose, lead to further implications for, say, business, military, life, conduct in large-scale societies, and so on. Or, maybe it just has to do with an autobiographical recounting of my refusal throughout life to follow instructions. Or, maybe it's just a simple statement of facts as they occurred. Readers should make such interpretations on their own.

And what about the **S**nippets of writing and poems that pre**C**ede **A**nd fo**L**low each chapte**R** **I**n Tinman and Tinman T**O**o? i d**E**s**CR**ibe these as i**N**teresting explanati**O**ns and expansions of the associated chapter's contents. The poems in **W**hich these codes appear are computer-created and include quotes from what I find important literature from the past. And yet I still mean them to explain and expand on the material of the chapter itself. Again, I leave such interpretations to readers. The macrostics here, as in *Tinman* and *Tinman Too*, continue to be fonted codes that provide further information about the un-named individuals, places, and circumstances of the chapter's story. Nothing has changed except the actual content. As for the larger code that the boo*k* *a*s a whole co*n*tain*s*, it differs from th*a*t of the first two Tinmans, but can be di*s*covered in like manner. I should also mention that these hidden messages follow my plan to control the tempo at which the text and poetry reveal information. In this way, I feel reading these excerpts can be a more intrinsically musical experience.

Some of the individuals I have known over the years will expect to read of their exploits here, and be disappointed not to find them. I did not, however, choose stories based on friendships, but rather on the interest of the adventures themselves. Those left out may then consider themselves saner and more mature than many of those I included. These left-out individuals might also understand that these three books are only the beginnings of a continuing saga.

I wish to thank every one of the people who wittingly and unwittingly helped create the events I relate in this book. Many of them are now dead and unable to read of their adventures. Some remain alive and will no doubt agree or disagree with my characterization of their actions. This is understandable. I argue only that these are my recollections and do not necessarily represent the recollections of others.

Autobiographies, memoirs, and personal histories such as this are usually written by elder statesmen and stateswomen. Important people about whom the public clamors for more enlightenment. I am not one of these people. Thus, as someone in the audience of one of my recent lectures charmingly asked, "What makes you think you're so important that you feel the need to write a book about yourself?" It's a good question, deserving a reasonable answer. I shall provide two. I have lived a fairly eventful life, whether by accident or by providence, I don't know. Unexpected circumstances—not necessarily of consequence but of interest—have followed me wherever I have gone. Probably less important, I have a good memory of these events, and even though I admit to slight slips and embellishments here and there, I can recall them in proficient detail. I have even at times recounted these memories in diaries, parts of which I include here.

(1941-1956)

1

Rose Bowl

for me who h**u**nt**s** for the c**a**u**s**es of thi*n*gs,
no other path will lead them apart.

for the same vigoro**u**s **C**omputatio**n** and logi*c*

as a mind para*l*e*l* **t**o **t**H*e* movement of the world,
th**E** t*I*me is **C**ome for t**HE**e to **R**eap.

1941

My mother took great pride in recounting the story of how
she appeared as a cheerleader in the Rose Bowl when she
was in her late teens. She'd describe how she and her fellow
dancers waited under the stands of the stadium in Pasadena
until heralded onto the field for the half-time show. How
they kicked their legs in air and demonstrated the various
maneuvers they'd been taught. And, after the show finished,
how they were shepherded back under the stands again.

She couldn't recollect which teams played in that game,
who won, or even the exact year in which it had been played,
though by guessing it would have had to have been sometime
in the late 1920s when her family still lived in El Monte near
Los Angeles.

It was difficult to imagine my mother as a cheerleader. By the time I got to know her, she'd become hard as nails, and no doubt quite different than in her earlier years.

But, whenever she'd tell this story, usually at the least opportune times, she'd get a little gleam in her eyes and seem to remember back to that glorious era when films had just gained sound and Hollywood had only begun to show what it would eventually become.

I've always wondered if it had been me that had changed her. A sickly boy whose life could only be saved by moving to an arid climate like Phoenix, Arizona in order to survive. A long way from Hollywood. In her mind, no doubt, she could have been in pictures. Both she and her sister Lois were certainly attractive enough as we'd seen in photos of them at the time.

the harvest of the vesse**l**

*c***O**nt**I**nue**S** for some time in t*h*is motion.

it is *a* so*r*t of skin which we must strip off

if we are to find the rea*l* mind.

it was th*e*n that i *s*aw the horse

compared to a colossal puff of flame.

2

Baldwin Hills

but they were all locke**D.**

i**T** wa**s** n**O**t *i*n us

but w**E** a**R**e in it.

it i**S** of**T**he make**R,**

n**O**t of wh**A**t **I**s made.

1945

I have written elsewhere that I was born with severe asthma,
so severe in fact that it ultimately forced my family to move
to Phoenix, Arizona, to save my life. And of the sulfa drugs
that were the prescription *du jour* of those early years of the
1940s that allowed my lungs to capture and integrate oxygen
into my bloodstream, giving my heart the will to continue
beating, and my body a reason to continue living. What I
did not mention was one of my earliest memories, that of the
twice to three times weekly early morning visits to a hospital
south of Culver City near Los Angeles located somewhere
near Inglewood, where I would later live and do graduate
work at the University of Southern California.

The trip south was inevitably shrouded in fog, and wound through the Baldwin Hills. Knowing what awaited me—a visit to the hospital, the doctor, his nurse, and at least one long needle—made the trip through these hills almost unbearable. Not so much for the pain of the shots nor the dour expressions on the doctor and his nurse's faces, but that I was allergic to sulfa drugs, and knew that for at least two days following I would be sentenced to literally writhe in pain from the reaction of my body to something nearly as lethal as the asthma they were intended to temporarily cure.

The Baldwin Hills, in those days at least and probably still so, were barren and brown, with grass and other small plants clinging to the same life as I. And on top of that grass and those plants stood several hundred, or so it seemed to me, teeter tottering oil rigs that looked like those gizmos that you place on the lip of drinking glasses that continuously dunk their heads into the water. Back and forth. Forth and back. Not even then knowing what these things I saw actually were, they, along with the fog and the dying grass and plants around them gave me the impression of what death must be like. And, try as I might, I couldn't think of a way to avoid feeling as I did.

As the decades passed, I realized that, compared to the many other things that children can face when growing up, my situation hadn't been so bad after all. Yet, when saddened by something occurring in my life even now, my mind jumps immediately back to those times when we passed through those hills in the early morning fog, and the hopelessness that crept upon me without a single opportunity to defend myself against it.

it was a moo**N**less **N**i**g**ht,

bla**C**k **E**xcept for a redness near the horizon

becomin*g* redder.

if equall**Y** falli*n*g bodies

have thought th*a*t this method

may be mechanica*l*,

it is really rat*h*er base

and *i*t must be burning

as it were not a *l*amp at a*l*l.

3

Gorkies

they have thei**r** little **a**ffair*S*,

but i <u>H</u>o*pe* th*A*t re<u>A</u>de**rs** equal ***t***o both

will thi**n**k about m<u>Y</u> wo**r**k
for the good of both

but ***i****N* the verity o*F E*xtolment.

1946

Like most youngsters, I had trouble learning words along with their full meanings. For example, very early on I called horses 'gorkies' for some strange reason. How I exchanged a 'g' for an 'h' seems hard to fathom now, but then it came naturally. Probably more fun to say the word. Nothing whatsoever to do with the meaning.

But I realized the foolishness of my gorkie ways when one day while driving through town, we stopped at an intersection and I asked my parents why Presbyterians were not allowed to cross the street. It took a while for my father to put what he saw together with my word and realize that my penchant for malapropisms had reached a new high. "That's 'pedestrians,' son," he told me.

i t*a*ke him to be a soul of g*R*eat arti*C*le,

but you mig**h**t see a bat.

but i*N*sight is *n*ot,

nor i*S* *A*ffectio*N* will,
because he knoweth that he hath
but a short time,

and such a machine is *D*escribed
as having n*O* free will.

4

Father, Mother, God

a good h**a**nd for drawing,

a goo**D** foo**T** for dancing,

an at**HlE**tic frame for wide journeying.

t*h*at i**S** **V**_ery_ *l***K**e a mou**S**e,

a**N**d *t*hat th**EY** **CA**n, in fact,

mimic the acti**O**n**S**

of a hu**M**an comput**Er** very c*l***O**sely.

1946

One of the first times I remember my parents actually parenting me was when I was very young. They'd come into my room after I went to bed and make me say the following little poem along with them. It went,

Father, Mother, God
Loving me
Guide my little feet,
Up to thee.

That was all there was to it. Short and simple.

Though I haven't had to speak it with them for nearly seventy years at this writing, I still find myself lapsing into it whenever any of its opening words occur in everyday conversation.

The thing about this poem was that I didn't really understand its meaning. The first and second lines seemed all right, but the last two were vague. After all, if my little feet were being guided up to God, wasn't I dying? Or was it when I was sleeping I went to heaven, only to return to earth when I woke. And then I went to heaven again when I really died. In other words, the poem was momentary rather than permanent.

But that didn't make any sense either, since I had nightmares most of the time. These surely didn't represent heaven. So, had my prayer not worked? Had I gone to hell instead?

Thinking of this did not occupying much of my time, but when you say something every night for a few years, it tends to stick and makes you pause. And this little ditty made me pause often and, because of its endless repetitions, makes me pause occasionally now.

it has bee**n** sc**o**rne**D** and thrown aside

                    alon**G** with euclid s tenth b**O**ok.

it is **D**one.

                              a **m**ass**y** wheel

crowded onl**Y** with what they regard as inferior animals.

5

San Francisco

he did no*t* go off on *h*is own

an*d* ass*er* t *i*t in isolation

from the first *c*ourse

t*i*ll he *t*hat died

from a pla$\mathbf{C}$e in m$\mathbf{O}$t*l*on lead.

1947

My first trip back to my birth city of San Francisco took place when I was roughly eight or nine years old. My father had driven us from Los Angeles, and taken the main route into the city via the El Camino Real, the 'royal road' in Spanish. Since this trip was long before freeways, our journey from San Jose to San Francisco took nearly half a day, even though it's less than sixty miles in actual distance.

We spent our first night in a motel on the Great Highway near the shores of the Pacific. I remember the particular room we rented by the fact that it had pay television. Since we did not own a television at the time, my sister and I were drawn to it as moths to fire. Irresistible, while at the same time nearly impossible to watch for we were on a strict budget.

Fifteen minutes per dime seemed like a lot of money to my parents in those days, the source of any chance we had to watch. At the time, the only television we'd seen prior to that was my grandparent's set which was so small as to require a self-standing Fresnel lens in front of it so that human images could be separated from the backgrounds through which they supposedly walked, crawled, or, well, whatever they did. All black and white, of course.

So there my sister Susie and I sat, attempting to decide at which point we'd turn on the TV with the two dimes we had, one for each of us. All the while, right outside our door, the great Pacific roared and behind us the San Francisco Zoo.

The second and last day of our visit to the city of my birth was equally strange. We'd visited Chinatown, a wondrous place full of exotic clothing, chickens hung upside down in windows sans feathers, and extraordinary kites. For lunch that day I had, of course, Chop Suey, as it turns out and in defiance of its Chinese-sounding name, an American dish. And I got sick. Really sick. So sick in fact, that once in the car, I couldn't imagine ever feeling worse.

Since my mother could never believe I wasn't faking it, I dared not tell her of my illness, but instead silently watched as we drove across the Golden Gate Bridge and up the switchbacks on the road toward the top of Mount Tamalpais.

I can still feel a little bit of what I felt then. The nausea permeating every inch of my skin, the surface of my eyeballs, my fingernails, the ends of my hair.

After that, I remember nothing more of that trip. We made it safely back to Los Angeles apparently, and my memories are what they are.

came a sof**T** sound

from near a ***vin***e covered **T**ree,

and fire came d**OW**n from **g**od out of h**E**aven,

and devou**R**ed them.

But fat**E** h**A**s lo**R**d it**S** limits,
being different from that above.

6

Humming

and *t*he*re* was s**e**e**n** in hi**S** t**e**mple the ark of his testament.

it will **BE A**nother part of the same,

and so absol**UT**el**Y** understood.

1947

When I was very young, my mother told me that hummingbirds never stopped flying. This image, realistic for me since I'd never seen a hummingbird do anything but dart through around, became fixated in my mind. So much so that I called them "helibirds," tiny birds that constantly flew and sometimes did so while remaining otherwise motionless in the air. Birds that never left their native habitat—that same air.

As time went on, however, it dawned on me that while my helibirds could eat, poop, and seemingly relax while flying, that there were some things that might require them to stop moving their wings. Sleeping, for example. It was hard to imagine a hummingbird sleeping while flying. Or propagate their species, to put it delicately, while on the wing. Or lay their eggs and sit on their newly hatched young in the air. And on, and on.

So I began to suspect that my mother was either ignorant of such things, or was pulling my leg. Since she was prone to the latter, it was leg-pulling that got my vote.

By the time I saw my first hummingbird perched on a branch, some forty years had passed since my mother had tried to convince me of their airborne eternity. And this first time came with pronounced anxiety, for as I watched this hummingbird sit, no doubt staring back at me through almost invisible eyes, I realized that my helibirds were, at least when sitting, rather normal birds after all. Until, of course, that same bird took to the air, hung in it for a split second, and then flew away at some obscenely high speed, all the while making sudden right and left turns.

I now realize that my mother's view of hummingbirds as impossible beings that never had to land on planet earth or anything attached to it, had been right after all. For every photograph I'd ever seen of a hummingbird included motion, flight, in stasis while flapping its wings when eating, drinking, or diving, and somehow making ninety-degree-angle changes of direction in no time at all.

Who cared if they landed a few times during their lives? Helibirds are the most beautiful and wonderfully strangest of all creatures.

And they never land.

it glaZed past the sliCk windOws
Once or twice.
she hAd peeped into the book,
and the spectroscope
to which he had at once resorted.

7

Five and Dime

go quite roun*D* the who*L*e e*AR*th
bef*O*re it falls,

which rudely or softly educates hi*m*

t*O* the *P*erceptio*n*

t*HA*t th*eR*e are *K*ept *N*o contin*gE*nci*eS*.

1948

How I figured out the economics of my idea, even at eight years old, remains a secret to this day. In brief, the idea was this; I buy as many comic books as I could afford—likely two—from the local five-and-dime, set up a stand between that five-and-dime and the furniture store next door, and then resell the each comic book for five cents more than I paid. For some reason, at that age, this made sense to me. A kid would come by, like both of the comic books, buy them, and I'm ahead by ten cents. Keep it up, and I'd soon become a millionaire.

Of course, my idea didn't last long. The first potential customer, a young lady a few years older than I, stopped by my stand, leafed through one of the comic books, looked at the price, and asked me why she should buy either of them since they were five cents cheaper in the five-and-dime next door. Her logic was so compelling, that I quickly realized the error of my ways.

I then considered my situation and realized that I either had to buy out all the copies of the same comic books the five-and-dime had, thus making mine the only place in town where they could be bought, or sell my copies somewhere else, where potential customers would think twice about the extra trouble they'd have to take to get to the five-and-dime to buy copies there instead.

The first idea, that of buying them all up, was difficult to accomplish since I didn't have enough money to purchase all the copies. The five-and-dime had comic books in groups as many as ten—especially *Archie*—and that was well beyond my means. Those they had only one of in stock, were unpopular and less likely to sell.

The second idea, that of moving my business out of town, was ridiculous. The town of Goodyear, where I'd set up my stand, was very small in those days, and the only place I could set up business a distance away was in the boonies. What adult, driving at sixty or more miles an hour, would stop to buy a comic book from a kid obviously trying to make extra money by overpricing the stock that he or she could buy within a few minutes or less driving time? Worse yet, since kids couldn't drive, what interest would such a driver have to stop in the first place?

Pity—the emotion that served me fairly well in a later venture in Phoenix and of which I describe in a previous volume of the Tinman series—would not work either. People seeing me crouched behind a table in the shadows if a small alleyway between two stores were not likely to take pity on me, busy as they were buying essentials. Besides, what the hell was I doing there anyway?

So, I closed up shop and took my two comic books home with me not very long after I had opened for business that day. I was not all that depressed for, after all, I'd enjoy reading the comics myself and hadn't actually lost any money. Maybe even gained a bit of humility for having tried something without having thought it through.

Strangely enough, however, the young lady who'd taught me my lesson so quickly that morning, met me on my way home and asked if I still had those comics to sell. I told her I did. And she bought them from me. I was now ten cents richer. Wow.

What had changed her mind? She could have easily walked back the way I'd come and purchased them for less money.

She smiled.

I smiled.

And I left her, and walked the rest of my way home.

None the wiser.

In fact, more confused than ever.

that law rule**S** existen**C**e

b**y** which it either carried **M**e **A**way
in the spirit,

or **C**alls
into the wilderness

so blinded b**Y** his vanity.

8

Marbles

the world was bein**g** wat**C**hed

*K*ee*N*ly **a**nd cl**OS**ely.

She felt she was dozing
if it sho*U*ld break as a savage a*C*cident.

our ato**m**s are as resistance
li*K*e unto fine brass,

as if they **p***Lay***e**d in a furnac*E*.

1949

When I was quite young—maybe five—I got good at playing marbles. I had my own set consisting entirely of clearies with strings of a single color shot through them. My friends and I played the traditional game beginning with a ten-foot-wide circle and thirteen marbles three inches apart in a cross in the center. We required knuckles down while shooting, the usual beginning outside the circle, and when someone knocks another marble out of the ring while their shooter stays in the ring make their next shot from that point. The winner is the one with the most marbles when no more remain in the circle. Simple. We had all the terms down as well. Mibs were the marbles in the center of the ring, for example.

Up until our little club of marble players got together the game was primarily for the opposite gender. Girls. Like hopscotch, marbles was non-violent and certainly no one could doubt that the thumb and forefingers of girls were as strong and accurate as those of boys. Therefore, we boys began our own club. No girls allowed.

One of the fascinating aspects of marbles is that there are several thousand variants of the game. The one that caught our attention the most was using boulders. Boulders were more than twice the size of regular marbles and created a loud cracking sound when striking one another. While we were never actually sure of this, it seemed that hands of boys grew faster than girls and thus, we were alone in our use of boulders.

Like with regular marbles, I had my own set of boulders. Again clearies, with single shots of color through them. With a well-placed opening shot, a boulder could clear two or more mibs from the center cross, and leave the opening shooter with a chance for a complete sweep of the circle. I remember my first such sweep like it was yesterday. Sweeps, especially with boulders, were difficult, so it was a special occasion indeed. Unfortunately, my mother broke my victory celebration by calling me in to do my homework. Right in front of the other boys as they set up for another game.

*t*he robot*S* danced and sang

and *i*s,

according *t*o the s**P**ace,

e*i*ther abs**O**lute or in relat**I**ve *n*os.

9

Prince of Foxes

and the swi**F**ter the **mot**on beco*Me***S**

*A*t t**h**e necessity of be**a**uty

un**d**e*R* which *T*he un*I*verse **Lies**,

th*A*t all is a*N*d **M**u*S*t be

pict**O**rial.

that the rainbo**W**
and the curve of the horizon,
and the arch of the blue vault,

only re**S**ults fro**M** the organism of the eye.

1949

One of the most impactful experiences of my early life
occurred in 1949 in a movie theater in Avondale, Arizona.
There I saw a film titled *Prince of Foxes* with Tyrone Power,
Orson Welles, and Wanda Hendrix. This film, in black and
white, literally changed my life, both because it was in black
and white and somehow emphasizing violence, and because

25

this violence overpowered me because so much of it was implied rather than seen.

This film, based on a period novel of the same name by Samuel Shellabargers, is based on the betrayal of a young nobleman by both his wife and the court of the Borgias. At one point in the film, Belli (Everett Sloan) is asked to remove Andrea's (Power) eyes with his thumbs in front of the court. This scene, at least to an eight-year-old, was so realistic that I couldn't imagine anything worse. I slept very little for days after that, and the scene recurred to my mind over and over again during the years to follow. I still remember it to this day.

What was so curious to me at the time—and even now—is that I knew these were actors, and that no eyes had been removed. Even in the story itself, the gouging out of eyes was to be faked by the characters. But none of this helped me solve my problem. I had, apparently, seen what humans could do to one another, and even the idea that one could think of doing this seemed impossible to imagine, no less be shown in a film projected on a large screen in front of an audience. Not even the final scene of Hitchcock's *Psycho*, which had a significant effect on me later on in my life, rivaled this horrific act.

bUt failed to interpret

the fluctuating appearanceS

of the markIngs they mapped so well.

but no,

they were all loCked.

10

Short Order

the wind *b*egan to blo**w**,
and remoter **F**rom t**h**e
SUN *i*n form,
and mov**i**ng
ex***P*** r**E** ss and
admira*bl**E***.

1950

The old route to Los Angeles from Phoenix—before Interstate 10 was completed—involved taking US Highway 60 through Wickenburg, Arizona. My parents would pack up our car and head out for 'Wicky' before dawn, and we'd traditionally eat breakfast at a small diner along the road there.

On one such occasion, while waiting for our breakfast to be served, I remember watching the cook, complete with his white outfit and stand-up cook's hat, demonstrate his skills in fixing four different orders simultaneously. He was great. Almost like a ballet. Flip the pancakes, check the sunny-side up eggs, stir the hash browns, butter the toast, all almost, but

27

not quite, by rote. It seemed impossible really, for he had to fill many orders during the day, and the likelihood of four identical to ours was very low if non-existent.

As I watched him slide the various meals onto our plates and place them on the counter for the waiter to serve, I was hooked. This was what I wanted to do in my life. Be a short-order cook. No doubt about it. And so I announced this to my father, mother, and sister as we sat at the counter and ate our breakfasts. The world had millions of diners, and many would need such people. Cooks of great skill and many different talents.

As I devoured my buttermilk pancakes smothered in butter and maple syrup, I couldn't believe my good luck. Not only did the cook have fun creating the food he served, but the costumers really enjoyed eating it. A more perfect job I could not imagine.

And, thus, that is all I talked about on the rest of our journey.

Of course, as time passed and our trips to diners decreased to one and then none, I forgot about by flirtation with being a short-order cook. I'd tried to boil an egg. And my attention waned such that my mother had to rescue the egg before it became what it did later in my life, an archeological artifact. A calcified remnant from the dark ages of my youth.

an**D** **the** earth was reaped,

and an*o*ther angel came out of the temple
which is in heaven.

and as soon as ever it flies awa*y*,

and we sit and ru*l*e,

*a*nd *t*hough w*e* sleep,

ou*r* dream will come to pass.

11

Cement

but this re**A**lly only means
that we think it would be

less likely he would **CO**nside**R**

the **C**i**R**cums**t**ances suitable

f**O**r c**On**ferring a **S**oul.

1950

When I was nine years old and still living in Goodyear, Arizona, my father drove his family to see our new home still under construction in a subdivision to the northwest of downtown Phoenix. The trip was full of suspense, as no one but my father had any idea what it might look like at this stage.

When we arrived, my sister and I were disappointed. For, rather than seeing a house without its skin as we expected, we found nothing but hundreds of cement foundations with small pieces of wood lying on them, nailed in place as indicators of where walls would eventually rise. How we even found our own new home within this maze of subdivision layouts was beyond me.

But, when our father stopped the car at a sloping curve on one edge of the numerous slabs and introduced us to our new home, we knew we'd found it. Sort of. We jumped out of the car and ran across what would become our front lawn and through non-existent walls to its interior.

The word 'disappointment' no longer covered what I felt. The rooms were tiny. So tiny, in fact, that it didn't seem possible we could sleep in any of them. Nothing but closets of varying sizes, I said.

My father countered by telling us that all houses at this stage of construction looked this way. That the pictures we'd seen, the drawings of how the final product would look, were true to scale and that we would indeed find the final results spacious and easy to sleep in.

I remember standing where the kitchen would be, staring out across the flat once desert landscape, and wondering what I'd done to deserve this. An apartment in Goodyear with a large scorpion living beneath my bedroom was bad enough, but this was intolerable.

Of course, my father had been right, and we lived in that house for many years thereafter. For me that meant eight years. For my parents that meant over fifty years. And there was enough room. Sort of. It hadn't seemed possible when I'd first stood there without the walls, knowing that they, too, would take up what little space the plan indicated we would have, and that we couldn't possibly survive in this space, but there it stands to this day, its cinderblock outer walls and swamp cooler on top for all to see.

And I miss it.

Sort of.

but look wHEre sadLy

the poor wretch comes

reAdINg.

and iT camE from

dEep in the ground.

and well Combined wiTh stone.
but could not hide from his fires from me

and from the sun.

12

Photo

crying wit**h** a l**o**ud voi**C**e to him

th**A**t **S**at on the clo**U**d.

no u**S**e **I**n c**R**yin**g** lik**E** that.

n**O** **we**eds,

n**O** grass,

no tongues,

e**l**se turn and

poure**d** into the sou**l**s of all men.

1950

As I remember it, the situation began like this.

My father came to my sister and I to tell us that he wanted to give our mother a birthday gift of a photo of the three of us. Husband, daughter, and son. And not just a photo, but one taken by a professional photographer in a studio. We liked the idea and he swore us to secrecy.

Time passed as he set things in motion. Mostly by calling and making an appointment with a photographer for an evening shoot because of my father's daily work schedule. We waited eagerly to hear the excuse he gave my mother for the three of us going out together on a school night. Unfortunately, he never revealed that excuse to us, just that it had worked and off we went.

Since I was only eight or nine at the time, I don't actually remember the details, but I do recollect that it took quite a while to set up the camera and arrange the backdrop for our threesome black and white photo. It took even longer to get us to pose in just the right ways for the photographer to take his pictures with a very large camera. Then he posed us holding smiles for which we got very tired of hearing the word *fromage*—'cheese' in French—spoken each time by the photographer before clicking the camera shutter. But we survived, and returned home without a comment from my mother.

What we didn't know then, but soon found out, was that this particular photographer was a perfectionist. He wasn't at all happy with the results from our first session, and he required two more before he got it right. We also had to return to give him our final approval of the photos and then separately pick them up. After all, my mother would see them if they came in the mail.

This, then, meant four or five school nights off and, of course, my mother becoming more and more curious about what was transpiring. A month had passed between when this series of visits began and when they finally concluded.

On several occasions I heard my parents discussing what mother had variously surmised had occurred. One night, for example, she was convinced my father was having an affair, a word that came up multiple times during their conversations. He, of course, claimed his innocence, and asked her why in God's name would he take his two children along if he were having an affair. She'd argue that he might be attempting to convince the imaginary other woman to take us kids as well as him in the bargain. On another occasion, I remember him trying to convince her that we weren't involved with an illegal scam to make extra money. We weren't doing very well in the money department and, to her at least, it seemed reasonable we might be involved in some scam to make more. In fact, I once heard her make a remarkable inference that he was attempting to sell us to Mexicans for what the market would bring. While I knew it wasn't true, I remember thinking how confusing that would be.

But time passed, and eventually her birthday arrived. When she opened her sole present—remember it was from all of us, not just from my father—she opened the envelope and stared at what apparently was the last thing she expected. While it should have immediately explained the multiple nights we'd spent having these photographs taken, she did not make that connection. For what she said first was, "How much did these cost?"

He explained to her that her happiness in having the photos was worth everything to us, and what it cost was not important. Of course, she still didn't look happy. While she liked the photos—all three of them plus copies—we couldn't believe that all the time we'd spent having them taken did not immediately make her jump for joy.

But she didn't jump for joy.

Eventually, of course, these photographs found there way into frames when we could afford them, and onto mantles, bookcases, and other places where such photos were usually placed in those days. And eventually the whole affair was forgotten—I use the word 'affair' here with some reticence.

Many years later, after my mother died, I went through the effects of my her life and once again came across the photographs that had survived well over the intervening years and smiled to myself. The story then seemed innocuous, but still had taken up a definite place in my memory. Everything about it seemed to explain the personalities of my mother and father, and the impression those personalities had on their two children.

in the upper region of our atmosphere

a permanent westerl**y** curr**e**nt.

and it would seem that this too
is the belief of the minds

upon ma**r** s.

13

Bethany Home Road

there are many questions
which have been proven

anD notIce**d.**

1952

When we first moved into our new home in Phoenix when I
was ten, the first experience I remember involves one of the
various farms and ranches cluttered around the intersection
of Bethany Home Road and Twenty-Seventh Avenue,
the nearest cross-streets of consequence to our house. The
southeast corner to be exact. This plot of land was remarkable
for its tall palm trees, the shorter deciduous ones that
occupied the shade from those higher trees, and nothing but
dirt below all that.

One day, a friend of mine and I chanced upon that plot
of land to witness an absolute carnage. Neighborhood cats
had assembled there as a huge number of baby birds made
their first attempts at flight. This meant these birds lay mostly
on the ground attempting to regain their breath and strength
before making new attempts. The cats, of course, were
feasting on the baby birds as quickly as time would allow.

I don't know how many birds I tried to save that afternoon, while probably saving none. I screamed at the cats. I cried. I couldn't believe that the world could be so cruel. That God could be so cruel. That evolution could be so cruel.

But cruel it was.

When the horrors eventually ceased, and the now overweight cats began returning to their homes, not a single live bird remained. Their picked clean bones and feathers lay here and there. And not many of those, since for the most part the cats with their raging hormones had gobbled most of the chicks whole as the birds died.

that t*HE*y weRe fi1Led.

buT reLation
and connection

are everYwhere.

14

Zuma

are n**O**t new men,
  but zeno,

    anaximene**S**,

      h**Ip**parChu**S**,

        emped**OC**les,

          ar**I**s**T**archus,

            pythag**O**ras,

              and o**En**opides.

1953

In my early teens, my Aunt Lois would occasionally took me, my sister Susie, and my cousins Paul and Jeannie, to Zuma beach west of Los Angeles. She most likely took Malibu Canyon Road south, and then west on Highway 1 toward Malibu to get there. I remember the views of the Pacific from high up on the Santa Monica Mountains ridges.

When we arrived at Zuma Beach, it was fun and games for all but me. Not that I was left out, mind you, but I had other plans. Sand crabs had captured my imagination so

39

completely by that time, I would simply sit at the tide line, watch as the surf came up and then recede, and see the bubbles indicating where these crabs had dug their temporary homes. I would then cup my hands deep enough to surround them, and pull the little guys up and into a little plastic bucket I'd brought along for just such purpose.

Sand crabs are amazing creatures. To the unsuspecting eye, they look like seafaring scorpions, especially to those like me who had come from more desert climes. But these sea scorpions are harmless and even cute when you get to know them. Barely weighing anything, they're only duty it seemed to me was to dig as deeply as they could in the sand, soft with seawater that brought them to shore, and wait until the next wave came to give them another ride and another home.

I had no idea at that time what sand crabs consumed to stay alive. I have since learned they ride the waves, move backwards, and use their antennae to catch and consume plankton. All this action, then, seemed amazing and mesmerizing to me.

Sometimes as big as a thumb and almost translucent, sand crabs are ubiquitous on the shores of Zuma. Watch a wave come in, count the locations of bubbles that rise from the sand as the wave recedes, and you'll get the idea.

Amazingly, you can see them at work in a bucket. A small layer of sand and a two or three inch top layer of seawater, and, while slowly rolling the bucket back and forth to simulate waves, the process is yours to see and make believe you own if only for a brief time.

I never killed or permanently removed a sand crab from the beach during my discoveries of their personalities. It seemed then, as it does now, that they deserved their rights to life as much as I did. And, who knew, maybe they added in some small way to the ecological balance of many other species, including humans.

On the other hand, I enjoyed naming and keeping track of their individual motions in order to discover whether their brains, if they had any, made deliberate choices, or if they simply reacted to their DNA which I'd just discovered in the books I'd read.

And, before I knew it, my Aunt Lois was collecting us for our trip back to North Hollywood. My little studies of sand crabs typically took more than four hours.

She'd likely scold me a little for my sand-covered swimsuit, legs, and arms, and sent me into the water to wash off. While my sister and cousins had bodysurfed their collections of sand away, this then would have been my first dip into the water of the day. Cold, but not refreshing.

they a**R**e *U*gly.

each i**S** des*I*gn̲ed

for a very limited purpose,

a**N**d a**S** parts of revolving wholes.

15

Joann

and she had never F<u>O</u>rgotten **y**ou.

you were the fIfth ange**L**,

soun**DE**d and **m**ay **b**e conside**R**ed

both to have Re**S**is**T**ance

and impu**l**se t**H**at is a little **o**verstated.

b**U**t that will pa**S**s.

1953

My cousin Joann—daughter of my Aunt Lois with her first husband—and I got along famously when we were both young. She loved classical music, studied the violin, and we'd trade stories of classical composers and listen to their music together. We only saw one another during the summers when my parents would drop my sister and I off in North Hollywood while they took vacations from us. But we remembered what we liked and then talked about it the last time we'd meet.

Then things changed. One summer when I arrived, all Joann wanted to play for me was the music of Barbra Streisand. I listened carefully and admitted that Streisand's voice was amazing. I, too, was quite taken with it. But, I reminded her, Streisand had not actually composed the music, someone else had, and that Streisand was the performer only. She didn't seem bothered by this. In fact, she seemed more bothered by the fact that I would notice such a thing. This confused me, for I'd always considered composers as originators and performers as necessary recreationists.

We agreed to disagree and, though it was clear our tastes had changed somewhat over the intervening year, we could still admire music in much the same ways.

By my next visit, though, things had changed more dramatically. First, Joann had a boyfriend. A good-looking and very nice guy that I didn't blame her for liking. At the same time, she'd not only lost her interest in the music we both loved, but had taken to attending wrestling matches at a local arena, one of which she made me attend as well.

A reclusive young man, lost in chess, classical music, practicing instruments, building telescopes, and so on, I was completely out of my element in this arena full of yelling people staring at nearly naked grown men attempting to beat the shit out of one another. And, what's worse, we sat in the first row, where the sweat rained down on us like spit on its way to a spittoon in the Long Branch Saloon.

When asked if I had enjoyed myself, I smiled and said I did. However, nothing could have been further from the truth. As far as I was concerned, my cousin Joann had visited the dark side, and had apparently liked it there.

Many years later, something like fifty, I met Joann again. She had developed an Oklahoma-type accent and spoke in combinations of aphorisms rather than original thoughts. She smiled readily, even though her husband now of many years had recently died, and spoke of her career as a photo laboratory technician and her years visiting a ranch where her family kept a horse. A far cry from Beethoven, but it was good to see her. I imagined, though, that her tastes by then had further shifted from Barbra Streisand to Dolly Parton.

and **O**ne too easily forgets
that you are true,

But crow**d**ed only
with wh**A**t they regard
as i**N**ferior thoughts.
but no, the ol**D** land was gone.

16

Cartoons

and there was f ound

no Place fOr them.

there may Be many such questions,

and questions which

cannot be answered satisfactoriLy.

1954

Sometime in my early teens I decided I wanted to be a cartoonist. Like every other kid I knew, I loved the comics, whether in books or newspapers, and it seemed so natural, so easy. After all, I'd trained in art school for a couple of years by then, and knew a bit about drawing. At least more about it than any other kid I knew.

So I set about becoming the best cartoonist I could imagine. Unfortunately, without the Internet and, for that matter any how-to books, I was pretty much on my own as far as how to proceed. Thus I began with imitation. I picked a few of my favorite cartoons and copied them without tracing. I used a ruler for framing and to keep the lettering of the captions level, but otherwise did everything freehand.

Not as easy as it looks.

When I finished, I found the characters in my cartoons, the ones that repeated from frame to frame, seemed different each time I drew them giving the suggestion in the three or four windows of repeated scenes a strange preoccupation with contorted heads, variations in haircuts, ears of different sizes and shapes, and so on. After further study of the comics I was imitating, I realized that cartoonists used the same drawings for the most part to avoid the problems I was having, and only varied the mouths as the characters spoke. So I eventually bought some tracing paper on which I drew the initial background and characters and then concentrated only the moving parts.

As time progressed, my character, a boy with a round head, a smallish body, and a good grin that changed position on his face depending on what he said at the time looked fine. I made the backgrounds simple to save time and keep the reader's attention on the central character.

Of course, it then dawned on me that I'd begun the wrong way round. I needed something funny to have my characters say. After all, that's why they were called 'funnies.' And that's when the real problems began. Newspaper cartoons seem naturally funny and not mere rehashes of old jokes. How did they do it? What made things funny?

I did my research by reading hundreds of cartoons and numerous comic books. Didn't help much. The cartoons seemed to be mostly plays on words, exaggerations, or ironies of some sort. Like one I remember that had a boy telling his mother, "We just got a phone call," and she responding, "What about?" and him saying, "Told us why our phone was out of order." It wasn't that funny, even to me, but in combination with the pictures, it worked okay.

So I tried to come up with some of these myself. Not easy. And, of course, as I did, I kept thinking that I'd then have to draw the pictures to accompany the words. And make them funny somehow as well.

I tried again and again without success. I didn't show them to anyone, since I was fairly sure if they weren't funny to me, they wouldn't be funny to anyone else either. I never got around to comic books. If I couldn't get three or four frames to work, how could I manage several pages of them with similar characters and a full story that would end up being funny? And then what about color? Comic books were in color. Cartoons in newspapers were not. At least not the ones during the week.

Eventually I returned to the single frame cartoons on the editorial pages, though I didn't know much about politics at the time. Only one picture with usually one balloon for the words. A cinch! So I tried my hand at these. So easy. The only problem was that my versions again weren't at all funny. Black and white, no character continuity necessary between frames, and I still couldn't do it.

So I gave up after two months or so. I could compose, paint pictures, write poems and short stories that made sense, but I hadn't come close to creating a true cartoon or comic.

the shadows from the moon were there.

the motIons of The gLObes

mIght be most augmeNteD.

that Is that affECtion

thst iS essential to

wIll that spirit

upOn whOse wealth depends
on the volume of the earth.

17

Soda Shop

whic*h* rudely *O*r sof*t*ly
educa**T**es h**I**m
To the pe**R**c**E**ption
th**a**t the**R**e **A**re no contingencie**S**.

1954

Around the corner from my aunt and uncle's house in North Hollywood, California, was what we then called a soda shop. This mom and pop business was very small, with nothing but a counter running from the front to the back with room behind it for the soda jerk, and room in front for the backless kind of swivel stools they used in those days. And, of course, room for people to slip by between those stools and the wall.

The magic of this place for me was that it served the most incredibly delicious vanilla malted milkshakes known to mankind. Since I'm not particularly fond of chocolate and am also allergic to it, vanilla was and always has been my flavor. And this store sold these malts for the incredibly low price of ten cents apiece. Thus, the store became the focus of every single day my sister and I spent in North Hollywood during the summers when my parents escaped us to take vacations.

It was thus my habit to spend my days begging for money to buy a malted milk shake at this soda shop grew. I'd begin with my sister and then move on to my cousins if she couldn't or wouldn't loan me the money. If still unsuccessful, I'd then start on my aunt and uncle. Worse come to worse, I'd end up standing outside the soda shop looking as forlorn as I could in hopes that passersby would feel sorry enough for me to give me the dime.

Most days were successful. I'd get my malt and find a place outside somewhere to sit down and drink it before the summer's heat made it warm. Most of these sit-down spots were near the soda shop where, across the street, stood a very large Pep Boys Tire Store. I mention this store because, though I never entered it before, by the time my summers were over I had memorized almost every aspect of it. The signs advertising the sale for the day. The heads of the three Pep boys, or so I assumed. And the paintings of scantily clad women on signs that for some reason were always selling tires.

Since my dopamine undoubtedly climbed to the stratosphere during these moments of nirvana, I no doubt got my first true taste of natural drug abuse. Maybe why my desire for endorphins forced me to run so much in my later years. But I didn't care then. I don't care now. For the habit of searching out and finding shops that sell vanilla malts continues for me to this day.

A city is not a city until I've discovered their malt shop. Just like a lake is not a lake unless it has fish, or a town is not a town unless it has a bookshop.

Just ask my wife.

that law rules thr**O**ughout **e**xiste**N**ce.

a **L**aw **d**eep hidden.

Far **F**ro**m** l**I**fe or death.

dr**i**pping **Cl**ean out.

and the **Y** heard a great voice from heaven
saying, i can reach the **k**ey.

18

Guide

with which he deCeived
them that had received

the mark Of the beast,

the stars blinked with red fire
in the night sky.

1955

During my last lengthy summer visit to my Aunt Lois and
Uncle Frank's home in North Hollywood, I discovered
something amazing. The back of their garage stored
approximately three hundred plus *TV Guide Magazines*.
These weekly pocketbook-size issues were all neatly stacked
and in reverse chronological order. Therefore, the most recent
one lay on top of the rest. This was intriguing given that after
four or five days each of these magazines—thick because it
was the Los Angeles area after all, and there were it seemed
to me several hundred television stations at the time—went
completely out of date within a week. Useless for anyone
except those who might be interested in what had been on

television at a certain date and time in the past. Likely no one at all.

I considered asking my aunt and uncle why they kept such things, and why they'd kept them in such neat order, but didn't for I could think of no good reason that wouldn't embarrass them. But, of course, these magazines might be useful as kindling in fireplaces. Except they didn't have a fireplace at that time. Or maybe they had a fondness for certain shows, and looking back for a short description of one of these shows brought back fond memories. Or maybe they thought these magazines would eventually become rare and be worth more than they paid for them. However unlikely these reasons seemed to me, one of them might be possible. Probably not. My last guess was that they simply couldn't bear to throw things away. Collectors at heart, as were most of my mother's family. And she herself.

I never did discover the fate of the *TV Guides* when I later discovered they had turned their garage into a large new family room. With a fireplace, no less. And, interestingly, in front of which they'd placed a large television set.

They eventually moved to Las Vegas, Nevada, where I never had the opportunity to visit them. If I had, I'm sure my first order of business would have been to ask about their *TV Guides*, suspecting that in the intervening years since I'd originally found them, the number would have increased by the thousands.

y<u>O</u>u**r** crib shall stand

at the kin**G**s m**E**ss

til a ch**OU**gh,

an **O**bje**C**t of de**R**ision,
and did not continue

his c**O**mmentary
up to the tenth book.

until **ve**ry recent<u>l</u>y,

a stora**GE** capacity

of e**VE**n a tho<u>u</u>sand digits

was ve**R**y rare.

it**S** o**C**eans have shrunk

until the**y** cover **BU**t a thi**R**d
of its surface,

whe**N** a race ha**S** lived its term.

19

Symphony Fantastique

theres a letter for you sir.

it comes from the **v**ery am**B**assa**d** o**r**

that was bo**U**nd for En**g****L**and

w**i**th **S**ca**R**ce**L**y a quarter

Of the superfl cial br**ONZ**e area

the**n** filled with water.

1955

As a youngster, I loved Berlioz's *Symphony Fantastique*, a work
of much charm, and, for its time, a masterwork of innovation.
But, as all things go, I grew tired of it, and one day in my
early teens I decided to prove to myself how my record
player—of vinyl recordings—worked.

I knew that record players, as complex and as large as
many of them were at the time, didn't do anything beside
amplify and provide speakers to sound that was already
present in the groves of the record itself. No big deal this, but
for me a challenge to prove empirically.

To demonstrate, I took a large piece of paper—any paper would do I'd heard, but I used thick paper just short of being cardboard—and curved it around one of its corners making it cone shaped. I then borrowed a pin from my mother—I shouldn't have because that made her curious as hell—and stuck it through the smallest end of the cone. I placed the record on an upside down top so I could manually spin it, and as I did, I stuck the needle into the first grove of the record and, *voila*, I heard Berlioz's *Symphony Fantastique*, albeit wobbly due to my uneven manual spinning. The cone did its simple job of amplifying the tiny sounds the needle made as it bounced around on the various bumps within the grove. All in all, a wonderful experience, despite its lack of acoustic resonance.

With modern day laser technology, however, this experiment cannot be replicated. I imagine that all manner of other tests are being made by today's brand of curiosity seeking ten-year olds that make my *Symphony Fantastique* experiment seem incredible tame.

he created thin**G**s.

and then di**P**ped sudden**Ly** down,

spinning **A**nd then cracking

the **Y** lay lifeless in the earth.
and the earth was reaped,
and another angel came
out of the temple,
which is in heaven.

20

Turquoise

waged   by   europea**N**

i***m***migr**A**nts in t**he** spa**c**e **O**f

fif***t***y years and by increasing

t***he*** **v**elocit**y**, a body is limited

ci***r*** cumscribed, and **J**ust by

surfac**E**s, but on a population of

t**WE**nty   or   two   hundred

mi**L**lion**S**.

1955

In my mid-teens, I was struck with the geological bug, bought a special rock hammer, a good book with pictures of lots of different rocks, and spent almost every second I was allowed out of my house investigating and identifying each rock-like thing I could find. Trips in our car called for special stops when I saw a particular color or outcropping that seemed promising.

On one very special day, I was out walking in the far reaches of our general neighbors—which at that time was mostly surrounding deserts—and came upon a new house being built at the end of a dirt road. What attracted me to this house, even from a distance, was the sight of turquoise. Lots of it. In fact, all in a large pile stacked in front of the house, obviously brought from somewhere else to use here as some kind of decoration.

Now this was not pure turquoise, but the more plentiful type laced with quartz, or, more likely, quartz laced with turquoise. Didn't matter to me, though, for within each near bowling-ball sized rock enough pure turquoise was evident that it could be extracted and used, if one wanted, to create all manner of jewelry, decorative ornaments, and so on.

One of the workman digging around the base of the house at the time noticed me wondering after this pile of stones, wandered over, and asked me about my interest. I told him I was a 'rock hound' and was curious as to what the stones were going to be used for. He told me then that more were on the way, and that they were destined to become a decorative ring around the base of the building, standing maybe three feet high continuously on every outside wall like wainscoting.

'Who could have enough money to create such a wall of rocks over stucco?' I thought.

He watched me carefully and said, "Why don't you take what you can carry just this once?"

I looked at him carefully to see if he was joking. He wasn't.

"Won't the owners miss it?" I asked him.

"Not a chance," he said, "they've ordered far more than we'll need and it can't be returned. Take what you want."

And so I did exactly as he said, and filled my arms with as many of the rocks as I could carry and returned home.

Once there, my mother asked me where I'd gotten them. Or stolen them. My father trusted me implicitly, but my mother never trusted me at all. A strange mix, but I was used to it by then.

I told her the truth, as usual, expecting her to disbelieve me or once again call the cops as she'd done before. For some reason, however, probably because they were so beautiful, she accepted my answer.

Strange thing was, the rocks then lay in a small garden near the west side of our house for as long as I can remember. They may still be there, for all I know.

The reason for this was that, try as I might, I couldn't bring myself to use my geological hammer on them for fear the rocks might shatter and become less than what they meant to me as is.

Of course, I showed them off to whoever would listen to me. 'Incredibly beautiful,' I told every visitor I could drag outside in the heat to see them.

but   the   rabbit   has   to   be   so constructed,   that   e**V**ents   that shortly   preceded   the   occurrence of **A** **J**ustified   punishment   are unlikely t**O** be repeated.

(1955-1963)

21

Ernie

whitewash all the more so,

in that **B**esides eu**C**lid

And his **com**ment**a**to**r** p**r**O**clu**S,

w**e** a**r**e arran**t** knav**es**.

all **B**elieve none

fu**rthe**r our superiority and

c**a**n only **B**e fel**t** on such an occas**I**on

in r**e**la**T**ion **T**o the one

ove**r** which we have

ponged off the roof

only to **B**e blown onwa**R**d

again by the wind.

1953

I had a serious fixation on the comedic talents of one Ernie Kovacs in my teens. His Sunday evening television show was a must to see. Most important in that show were three gorillas wearing derby hats called 'The Nairobi Trio.' These gorillas—actors dressed in that fashion including Kovacs with his trademark cigar along with various showbiz friends such as Jack Lemmon, Frank Sinatra, and Kovacs's wife Edie Adams—animatronically performed in mechanical fashion to various pieces of classical music. One of the gorillas had a pair of mallets that he often used on Kovacs's head, particularly at cadences. Another played the piano, supposedly, and the third—Kovacs himself—conducted, or at least attempted to do so. Typically, the laughs began when something went wrong, and one or more of the characters began the 'slow burn.' Every show had one of these skits, possibly two, and I loved them.

On one trip with my family, we had lost track of time and it was clear that we might not make it back in time for the Kovacs Show that then aired at 8 o'clock on Sunday evenings. I exhorted my father to drive faster, that we were going to miss the EK show. This was indeed a big deal. Luckily, we arrived just as it began. I watched—in poor definition black and white—as a timpanist made his way slowly up to his instrument, took very slow aim by bringing both his arms upward and back to nearly behind his head, obviously preparing to give a percussive fanfare as introduction to the show. But when his hands and the mallets came down to hit the drum, they didn't bounce. They didn't even make a sound. For someone had filled the drumhead-less instrument with white pudding. I suspect, by the shock on the performer's face, that he'd not been told. The mallets kept diving deeper and deeper into the mush until the performer's head almost disappeared as well.

I howled with laughter as my family stoically looked on. Apparently I'd crossed a line somewhere in my love for this comedian's work. Yet I couldn't stop laughing. And the timpanist slowly extricated himself from the pudding, dripping now from head to toe in it, and began to laugh.

When I heard that Kovacs had died in a car accident, I was grief stricken. This was sometime in 1962 by then. The story was that he had lost control of his car while attempting to light a cigar which, when his body was found later that night, lay just beyond his reach on the pavement near his extended arm.

it will be an**O**ther p**A**rt
of the same,

an**D** so absolutely understood

it **W**ill be perpetu**A**ll**Y** mutable

and not generally understood.

22

Yankees

i can rea**C**h the key,

s**ee*ING* I**ts i**mmort*A***lity.

he says i am immortal seei**Ng**,

i**TS** i**n**vin**ci**bility.

he says i am stro**n**g,

beyo**nD** its e**a**r**t**hly level.

namely h**O**w heaven woul**D**

have acce**p**ted h**a**rmon**i**ous forms
for **i**ts particular parts.
for this was certai**n**ly no**t**
th**e** fir**r**st time.

1955

In my early teens, my Uncle Frank bought me a present, a
baseball signed by most of the New York Yankees of the day.
Since I was then a Yankees fan, this was an incredible gift.

Here I could see the great players' signatures. Elston Howard, Yogi Berra, Mickey Mantle, Whitey Ford, Bob Turley, Hank Bauer, Billy Martin, Don Larson, Moose Skowron, Bill MacDougald, Enos Slaughter, Tony Kubek, and many others.

I'm sure I didn't thank my uncle enough for the gift, for it was certainly a treasure. And still is, since I now hold it in my lap as I write these words. Though it's far from mint condition, being nicked and chipped during the many moves and storage containers it's been in, it's still a wonderful reminder of when baseball was a game not just a business.

Now, I root against the Yankees, since they have the league's most money and buy their way into the playoffs by collecting the best stars from teams who can no longer afford their player's salaries. The best team money can buy.

it is equal to the square
of the sum

of its di**G**its.

w**E** might sta**R**t
and go on until we got a number
that worked.

the time i**S** come
for thee to reap,
for the harvest of the earth is ripe.

23

Alaska

for thoSe dISTinctions

   of conceptuAl Existences

      weᴙe known well enough

         by hiM the limp.

            still yOung bᴙown body

               waiTing foR life,

                  ears dead to the sound
                     tongue motionless.

1955

During my freshman year in high school I spent a lot of time reading. High School bored me, and I gathered bored many others as well. I remember one particular chemistry class where the order of the day, every day, was seeing how many spitballs could be thrown without hitting the teacher who spent the class writing on the blackboard with his back turned toward us. In my history class, the teacher circled the students around him as he told stories. Some, I guess, had historical value. I don't actually remember.

One of the things I often read was Popular Science magazine. Mostly, I think, because of the various advertisements for rocket fuel. One day, I encountered an ad that offered one square inch of Alaska for one dollar. The square inch came with a deed and a map of the approximate location—actually the ad said exact location, but that would have been impossible. This seemed wonderful to me. I could become an actual landowner in the wilderness of the great state of Alaska. It was too much to pass up.

And so I sent in my coupon and, after waiting a few weeks, received the proper document claiming my ownership and a map that suggested a location of my square inch of property. It probably should have also come with a photograph so I could tell whether my square inch was in a forest or at the bottom of a lake. After a time, though, I suspected the latter. But without such a photo, all I could do was imagine what it must look like. In my happier moods, I envisioned an open area next to a copse of trees with stark snowcapped peaks in the distance. In my less happy moods, I imagined it under a tree.

I knew I couldn't stand on it, at least not without trespassing on my many neighbors' square-inch properties as well. I certainly couldn't build anything on it, except maybe a toothpick cabin fit for a flea. But it didn't matter. It was the principle of the thing.

As time moved on, I forgot about my square inch of Alaska. I forgot about the trip I'd planned to find it one day and discover somehow what the view held for me from there. Now, as I age, I've remembered my property. Of course, I no longer have the deed. Nor my map. And they never sent me a photograph, so I have no idea where it is. Nothing left but memories of a great adventure I never had.

HE looked out ac**R**oss the me*a*dow
       sealed up *t*hose th*i*ngs
          which the thunders uttered
             dissolving the material u*n*iverse
              by carrying the mind
                up into a sphere
                    where all is plastic.

24

The Monster

determine whiCh Of the other
two, the IntelleCtUal side OF
man already admits that lIFE
is an incEssant struGgle for
existence.

1955

I have previously mentioned the "hand-me-down AM/FM
shortwave radio that stood four feet tall—mostly to house its
large single speaker." What I haven't mentioned before is the
name, "The Monster," I gave it due to its size in relation to my
own and the importance this radio held for me in my teen
years.

When I first encountered The Monster, I was most likely
six or seven years old, and it was the lone entertainment
center of our household. It was an extraordinary piece of
furniture as much as a producer of sound. It stood four plus
feet high, two-and-a-half feet wide, and at least that in depth.
All beautifully handcrafted wood, bamboo-thatched covered

speaker, and large multi-channel non-digital dial that lit up from within when we turned The Monster on. This light gave our front room an eerie glow when otherwise dark.

The top of this radio was not flat, but rather gently curved inward from its sides in a kind of exponential way so that it came to a point at the very top. All its wood was wonderfully varnished to a glow showing a rich vocabulary of grain that I often found myself staring at when bored.

The Monster began its life, at least for us, as our main source of family entertainment. But it soon became mine when my parents purchased a much smaller and more portable radio. It's second home then became the washing machine or utility room as it was called, where I set about to begin to understand how its magic worked.

I turned it around, took off the black tar paper rear, and was dumbstruck when I realized that it contained mostly nothing. Empty space. At the top, of course, directly behind the dial, was an accumulation of vacuum tubes and various resisters, capacitors, and so on, that I was soon to become intimately acquainted with. Below that level was the single huge speaker that belched it sound from behind a wonderfully designed shield of protective porous material. And, of course, lots of that empty space designers must have thought gave the sound further resonance but did not.

I remember watching the open backsides while the radio hummed with the sounds of static on its shortwave bands, and marveling at the complexity of the wiring and vacuum tubes not knowing as I soon would how brutally simple the damn thing really was.

The Monster then migrated to my bedroom where it stayed, I presumed, for many years until its death. There, I listened to Nome, Alaska, as well as stations in Africa, South America, Europe, but not Asia, unfortunately. And it was here that it gave me protection from my mother's bouts of heavy drinking, occasional slapping-me-around sessions, and senseless derision and comments about the pointlessness of my life. I would huddle around this radio in my bedroom as if my life depended on it, which it may have, and as I could hear her walk by my bedroom door, hope and pray she'd get the idea I was on to something important and leave me the hell alone.

I remember The Monster with fondness. Not only for the incredible things I learned about radios and their operation, the amazing things I learned from around the world, but the protective qualities given me at a time when I needed them most.

*A*nd i saw an angel standing in the sun. a

so*R*t of mixed flavour of cherr*y*-ta*r*t and

cu*S*tard pine-apple r*O*ast turkey. t*O*ffee and

hot buttered toast. a *m*an speaking from insight affirms himself. what is true of the mind.

25

Marching Band

but the dogm*a*

makes a **Di**_F_ferent **I**m*p*r**E**ssi**O**n

When it is he**LD**

by the we*a*k and lazy

that no man knew b**U**t he him**S**el*f*

1955

In my first year of high school, before I discovered the cello but having divorced myself from the piano, I sought an outlet for my musical performing needs by joining my high school marching band. Not playing any instrument in the band but aware of my great desire to join the group and its need for volunteers, the conductor agreed to let me play trumpet.

From that experience, I now consider the trumpet the most difficult to play of all instruments. And I have now taken lessons on every standard orchestral and band instrument. Something about the embouchure, the devilish fingering, breath control, or all three, prevented me from getting very far with it. But I learned the tunes,

75

and eventually marched along with the group with my music stand protruding upward from the instrument itself, my uniform well cleaned and properly displayed, and my body rhythmically swinging in rhythm to the meter of the music. It was, after all, great fun. Not particularly musically interesting, but indeed great fun.

I marched with the band on the football field beginning at halftime, performed two or three pieces during it, and left the field at the end of the game. And I performed with the marching ensemble during parades. In short, for the fall of my first year in high school I was a member of a group of performers needed by the community to continue school tradition.

The low quality of my playing, however, became clear when the conductor switched me unexpectedly to percussion after the holidays. But I didn't care. I wanted to play something, and the louder I could play, the better. Therefore, I gladly took up the snare drum, bass drum, and crash cymbals, the first of these instruments being the more difficult to learn. So I practiced the single stroke, double stroke, diddle, paradiddle, drag, flam, and roll. What made practicing really fun was that I could do it even without a drum. So I practiced everywhere using just my sticks. Or even pencils. At the dinner table. On my desk during classes. In bed at night when I couldn't sleep. On the bus on the way to school. Just about everywhere. Even on toilet seats in the restrooms.

Maybe this was the reason my parents so quickly decided to buy me a cello when the orchestra conductor needed cellists for the high school orchestra.

we are **Bo**U**nd to think

a goo*d* de*a*l about the proce*s*s
which has brought it to the state
that it were in.

and thus do we of wisdo*m*
and of reach

and of fa**L**l ov**E**r.

b*U*t the face**S** wh*iC*h follow,

being known an**D** conseq**U**en**T**l**Y**
the opposite ones that precede it.

26

Herman

the **s**hip had **tr**u**L**y m**O**<u>V</u>ed
*T*oward t*H*e east,

        and **i**ts face was as the s*U***n**.

        a body **I**s li*M*ited circumscri*B*ed,

                and f**O**rmed by surfaces,

                and ready to we**l**come an
enter*P*rise.

1955

Like most people, I tend to name inanimate objects I like. My first and last cello I owned for seven years was no exception to this. Why I named this instrument 'Herman' will be forever lost. For the last thing I imagine I wanted to put between my legs while playing would be a 'Herman.' But Herman it was, and remained during my active performing days. During my three years in high school playing Herman, he got me into All-State Orchestra and many other lesser but nonetheless important to me ensembles. During my college days, Herman led me through the six Bach Cello Suites and several concerti of repute, along with a much needed scholarship.

But, as with many good things I owned at the time, I sold Herman in order to help me pay for graduate school. Since then, I've played several different cellos but owned none of them. Nothing could quite replace Herman.

Funny thing, though, while I was quite fond of Herman, he did not seem so fond of me. For example, during very loud orchestral passages, I often found it helpful to place the tuning peg of its low string C in my ear to help me hear my intonation better. For some reason, on more than several occasions, Herman decided that the tension that peg held should be released, and its quick circular loosening gave my ear quite a ride. I still remember the pain not so fondly.

On other occasions, the endpin, the one that cellists stick into the floor or some other kind of gizmo to keep the instrument in place, would suddenly give way and Herman would either slide to the floor, or leave me holding it between my knees in a most unseemly position. Though not particularly painful, trying to rectify this while performing was both awkward and rather embarrassing.

Another problem arose when the instrument abruptly and without warning decided it didn't like my bowing. To retaliate, Herman would make all four strings prickly as barbed wire having the effect of breaking bow hairs. Not one or two as is forgivable, but ten or more which is not. For as the many hairs suddenly pulled free of their moorings, I rather looked like I was using the body of a small gray-haired old lady rather than a cello bow.

While other strange events also occurred—such as bridges breaking or sound posts slipping—these did not occur as frequently as the most annoying of Herman's strange preoccupations.

You might ask, then, why I continued to play Herman for over seven years of my life. To that, unfortunately, I do not have an answer. Maybe it was because I couldn't afford a better cello. Or possibly I didn't want to tell my parents that they'd spend their hard earned money on a dud. Of maybe I just didn't want to break Herman's heart.

More than likely, however, it was due to my love of cats. Not because catguts were the source of strings for cellos at that time, but because cats do the damndest things to get your attention.

she tried t*O* quit a*S* she spoke.

for wh**a**t we know **m**ust be **Vi*E***wed

and *I*s common.

*ThI*s ar**g**ument is **qu**ite we**l**l expressed

in pr*O*fessor lister

or**a**tio*N* fo**r** 1949

from which i now quo**te.**

yes.

true.

27

Mommy Dearest

the pra**C**tical view is t**h**e **O**ther s**O**und re**La**tion to these facts is to use an**D** command, not to c**r**ing**E** to those ty**p**e**S** and d**i**fferences of **T**he su**B**ject**S** might b**E** , de**S**pite a **S**ense **an**d secrecy that rema**I**ns n**O** l**O**nger in **t**he body when **th**e ac**t**ion is o**Ve**r.

1956

By titling this chapter "Mommy Dearest," I do not wish to suggest that my experiences with my mother were anything like those described in Joan Crawford's daughter's book of the same name. I do, however, wish to suggest that my mother had her foibles, and that they made a big impression on me during my life. While most of these may seem negative, I do not mean to suggest anything other than this was my take on them. Maybe someone else might have reacted differently, or taken them in other ways. I also want to stress that many of my reactions turned toward the positive as I got older. Just by having endured, my survival skills are possibly more honed than they might otherwise be.

My early days with my mother seem to me in retrospect to have been fairly normal. By the time I was six or seven, however, I began to see sides of her that I'd not witnessed before. One of these was her penchant for stopping by my bedroom every night and, if I wasn't yet asleep, reminding me that if I didn't get there soon I'd be a failure. Not just the next day, mind you, but most likely the rest of my life. Of course, this had the reverse effect on me of not being able to fall sleep at all. Closing my eyes and not answering her, yes, because then she would stop her rounds. But sleeping no.

I wonder now if this might have planted the seeds of my lifelong battle with insomnia. But I don't blame her for that. She was doing what she thought best, and, like most of us as parents, having little or no instruction on how to do it. How was she to know that I had an evil alter ego who took every chance it got to disadvantage me?

My mother also smoked like a chimney. By this, I mean, two packs a day were not unusual, filling our house with smoke for, after all, this was Arizona, where the air circulated through the house, over and over again with rarely a peak outside toward the almost continuous three-digit temperatures. This led me to my first experience with smoking since, after all, I was literally smoking all the time anyway with her second-hand exhaust. But I don't blame her for that either. She'd not wanted to move to Arizona in the first place. That had been my fault for having terminal asthma, at least terminal in the sense that I was going to die if I didn't move to a more arid climate. Of course, her smoking didn't help that either, but so what? She'd been raised in a house with smokers, and on the west coast where temperatures rarely exceeded the seventies.

I could also never be sick. No matter that I had a temperature of over one hundred, was blowing my nose to rawness, or coughing up my lungs, I could never be sick. So, by her logic, I had to be faking it. Lying, in other words. With this bit of twisted reasoning, she actually made me sicker. This irony seemed to originate from her mother who had by then converted, if that's the correct word, to Christian Science. To this day, no matter how much I fight it, I'm always well enough to do anything, no matter how I really feel. Even though I believe myself to be a man dedicated to scientific thinking, I cannot help myself.

Of course, my mother's drinking was another issue entirely. She could empty a bottle of whiskey faster than most people could empty an equal size bottle of water. And when she drank, she began slurring her speech and changing personality before the first glass was completed. I'd never seen anything like it, but my sister and I didn't wait around for a second swig before we headed for our rooms—remember it was too hot to escape outside, even at night—and lock our bedroom doors. What a race that was. Though my mother soon figured it out and the locks were removed on the pretense that a fire might break out and we could find ourselves trapped. In any event, it was during these episodes of drinking, occurring initially two or three times a week and then escalating from there, that I learned that her having children was something she'd never really wanted and that I, as the oldest and therefore the most responsible, was guilty as charged. I had caused her twenty-day labor—a duration that grew larger as time passed—and the pain that went along with it. My lung problems had caused all manner of worrying on her part. Our trip to Phoenix and my Dad's need to find a job, and on, and on, all exacerbated her problems. Oh, and yes, were she still with me as I write this, she would strike the word 'contributed' and written in 'caused.'

As she drank, my mother also became physically abusive. Not so much that I needed medical attention, but more than enough that at the time I probably needed psychological help. She'd slap me around a bit, which, as time went on created difficulties due to my growing size. In short, I grew larger than she and the risk that I might retaliate became more and more conceivable. On one occasion, when she'd began drinking earlier in the day, I ran away from home, an experience that led me to write my first children's book called Away Again Home. That book is fictitious, but nonetheless accurate in its basic concept. I remember my wagon that held food and clothes for at least one night in the desert and my sister begging me to return home.

In the end, my mother never discovered my attempt since I thought her retribution would be worse than any lesson learned.

It got so I dreaded the night when her drinking began and looked forward to her passing out. I never could figure out why my father put up with it, except that he was a good man, felt lucky to have married my mother who in her younger days was apparently a 'looker,' and he needed to work virtually seven days and nights a week in order to keep up with the rent, food, and house payments. Whatever the reason, however, put up with it he did.

Time passed, however, my sister and I went our separate ways. She moved to New York City and eventually North Carolina before getting divorced and moving back to Phoenix. I toured the country with various teaching jobs until arriving for good in Santa Cruz, California, where I taught at UC for over thirty-five years.

One event that sort of sums up her point of view involved my wife Mary Jane who then happened to be pregnant. Sitting in our kitchen at the time, my mother was thoughtful enough to ask my wife if her smoking would be a bother. Mary Jane responded that she was pregnant and that alone should make it obvious that my mother shouldn't smoke. My mother responded with an "I'm sorry," and lit right up. As if her saying she was sorry made it all right.

These events led to a kind of problem that neither of us could have predicted. My sister's close location to my parents in Phoenix put her more or less in charge of my aging parent's lives, my father's funeral, and eventually living with my mother for a couple of years, something I wouldn't wish on my worst enemy.

My mother, ever the outspoken teller of truth according to her own views as a racist, drunk, chain smoker, and continuing wallower in self pity, poured it on with her hosts—my sister and new brother in law. When all else failed, she would attempt suicide by hunger or some kind of drug overdose, sending everyone into total confusion, she loving every minute of it. These bouts were separated by her cackling over the fact that another one of her friends had died, and she'd outlived them. A striking oxymoron given her predilection for apparent suicide.

Once, when my wife and I visited my sister and her husband, my mother showed me the room where she then slept and secretly took me to the closet where she'd hidden her whisky and several bottles of Excedrin. I did what she would have done in similar circumstances; I turned her in to my sister.

When we visited my mother during her last years in a rest home where she would often beg for us to come, she'd then sit stoically for half an hour ignoring us.

One afternoon she decided to maintain an element of composure during our visit. She announced out of the blue that we should know that life was all about her, and no one else. This said with the calmness, determination, and pride of someone having been fussed over all her life.

I remember her funeral. She, like my father before her, had opted for cremation and so the few of us there, my wife and me, my sister and her husband, my cousin Jeannie, and my sister's available sons and daughters and their spouses, maybe ten in all, read the twenty-third psalm and called it quits. Maybe lasted six minutes.

That afternoon in my sister's home, she and I fell into our youthful rhythm of what had been wrong with Mother (she always insisted we call her that; no nicknames or other fond attributes allowed).

Please do not get the idea from my writing this that I did not love my mother. For I did. And, all things being equal, I wouldn't change a thing about my youth or her. She taught me how handle the world's cruelty and how not to live my life. And those are large lessons, let me tell you.

and its light reflEcted and looked at it and Cried with a loud Voice saying to all the fowls that fly in the midst of heavens route.

28

Sometime in my Teens

what **P**oor m**a**jesty sho**U**ld **B**e.
what duty is.
Let **I**t be your lot
to sla**n**der what you do
not u**Nd**e**rs**tan**D**.
l**e**t me **S**ee.

1956

Sometime during my teen years, I apparently suffered a serious injury to my eyes. Interestingly, though, I didn't know it at the time. Or maybe I've spared myself by conveniently forgetting the incident.

When, much later in 1977, I got an eye infection, it prompted me to visit a local ophthalmologist for a complete exam, which I surely needed in any account. After thoroughly studying my eyes and accounting for my recent infection, this ophthalmologist invited me into his office and asked me to sit down. This being somewhat unusual for an eye doctor's visit, I immediately suspected that something was amiss.

The ophthalmologist then startled me by asking if my family had any history of blindness. I thought not, which I later verified with my parents. He then apologized for having to deliver such bad news. Within the next five years, he predicted, I would go completely blind. Of this, he added, he was ninety-five percent sure. My retinas had, most likely in my youth, become seriously puckered, he told me, and they would worsen until they detached permanently. At the time, such a condition was not rectifiable. To say that I was thunderstruck would be an understatement—I had simply come for a routine eye exam. This kind doctor then supplied me with a series of self-diagnostic vision charts, which, he said, would indicate over the following year a slow deterioration of my eyesight. He then sent me on my way.

My post-ophthalmologist life, of course, no longer followed its typical energetic habits. I constantly checked my eyes and then my charts for vision changes, and I generally drifted about feeling dreadfully sorry for myself. I even occasionally walked around blindfolded in order to experience my eventual way of life. My respect for those so afflicted, as well as those with similar conditions, grew intense during this time. My creative work, in fact my entire life, ground to a virtual halt, and I maintained only the minimum of my other duties—teaching and attending meetings and concerts at the university.

About three months after my fateful eye exam, I awoke one morning and, as usual, checked my eyes for change. They seemed fine. This particular morning, however, probably due to some predictable stage that psychologists have named and figured to the hour, I took my eye charts and stuffed them into a nearby wastebasket. I'd simply had it with this way of living. If I was going blind, so be it. However, I had to continue on as if nothing were wrong until prevented from doing so.

As of the year 2000, and almost twenty-five years since my exam, my eyes had improved to almost twenty-twenty vision. Apparently I belonged in the five percent margin of error with which my ophthalmologist qualified his diagnosis. It's also possible he was wrong, or that I had simply overcome my condition with vitamins or positive outlook, or even by ignoring my condition—though of this latter possibility I had serious doubts. Whatever the reason for my continued good eyesight over those years, I was grateful. I was also thankful for not having spent that time so long ago continuing to mope about feeling sorry for myself.

Since the turn of the century, however, my eyes have deteriorated to the point that in 2011 I could no longer pass the visual part of a driving-license test. Desperately needing to drive, I visited another ophthalmologist in hopes that glasses would do the trick. She informed me that I had developed serious cataracts in both eyes, no doubt due to my childhood in Arizona and not wearing sunglasses. Hence, extensive diagnoses took place between both my new ophthalmologist and retinologist. The results of the various tests they conducted put me once again in jeopardy for blindness. I now had two things wrong with each eye. With a lot at stake, my two specialists agreed that my cataracts should be repaired first, and, given that my retinal puckering had not deteriorated since its first diagnosis, wait and see if it would now worsen.

I'm sure that doctors who've never had the surgery they inflict on their patients and view it as 'no big deal' are sincere in their beliefs. But no one can tell me that cutting into your eyeball, demolishing its lens with sonic booms, vacuuming out the remains, and then replacing that lens with a virtual one, all in fifteen minutes, should be considered 'no big deal.' But they do tell you that. Along with a series of potential complications, including the small chance you'll die.

My left-eye surgery narcotics made me unaware of what had occurred during surgery, for which I was thankful. Apparently I'd done what my surgeon ordered me to do well, and the results proved extraordinary. For my right-eye surgery, some two months later, I determined to remain awake and thus witness all the aforementioned horrors first hand. And I did. Don't try it. Even with narcotics it isn't fun.

Now, thirty-five years after my original diagnosis of going blind and more than fifty years since my long-forgotten injury, I can see fine, even without glasses. And, according to the California Department of Motor Vehicles, well enough to drive my car. But I do wear glasses, just to perceive the details of what I'm seeing.

aNd i hEard a v**oiC**e from heaven

Sung unto me aS **d**escribed

by a **K** ind that s**E**es it,

and moves on that wo**R**ld

und**E** r him

for root an**D** suppo**R**t.

h**E** is **T** o others as the k**I**ss of the world.

o**N**e seventh of the soul of these e**A**rth**S**.

29

Bayless

burning as it **WE**re a lamp

that fell upon t**h**e third part **O**f the river**S**

and therefore a**S** is **p**oss**i**b**LE**

th_a_t present**lY** bid the players
make haste.

and in the making of the world from pro**C**lus

spinning, and t**h**en cr**a**ck as they lay l*i*feless i**n** the earth.

1956

In my teens I knew a young man that worked for a local
supermarket chain in Phoenix, Arizona. His job was to help
patrons carry their groceries from inside the store to their cars
in the parking lot outside. Unfortunately, this job entailed
packaging the groceries inside at a temperature roughly sixty-
five degrees—Arizonans typically overcompensate for the
high temperatures outside—and push these groceries in a
basket into the lot where it was roughly one hundred and ten
degrees. Doing this many times over a one-day period caused
his heart to stop beating and he died. At sixteen. Apparently,

moving from cold to very hot temperatures and back again maybe fifty times a day is enough to kill even an energetic young man such as he.

I did not know him well and can no longer even remember his name. I do, however, find it difficult to believe that the practice of sending young people to their deaths in such a manner is still apparently legal. At least in Arizona.

and she Jumped up On to hEr feet.
one could say that a man can inject an idea into a machine
that will respond to a certain extent.

30

Evelyn Wood

shE *t*ook t*he* male foRm
   of that kiNd,
until shE *b*eCame a T lAst
   a wOman and goddess.

1956

At some point during my teen years, I had the good fortune to take a course in speed-reading from Evelyn Wood. My parents thought this was a waste of time. Reading, they said, was something done for pleasure, and the longer it took the better. I certainly saw their point of view and understood their reluctance in paying for my tuition to this short—two day—workshop, but for some reason I had to take this course. So they put up with my obsession and forked over the dough.

From the very first moment, I knew I'd found something special. Wood told us that everything we saw or did entered our brains and was there for remembering if we wanted. That we'd been taught, either through watching our family and friends or through explicit expression by others, that this was impossible. This inadvertent brainwashing had convinced us that we could not access the information our minds naturally made accessible to us. The one example she gave was that of so-called photographic memory. She said that this was not a phenomenon for the lucky few, but basically the capability of all. That we should take advantage of it by doing our best to put aside our limited view of ourselves and learn everything we could.

This concept was both seductive and daunting. I remember my skepticism and feeling that I should leave the workshop before she convinced me that she'd just seen a flying saucer, climbed aboard, and witnessed wondrous things.

But I stuck to my guns, knowing of my parents' reluctant paying of the fee and that were I to leave, I'd have to spend a lot of time doing nothing before I returned home. And then lie about where I'd been. I'd tried that once before and the thought of doing it again disturbed me immensely. So I stayed put.

The next thing that Evelyn Wood told us was that we should pull out one of the books stored beneath our chairs— it didn't matter which one—and begin turning the pages at the rate of one page per ten seconds (though I am not sure of that exact figure, it may have been less). She said nothing about reading the book, just to frame it in our view such that we wouldn't be disturbed by the motions of our colleagues, and begin turning pages.

Whether she said 'read' or not didn't really matter, though, we all knew what was what and that she was doing her job. Getting us to read a novel in roughly ten minutes or less and remembering all of its salient features.

As I turned pages, I began thinking what a waste of money. I wasn't remembering a thing about what I wasn't reading. But I continued, now quite curious about what she would do next, especially since I imagined all the other people in the room, most older than me, were experiencing the same thing.

Interestingly, as I turned the pages, the timing and the physical motion began to relax me and even have the effect of mesmerization. As this occurred, I gave in and let whatever was going to happen, happen. And it did. As I stared transfixed at the book pages passing by, the story represented there came alive. Suddenly I was speed-reading. Realizing this, however, caused me to see myself speed-reading in a way that forced me to stop speed-reading. And I made a strange grunting sound as the images that had come to life disappeared. As my belief that I couldn't do what I'd just done recaptured my brain.

I stopped my page turning.

Interestingly, as I looked around the room I could see many others had done so as well, and those who had not soon did, usually making the same grunting sound as me.

What an experience! Magic! Transformation of a sort. I had briefly accomplished everything Evelyn Wood had advertised she would do. And we'd only just begun. I had peered into a different universe, or so it seemed to me. A universe of incredible possibilities.

When all the class finally looked up, Wood just smiled. She knew she had us. And had us she did.

She then told us to pick a second book from under our seats, and to begin the same process again, but not to expect too much. This speed-reading thing was a life-long pursuit, not a get-rich quick scheme.

When I turned the pages on the second book, nothing happened except that I continued to wait for the magic to occur again. This expectation, by my alter ego no doubt, was as bad as my expectation that the process wouldn't work.

Maybe worse, for this time no moment of 'ah ha' occurred at all. I merely went all the way to the end of the book with nothing much changing. Thank God it was a rather small book, for with *War and Peace* I might still be there turning pages.

Wood then passed out a small test of sorts, with general questions that could have pertained to any book we read. Questions like "What was the name of the lead character?" and "Did anyone die?" are examples I remember now. We filled them out with surprising speed as we discovered the test was easy. I, at least, could answer most of the questions, and I imagined many others in the room could as well.

She didn't make us hand in our tests. Instead she told us we should already know how well we did. And she was right. I'd discovered that a part of me did remember some important features whether I thought so or not.

To describe this process, she continued to use the word "access." It was not that we didn't remember everything we'd seen, but that we still didn't believe we could access that information in a meaningful way. Her job, then, over the next two days, was to encourage us to give up the mistaken notion that we *couldn't*, and believe profoundly that we *could*.

And so, we spent the next two days—including the one we were spending then—in reading book after book after book. Tiring ourselves to the point that we'd forget what we couldn't do, and just do it.

And, of course, it worked. When I returned home after the second day, I proudly announced to my parents that I could speed-read. That the workshop had been a complete success. Of course, they didn't have the time for me to prove it to them. In fact, it was a hard thing to prove in the first place. Especially to two hard-nosed skeptics.

To this day, I find the experience of speed-reading, whether I choose to use it or not, has had a profound effect on my life. In a word, that effect is *belief.* Belief that nothing magical had happened during those two days. But if it had, I realized that it had happened not only with reading, but with everything that entered my brain. I could pull any information out—access it—at least in the short term. This had the effect of making me believe that nothing was beyond my ability to understand. Or accomplish. And with that belief, I learned faster and more completely. I taught better, composed better, painted better, wrote better, and on and on. None of these occurring because I was better than anyone else, but because I could access the information in my mind that was unavailable to others because of their learned biases toward not being able to do so.

Interestingly, I now read about Evelyn Wood as the person who taught reading as a skill of working down the page rather than left to right, something I do not remember her mentioning in the workshop. There, she'd barely said a word, just had us read book after book in any order, turning the pages at a certain rate no matter how much we felt we comprehended.

Had I misremembered my experience? Made it into something much larger in my life than it warranted? Had she had a special two days of experimenting with us? Had I just taught myself something she'd not considered?

I will never know for sure, because some sixty years having passed since I took the two-day course.

What I do know for sure, however, is that wherever it came from, the knowledge that I can access at least a larger portion of stored knowledge in my brain than I can imagine, has been the single most important thing I have ever attained.

And this knowledge is not mine alone, or make me special in any way. Everyone possesses this ability.

and she he**r** self w**a**s a **JOY**

      to ha**ve** been bo**r**n

f**R**om th**E** oce**A**n spra**y**,

     an**D** of hav**in**g noth**IN**g to do

with that capab**I**lity a**N**d **G**odlike reason.

31

High School

he stood At the edge of the cliff, aNd AlSo To desTROy the NOtice when he coMes back, if he has the logic, he shall not expect propoents.

1956

I have written elsewhere about the great mathematics courses I took in high school. My teachers in this subject were wonderful, and my grades and understanding of the subject warranted my best work. To this day, my love of the subject has not waned for I still work at it whenever I get the opportunity. In other subjects in high school, however, I did not fare so well. Biology, for example, was almost intolerable. Not only was the teacher uninterested in the subject he taught—as if he'd been transferred from teaching English— but he knew little about the subject. At the same time, this teacher was a tyrant for details. Especially on tests.

So, I set my alarm clock for early rising and spent an hour or two every morning before classes going over the text and doing the assignments. I don't remember my exact grades in biology, but I know I passed. I still hated the subject, however. Dissecting frogs—already dead or not—was not my idea of a good time. Nor was memorizing human body parts, most of which I couldn't see, and most of which as far as I could tell at least, did their jobs and that was all I cared about.

As I mentioned earlier, chemistry was even worse. The teacher of this subject simply didn't teach. Occasionally he'd tend to an experiment in front of him and us, but never once, it seemed to me, looked directly at the class while he spoke. Enduring one of these sessions was like going to gym. By the time it was over, we'd spent most of the energy our breakfasts had provided us that day. For a while it was fun. Then it became idiotic. Finally, it proved impossible to bear, and many of us just skipped class since roll wasn't taken anyway.

I have no idea what grades I made in chemistry, but know I passed them as well. I might have even gotten straight As since the teacher did not demand homework and the tests were incredibly simple.

All I knew at the time was that I wanted classes in subjects that the school didn't offer. Chess, for example. Or astronomy and physics. And, of course, more mathematics.

In the end, I survived high school, and later in my life when my kids complained about their studies while in these same grades, I could hardly disagree. I think I may have argued with them about good or bad teachers and that life was too short to miss the opportunities that the subjects themselves presented. But by then I knew they'd most likely discover the ideas these classes presented on their own like I did. And it came to pass.

three hits he h**a**th la**Y** o**N** twelve, and was j**U**st in time t**O** hea**R** it say th**E** four beasts had each six win**g**s about h**i**m, and yet to investigate and sear**c**h

outwhattheiconogra**phy** was.

32

The Garden of Earthy Delights

under the name of v**I**va voce,

to di**S**cover whether so**M**eone

re**Al**ly understands s**o**methin**G**

or has learnt **I**t **pa**rrot fash**i**o**n**

u**N**der that which he sh**A**ll no**T**
choose, but fall.

1956

During my youth while I attended Arizona School of Art
as I describe elsewhere in *Tinman*, I found four paintings
described in library books that held my fascination to
the point of obsession. And still do. Each of these works
represents some kind of extraordinary enigma. Not only for
me, but for those who've studied them professionally.

The first of these, *The Garden of Earthy Delights* by
and created in the late fifteenth century, is a three-paneled
masterpiece that unfolds into birth, life, and death—or
heaven, earth, and hell—as imagined by the artist. Each of
the panels is replete with various images of humans engaged

in the most incredible activities that humans are wont to engage in. While most art historians seem to agree that Hieronymus Bosch, a name derived from his given name of Jheronimus and the town of his birth Den Bosch, meant something by his depictions of pleasure and pain, no one can agree as to actually what that meaning is.

The second of these paintings is called *An Experiment on a Bird in the Air Pump* by Joseph Wright from the eighteenth century. This incredibly detailed and realistic work shows men, women, and children surrounding a strange apparatus depicting a reverence for science. Uncharacteristic for its time, it represents another enigma for me and most others who have had the good fortune to know it.

The third, *La persistencia de la memoria* (The Persistence of Memory), is a surrealist painting by Salvador Dali that introduced his extraordinary melting watches. When asked whether it reflected his views on Einstein's theory of relativity, he replied that it represented his perception of Camembert cheese melting in the sun. Dali, also a philosopher of note, enjoyed keeping a secret.

My last fascination is not one, but 135 separate works of art by Gustave Doré for Dante Alighieri's *Devine Comedy* created between 1308 and 1321. I literally grew up with an edition of this book in which each over-size illustration was covered in special tissue paper to protect it from imprints of ink from a previous or following page of text. Like Bosch's *The Garden of Earthly Delights*, these illustrations represent heaven and hell so incredibly realistically, that as a young man they mesmerized me in ways both horrific and pleasurable. Unlike Bosch's *The Garden of Earthly Delights*, however, the text of *Devine Comedy* helps explicate the meanings of the art. For me, though, not being fluent in Italian, these incredible works of art do more than simply reflect the poetry of Dante, they take it as a starting point only and move it far beyond the text and into the world of magical realism.

Each of these special works of art share many important things for me. One stands above all, however; that being *ambiguity*. No matter how horrible the atrocity depicted, no matter how lush or surrealistic the image, I come away from the experience with a sense of having gained more uncertainty than that with which I began. Surprisingly, this is immensely pleasing for me.

It is POssIble that the iNfusoria
under the miCroscope
do the sAme, the duSt whiSpered
as it glazed past the slick windOws.

33

His Dog Spot

they watChEd
how brAve
tHeY will all think mE.

1956

When my uncle's father and mother—Grandma Nettie and Grandpa Paul—went on vacations, they left their house next to my uncle and aunt's place in North Hollywood for me to guard and sleep there at night. This was great, for without the watchful eye of my aunt, I could stay up all night and watch movies. Even then the insomniac, I saw most of my early films alone in a spotless front room, interrupted by none other than Cal Worthington and 'my dog Spot.' Cal was famous even then for his unpredictable dress, strange sense of humor, and the various forms of life that 'my dog Spot' took. For example, Spot was often a tiger, seal, elephant, chimpanzee, or bear. In one advertisement, 'Spot' was a hippopotamus, which Worthington then rode. On other commercials, 'Spot' was a vehicle such as an airplane that Worthington could be seen standing atop the wings of while airborne. I often watched terrible movies just to see the commercials, something that one could not imagine today. 'My dog spot' was, however, never a dog.

According to some Internet sites, Calvin Coolidge Worthington (born in 1920 in Shidler, Oklahoma) made millions each year from his dealerships, and typically spent more than fifteen million a year on his own advertisements with him as the only star—excepting 'Spot,' that is. For those in disbelief of the extravagance of this character, a visit to the Internet will prove enlightening. His inventive characters live on in YouTube videos. All the major online encyclopedias list him as a major figure in the development of television commercials and automobile commercials in general.

Thank God for Grandma Nettie's and Grandpa Paul's house. Worthington now lives in Orinda, California.

*Author's note. Sometime during the day of September 8, 2013, Cal Worthington died in his home near Sacramento, California. He was 92. It was on that day that I wrote the above story, completely unaware of Worthington's condition. In fact, I had just days before checked the Internet to make sure my facts about him still living were correct.

and they were *f*Ull *Of* EyeS̲

withiN *Gre*en

of *ve*getAtion

and g*r* ey with water.

34

Howell

but i believe this is
        the aRgumEnt useD,

              but failed tO interpret

                  the fluCtuating appearrances

        of the markings they mapped
sO Well.

1956

When I was fifteen or so, my parents drove our family to Salt Lake City, Utah, where my father, Howell Nicholson Cope, was born. He'd been raised in the Mormon Church as the eighth of eight children, but renounced his membership in the church and moved to San Francisco in his early twenties. I'd heard that others of his brothers—most notably John and Frank—had followed soon thereafter, John to become a soundman for the Hollywood studios, and Frank a fairly well known painter in San Francisco.

    In any event, one of the points of our trip to Utah was to visit my father's mother who, at the time, lived in a home for the aged, her husband and my father's father having died earlier on of stomach cancer. I never met him.

The visit to my grandmother, who I had not met at that time either, has two versions. The first is my memory and the one I prefer. According to this version, my father parked in the lot at the home where my grandmother lived, and went in to visit her by himself. He exited not long after and rejoined us in the car. I remember it being a cold overcast day, with little to differentiate it from the others we'd spent in the city visiting my father's sisters and brothers who'd stayed home to tend to their inherited religion. Inheriting religions seemed like a strange idea to me. As if children were not allowed to have minds of their own.

The second version of the story, the one preferred by my sister who, in this case, may very well be right, had all our family going into my grandmother's room to visit her. In this version, my grandmother, who was probably very old at the time and most likely dying, shouted upon our entrance, "There's Howell," her youngest son, my father, but who was then standing beside her bed. Unfortunately, according to my sister, she had been looking in my direction when she'd shouted, and now pointed her aged bent forefinger directly toward me.

No doubt my father was very disturbed by all this. And, as the account continues, he began to weep, whether for being misrecognized as me, or by fully realizing how far his mother had slipped into dementia, I have no idea.

I didn't know what I then thought, for remember, this is not my memory but my sister's. As I say, her version could be right, especially since, if I'd understood the situation—being called Howell, seeing my father cry, and so on—I could have easily misplaced my memory of it.

Anyone else's version of the situation has remained unspoken, so I will never be sure. But given the angst it caused, I'm quite happy to have it stay buried somewhere in my subconscious mind.

bUt relatIon and connecTion

are not somewhere,

but eVerywhere

and always.

but inJury is wHat

inflicts On us so quick,

tHat No man kneW but he himself,

or lAstlY

so that it might NEver fall to the earth.

35

The Little Foxes

and that t**he**y can,
in fact,

Mimic the actions

of a h**u**ma**n c**omputer

ver_**Y** c l**O**se**l** y.

We go to **h**ero**D**otus

a**N**d pluta**R**ch

for **E** x**AM** pl**ES**
of fate.

1956

My maternal grandfather owned a fox farm near Big Bear
Lake, California, and when I was young my father took our
family there to vacation occasionally. On the way, we drove
the Rim of the World Drive, a highway that follows a crest
above the greater Los Angeles basin and in those days—
before smog—afforded extraordinary views of the cites
below. Once there, we stayed in a log cabin. During the day,
my sister and I scouted the various acres on this farm—or

was it a ranch—and once in a while caught glimpses of the fenced-in areas where the foxes lived. Lithe and young, they were beautiful to see. At night, things got quiet since we were at roughly seven thousand feet elevation, in a pine forest, and back from the lake and town. I remember listening to radio broadcasts of the baseball antics of the Hollywood Stars, predecessors of the Los Angeles Dodgers who would arrive later.

Once, after we'd not been to Big Bear for a while, I asked my mother how my grandfather made a living. It would, after all, take some doing to feed those foxes all the time. Rather than answer me, she went down the hall of our home in Phoenix and opened a closet door. When I looked into it I saw a large fur coat. I had no idea what such a coat would cost, but imagined it a lot more expensive than my parents could afford. I then realized what my grandfather did for a living. Occasionally now I fly over Big Bear on my way to points east and recall those vacations in the log cabin, the Hollywood Stars, the short-lived foxes, and my grandfather, long departed and no longer owner of the ranch.

but we are examples

qu**i**squ**e** suos patimur ma**n**es

and s**a**id go

and take the **l**ittle book
of the angel,

and b**u**bbling covered the noise.

i have never read an␣**Y**␣thing mor**E** confu**S**ed
and involuted.

36

Stan Laurel

absolutE **AN**d relative **s**pace

are t*h*e s**a**me in **F**i**G**ure and magni*t*ude,

mou**T**h**S** L**I**mp and op**E**n

wa**S** made an object of de**R**isio**N**

and did n**O**t c**ONT**inue.

1957

There is a short film made by the comedy team of Laurel and Hardy that, for me at least, seems to sum up their style in a single short scene. It seems that the two of them are driving an ancient car on the dirt main street of an old village without a name. As they do, they encounter a mud puddle in their way.

As was typical of their comedic process, they stopped the car and begin a discussion, argument, and then fight, a true benchmark of their characters. With Hardy ultimately winning this discussion/argument/fight, they slowly drive forward into the puddle. As they do, the car begins to slowly sink. Down, down, and yet further down. Just before disappearing completely, Hardy gives us one of those looks at the camera that says it all. How could this be happening? How could Laurel have been right? Can you believe this? And so on, ad infinitum.

This scene is, as was commonly the case, hysterically funny no matter how many times you see it. Especially since once they're completely submerged in the water, a few bubbles surface, and then slowly burst to add affect. And they never reappear.

My addiction to Laurel and Hardy has been lifelong, and I enjoy their nearly always unsuccessful pursuits as much now as I did when I was a kid.

Later on in life, I discovered that a friend of mine, Skip Wilson, had been lucky enough to visit with Stan Laurel only weeks before his death. It seems Skip had gotten an opportunity to interview him for some local paper and immediately grabbed the chance.

Skip told me his story of seeing a man, long past his prime and with his nearly lifelong partner long dead of old age, now calm and reserved, claiming in his wonderful self-effacing way that the partnership had been one-sided. That Hardy had been the source of the humor and that he'd been nothing but deadwood necessary as the foil. The straight man for the comedic exploits of his partner Oliver Hardy.

Hearing this made me return to watching the two of them and their exploits on the silver screen, and realizing the errors of Laurel's assessment. The two of them were perfect bookends, desperately attempting to keep the books shelved but never quite being able to do so. One without the other is impossible to imagine. It simply didn't matter who wrote the script—if there'd actually been one—or who directed the scene, these two were one. And, even with their failures, and there were certainly many of those, Laurel and Hardy at their best, were the best. The glances, the timing, the hopeless situations, and the reactions are the result of such honed skills, that the results are as timeless as the characters they played.

in His commentary in the book,

it was possible to elicit much

without describing their construction.

it would be of Very little use

withOut my shoulders.

if it were only
an hour separated from his will.

37

Stuck

rendings from earthquake

anD voLcanos.

this argumEnt iS

vERy wEll Expressed

in prOfessor jeffersons lisT er oration

from which i will quote,

althouGh not for this purposE.

1957

Near the confluence of the Salt and Verde rivers to the east of Phoenix, Arizona, lies a stretch of sand that bodes evil for those who deem it safe to pass over it in their cars or trucks. I discovered this while attempting to fish this confluence with a buddy of mine in the late 1950s. Most fishermen know that when rivers combine, fish are often plentiful, if for no other reason than that their chances for food seem to double. And so it was, that we parked in that sand and fished the single river the two made into one on a late summer's afternoon in August.

According to the maps I see on Google today, this spot is now part of a state recreational area. At the time, though, it was a bone fide wilderness for my friend and I. So we headed out that morning expecting to reel in a string full of trout or bass to show our friends, and boast of finding the perfect place on earth to fish.

Of course, as is often the case, the best laid plans of men and boys came to no good end, and we left the river mid-afternoon without a single bite. No problem, though, since the purpose of fishing—the real purpose of fishing—is to become one with nature, not to steal a part of its beauty.

When we returned to the car we found nothing disturbed, loaded our gear, and drove off. At least that was the plan. What actually occurred, however, was that I shifted the gear into drive, put my foot on the gas, and watched a plume of sand belch behind us as the car stood absolutely still. So I gave her more gas. Then, of course, the car began to shudder as the tires ground down into the extended beach on which we'd parked.

After a while of this, I turned the motor off and got out to take a look. What I'd done was create a hole in the sand, deep enough so that nearly the entire wheel was now lodged in it. The drive wheel. The other ones remained nicely placed on top of the sand.

We were stuck.

Not to worry, I thought. We were smart and could easily figure a way out of this mess. So I looked around for something to slide under the drive wheel so it could get some traction. After several attempts not to lose the location of the car while we searched, we found a slab of wood, strong and wide enough to do the trick, and brought it back to give it a try.

Unfortunately, each time we placed the wood under the tire—at least as far under as we could get it—the spinning wheel spat it out in disgust. The harder I pushed the gas pedal, the farther the wood flew. It was all I could do not to get out of the car and measure the distance by foot to see how far I could get the damn thing to fly. Maybe break some kind of record in the process.

In short, the plan failed.

Miserably.

We rocked the car back and forth to no avail. The hole was too deep.

I put the car in reverse without luck. A hole was a hole no matter which direction one tried to escape from it.

We hitched a rope to the frame of the car and tried to pull it out with the shift in neutral and the emergency brake off. By hand. No luck. The damn thing was too heavy.

After several other attempts that are too embarrassing to mention here, we sat down on the sand and stared at one another. By now it was nearly five in the afternoon with nothing much separating us from spending the night there. We'd told no one of our destination, and the odds of someone finding us were less than slim.

Walking or hiking out seemed useless, since the highway was several miles away and beyond our capability before dark. Might as well sleep in the car rather than on the desert where the scorpions and rattlesnakes hunted at night.

Without food or water, we paced and thought, thought and paced, pushed the car hopelessly, and paced and thought some more.

Nothing.

Finally, we made peace with our condition and settled in for the long haul.

That's, of course, when a desert ranger drove right by us on his way to the main highway. He then saw the fresh tire tracks in the sand we'd made on our way in. Figuring we were stuck in the muck somewhere nearby, he stopped, backtracked, and found us.

As he exited his vehicle, he smiled, trying not to laugh out loud.

"Stuck are we?" he asked.

No need to answer.

We found out after he'd used our rope tied to his truck to pull us out of the sand, that he regularly passed through this area looking for stranded idiots trying to fish the confluence of the Salt and Verde rivers. We'd just become his latest find.

Requisitely humiliated, we thanked him and drove back home, where our worried parents could see our sunburned faces again.

and that ye receive not

of her plagues

and will inhabit this earth,

saying yes to her very earnestly.

38

Cantata

the interro**gA**to**r**
    in the first line
        of yo**U**r sonnet
           which re**aD**s
          shall **I** com**p**ar**e** th**E**e to a summe**r**s day
      would **n**o**t** a spri**NG** day
d**O** as well or better?

1957

In my teens while living in Phoenix, Arizona, I heard of a composer who weekly wrote a cantata that was then rehearsed and performed on the ensuing Sunday. Much like Bach had. This seemed so incredible to me that, against my better judgment, I attended one of these performances.

Not knowing exactly what to expect, but believing the worst, I located the appropriate church on Central Avenue, and found a seat in the well-attended hall there. I figured the attendance was due in no small part to the lack of cost for the event.

At precisely three o'clock, a small orchestra and a sixteen-voice choir arrived on scene, tuned, the composer approached them with a great round of applause, and he proceeded to conduct his new work, or so the single-page program announced.

What I discovered was this. The music that I'd pre-ordained as bad wasn't so bad after all. That the composer had accomplished his goals for almost a year now with output soaring into the forties. And that the performance was not half bad either.

The cantata, clearly sacred not secular, had lyrics by the composer and pronounced the glories of God just as Bach's did. The style of the music, mostly modal and reeking of the consonant idioms of that time, at least in Arizona, still amazed me with its consistency and skills of counterpoint.

After about forty minutes or so, a huge amount of music for such a short composing time, the work ended on a major triad to thunderous applause by the audience. Clearly these people were followers. Not just of whatever God they believed in, but of this composer who was celebrating his own beliefs with his musical compositions.

As the audience filed out of the church, I waited in my seat hoping to get an opportunity to meet the composer-conductor and ask him why and how he did what he did. But I was disappointed. No sooner had the audience and orchestra/choir left, but so, apparently, had he.

I don't remember his name now, unfortunately, nor can I find any mention of these works or their composer on the Internet or any other place. Apparently, his music was a gift to God with nothing left behind for people like me to peruse more carefully. Not that I would spend much time at it, of course, but it would have been interesting nonetheless.

an**D** they as**CE**nded
up to heaven in a cloud.

and that i**f** you cut your **f**inger

very deep**l**y with a knif**e**,

Sho**u**ld it sus**t**ain the weights

with the **C**o**r**ds **ma** a**n**d np?

t**her**e wasn't even a shadow
on the **C**urtains, but th**e** light
remained there be player**S**.

39

Pulp Fiction

who adds this

doＥs not ｉＭpＬy

that it may ｎＯt bＥ pＯＳsible

ｔo ＣoＮstruct Ｅlectronｉc equipmeＮt

wＨich will think for itsＥlf,

Ａnd theＲefore in their ＳyＳtem

anＤ fＯrmed could not be Ｚero.

1957

During my teens, I read insatiably. And carelessly. From serious books on relativity to what were then called the 'pulps.' These latter books, called pulp because of the cheap bulk paper on which they were printed, and whose pages turned brown almost before you completed reading them, generally represented my fiction of choice. Mostly consisting of private detectives and science imaginings, these books could be quickly found in drugstores by their lurid and garish covers, typically including at least one buxom blond with her clothes torn revealing just enough skin to make potential readers—mostly young boys and men apparently—snatch them up with amazing alacrity.

Many eventually important writers got their start by writing pulp fiction with Raymond Chandler, Dashiell Hammett, and Ray Bradbury coming to mind immediately, though I also bought books by Isaac Asimov and Arthur C. Clarke with equal zeal. Many pulp magazines the size of pocket books also grew popular during this time including Black Mask Magazine and Astounding Stories.

Now looked upon by many as classics from the 1940s and '50s, these books and magazines tended to have two things in common. They were written fast, hard, and ruthlessly, and they paid no heed whatsoever to proper use of the English language. Typically full of sex and violence, they present a veritable field day for copy and content editors of today's literary standards. And most everyone, including me, loved them for that very reason, not in spite of it. We imagined the authors to be one of the characters in their stories. Rough and tumble men of ruthless character and wild of mind and spirit.

One of my favorites of the time was What Mad Universe by Fredric Brown, a true pulp genius, that had on its first edition cover a partially clad brunet, a moon of some kind, and a rocket ship, the later two sufficiently in its distance so as not to detract potential readers from the main thrust of the intent. In this book, the central character, and editor of—not surprisingly—a pulp science-fiction magazine, gets hit directly on the noggin by an arrant atomic bomb. He then wanders in an alternative future confessed with daytime imaginings of beings similar to his friends along with creatures from other planets and nighttimes of darkness thick with fog and peopled by wanderers in search of food an particulate deaths.

I recently fond an old copy of this illiterate nightmare so mangled that I could bearly make out it's cover nor it's soft-porn violence text.

And so,

he might even wake up sleepy minds.

and they **R**es**T** not day and night

saying, i cannot look without seeing splendor and grace.

40

Savant

it mAy he be conSidERed

aS a wedge beTween

the two inter*n*aL surFaCes

of a boDy spl*i*t by it,

and hence the fOrces
of the *zon*e,
*a*nd the mallet may be determined

by aUthority.

1957

In art school during my teens, I met a young man about
my age who had a singular talent. He drew cartoons.
The kind you see in newspaper comic strips and that I've
discussed my love for previously. His skills at producing these
were spectacular. And I was not the only kid in class who
noticed, for even the teachers were amazed at the agility and
speed at which he drew his amazing scenes and characters.

Unfortunately, he wasn't so good at painting or sculpting, the main reasons for attending art school, and thus he didn't remain with us for long.

During his short stay, however, I got to know him slightly. To say I was awed by his abilities would be a gross understatement. When I asked him how he'd learned to do the things he did with pencils and pens, he almost cowered and told me he hadn't learned them, the skill just came naturally. From the first day he'd picked up a pencil he could do it. He also told me he didn't use models for his drawings. That the figures he so easily created just seemed to leap onto the page. A kind of highly focused Mozart syndrome. He was the vessel through which his art passed.

Even more interesting was his speed at producing a full set of serial images. Then he'd add the ballooned text to explain the goings on. And, somehow, the words exactly fit the drawings.

I now know that I had met my first savant. Someone whose specialty seemed to come from his DNA rather than experience or knowledge. Naming it thus, however, does not really explain it. All I now know is that I wished then that I could have had some of what he had. My painting and sculpting came hard and took long hours. I envied him no end.

Later in life, when I encountered Calvin and Hobbes by Bill Watterson, I recognized something in the drawings and verbiage that reminded me of my friend in art school. Every figure seemed perfect and natural. The conversations between characters, while perfectly understandable, seemed philosophical in ways I couldn't explain. I doubt that my friend had blossomed into Watterson for the ages didn't match up. At the same time, however, my appreciation for my art-school buddy and Watterson's imagery made me realize that I'd had the good fortune to encounter two such prodigies in my life. Lucky fellow me.

and o**U**r monarc*h*s and *o*utstretched her*o*es,

the ***B***eggars of shadows,

and if i***T*** makes me grow sma*l*ler,

thn the wind*o*w stands o**p**en.
and o*f a* wa*r*m wind

whipped *t*he cur**t**ains p**ure**.

41

Vodka

what ignorant *l*ittle girl

solves pr**O**ble**mS** and ***t***he**o**rems

and is dis*CO*vered i*N* eu**C**lid?

*F*or all **the** diffe**r**ent kinds and q*U*antitie*S*

of t**H**e arts

b<u>**O**</u>und up ***W*** *I*th th**e**m?

1959

My first attempt to drink an alcoholic beverage came during my freshman year of college. I'd had sips of wine that people offered me before then, but not enough to actually get me inebriated to any degree. One Friday night, however, long before my twenty-first birthday—the legal age for drinking in the state of Arizona—I found the courage to visit a liquor store. I didn't have the identification needed, but hoped the counter person would let it pass. He did. And I, armed with a fifth of vodka in a brown paper bag, made my way back to my apartment with great expectations.

However, when I took my first sip I knew I'd made a mistake. No matter what friends had told me, it tasted like poison. Of course, it *was* poison. But people drank it and survived, why not me? I needed a mixer of some sort. I'd heard the word before, and knew what it meant. So I walked to the nearest place to get something that would cover the taste of the vodka. In my case, this was one gallon of root beer from the local A and W.

And so, sitting in the dark in my apartment again, with the radio tuned to the college classical music station, I mixed two parts root beer with one part vodka and took a drink. Not bad. It tasted mostly like root beer with a zing as a chaser. And with it came a nice warmth gurgling down my esophagus toward my stomach. I burped, and took another swallow.

At that time of my life, I hated Vivaldi, but that's what the radio was playing. One of his concerti for two bassoons. I remember it well. Not the actual music, mind you, just the general sound of it. What had been what I thought was badly regurgitated Bach previously, suddenly sounded quite nice. And I felt quite nice as well. Both the music and I felt quite nice. And so I drank some more. It pleased me in a way I'd never quite felt previously.

I drank most of the fifth of vodka over the next hour or so, feeling better with each belt. My mind lost its worries and everything was funny. Including Vivaldi. Including my life. Including everyone's life.

But then, it all went all wrong. I got dizzy. The room seemed to swim around my head. Then I felt nauseous. A need to toss whatever cookies I had in me, out of me. Vivaldi took on a sinister quality I'd never imagined his music to have had before.

To make a short story longer, I spent the rest of my evening praying to the porcelain convenience and flushing as much of the root beer and vodka out one end, and then switching position to flush it out the other end. It took me fifty years to come to enjoy Vivaldi again, and I've never had a single swallow of vodka since that day of my freshman year in college. Root beer, however, has remained a favorite. I know not why.

I staNd aloof,

and will no reConcilEment.

i know not what the word sublime meaNs,
if it be not the intimations
of a terrible force.

althouGh i do a calculation,
i do it in a hurried slipshod fashion.

42

Grand Canyon

There are stupid people

$$a$$nd many Such-like a$$s$$ses

of G$$r$$Ea$$T$$ cha$$R$$ge.

And n$$o$$w and $$T$$hen,

An amiable $$p$$ars$$O$$n

mig$$h$$t scrutinise

the transient creatures

that swarm and mu$$L$$ti$$p$$ly

in a dr$$o$$p $$O$$f water.

1960

During my second year of undergraduate studies at Arizona State, the university orchestra in which I played first cello took one of its two- to three-day trips, this time to the Grand Canyon. We spent our first day driving to Flagstaff through Oak Creek Canyon, at that time the only reasonable way to get there. The bus we traveled in took hours to go just a few miles as we encountered snow upon entering the canyon and that only got deeper the further north we went.

When we arrived in Flag, as most Arizona residents refer to Flagstaff, we found ourselves several feet deep in the stuff. Difficult to maneuver through to get to our dorm rooms at Northern Arizona State University, the location for our first night's stay. I remember this drive, my first real encounter with a snowstorm, as the view out the window slowly disappeared in favor of a blanket of white.

The next day proved quite the opposite, most of the snow having melted and the blue sky evident and filled with the famous blazing Arizona sun. We headed north with the magnificent crest of the San Francisco Peaks—so named by the locals imagining they could see the city of San Francisco from its lofty heights—looming to our left.

Approaching the Grand Canyon from the east as we were, the incredible view of the Little Colorado River chasm dove immediately down from a high mesa that provided a spectacular vista for those on the rim. Then, the views came and went according to the design of some highway architect using rationales known only to him. Or her.

We arrived at the Canyon Lodge with our musical instruments in tow, and found our chairs, music stands, and conductor's podium laid out ready for our noon performance. Unfortunately for some of us, these chairs, music stands, and podium were located perilously close to the lip of the canyon. But there we were and there we would perform, at least according to our conductor who, I might have guessed, was probably hoping for some gigantic resonant boost from the many miles across deep fissure near which we now stood.

While sunny, and with the snow swept clear from the stone deck upon which we were to play, the wind rode fast, harsh, and cold against our skin. In short, this was not an optimal place to perform Beethoven, whose *Egmont Overture* we were to play that noon. But, young in both body and mind, we unwrapped our instruments and prepared ourselves by warming up and tuning.

As we did, I remember my feelings of doom as I imagined us toppling off the cliff along with the rocky deck beneath us (and many such rocky perches before us from looking at the scree on various levels of the plateaus below). I'd have bet then as now that those rock falls had not had Beethoven as accompaniment as they loosed themselves into the mighty crevasse.

Nonetheless, we had promised Beethoven and Beethoven was what the small random crowd got, huddled as they were around our unmarked borders.

I can't imagine how we sounded that early afternoon. With our instruments going more out of tune with every note we played, and our fingers, lips, and mallets nearly frozen in our efforts to warm ourselves up in any way possible.

But we finished together, a good sign, and even received a free lunch for our efforts.

I still wonder, occasionally, how that concert came to be. After all, most performance venues for classical music are bad enough with four walls, a stage, and some kind of permanent seating. With our wood, metal, and skin instruments— plastic had not yet become popular—and our frozen digits and tongues and ridiculously out of tune fiddles and bones, we must have been a joke to anyone musical within hearing range.

But we did get applause. Maybe pity applause, maybe not. Maybe our audience was just glad to hear something out there not performed by the Chipmunks—a group singing four times faster than humanly possible and most likely an early example of electronically enhanced music very popular at the time.

Thank God our trip back went more smoothly, though I was certain I wasn't the only one on the bus asking if this performance was really worth three days of our lives.

perhaps this psych**okin**esis

mi**G**ht cause the **m**achin**e**

to guess right

more ofte**n t**han

would *b*e expected with a probab*i*lit**Y** c*a*lculation.

43

Party

and sLowLy and surely

they Drew *t*heir pl<u>an</u>s

*a*Gai<u>n</u>st us, and thE

nati<u>O</u>n hOlds it No

sin to ta*rr*e them to

cont***R***oversy.

1960

Almost every Saturday evening beginning around seven
during my last two undergraduate years, a group of seven
to ten students gathered at my apartment. Most would
bring some sort of alcoholic beverage—primarily beer, since
we were starving students after all—and once settled in,
we would discuss the serious issues which concerned all of
us. In brief, while the rest of the thousands of males who
attended ASU at that time were committing panty raids,
fraternity pranks, and attempting sexual conquests, we would
ponder Schopenhauer, Camus, Bosch, Sartre, Beethoven,

LeCorbusier, and on, and on. From philosophy to religion to radio astronomy, we dribbled out our excuses for reasoning as we slowly dribbled out our saliva, drooling as an excuse for forgetting lines from Beckett's *Waiting for Godot*. Sometimes the characters in our little ensemble changed. Sometimes our thoughts bordered on treason. Sometimes our tempers grew short. No matter, though, the party went on into the wee hours, guaranteeing the next day wouldn't really begin until the sun went down. And the hangovers lasted until midweek.

For anyone needing drinking water, visitors had to use the bathroom, for it was during those years that the kitchen was off limits (see the Saguaro Hall chapter in the first *Tinman* volume). Bottles and cans also had to be removed by those who brought them, for the management didn't approve of drinking, no less filling its garbage cans with volumes of empties. But everyone had a good time, proven by their returning the next week, and the next, and so on.

Women were certainly welcome at our soirees, but few came. When they did, they usually gathered their escort and left early, for the bawdy jokes became raunchy, and finally beyond the pale. They also did not want to accompany anyone in the condition they'd eventually be in after the *soiree* concluded.

It was a rite of passage, I suppose. Something we all remember some of, and wish we could experience again for some reason, but truly hope we never will.

Truth be known, I do not now know what exactly we discussed or decided at these parties. Of course, the *real* truth be known, I didn't know what exactly we discussed or decided at these parties even when I woke the next day.

the proposed use of the **WO**rk m*i***G**ht be
what the classes are about. and i saw an angel

standing in the sun, and r**O**un**D** the neck
of the bottle was a paper label.

(1960-1969)

44

Pigs

a**n**d wri*T*e them n**ot**

as the voice which i hea*R*d from heaven

s**pa***K*e *U*nto me a <u>**GA**i</u>n.

that wh*i*ch is vu*L*g*a*r*l Y* t*A*ken

for i**M**movab*L*<u>E</u>

s**pa**ce

as <u>**S**</u>uch, *I*s *t*he dimension

of a subte*r* raneaneous cave.

1964

I found my true pet of choice while in graduate school at
USC—Guinea Pigs—the longhair or shorthair varieties that
live in the moderately high regions of western South America.
There they act as both pets and, when the going gets tough,
food for the families to which they belong. For me, however,
I was just happy to have them around to keep me company.

143

Few people are aware of the wonderfully social benefits of owning and caring for Guinea Pigs. All that's really required is a fair-size cage, depending on how many you have, and food and water. The food is usually hay or alfalfa pellets. For this modest investment, you get an extraordinary payback. They'll talk to you, nip at your fingers without intent to hurt you, and jump up and down with happiness for no other reason than just being alive.

I kept Guineas for several years, including my first two years of teaching in Kansas and my first year of marriage. Many visitors found it strange until they too discovered the wonders of animals that celebrate existence the way the little furry pigs do.

I also brought several generations of them into the world serving as standby midwife. Their litters, usually four to five pigs in size, prove rewarding beyond imagination. The little ones squeak with delight almost from the time they're born, and as they grow they walk nose-to-tail behind their mothers. Watching these kite-tail-like single-file lines of them is a wonder. For as mother does, so do the little ones, each delayed by a fraction of a second so that it seems as if the group is a flailing kite tail behind mom. Mother leaps, and each one in turn leaps as well. Mother turns, same thing. It's really something to behold.

Since I have switched my allegiance from Guinea Pigs to cats as of late, I realize how much I miss my guineas. Their squeals of delight, their smell except of urine, and their eyes of forgiveness. I suppose the latter I miss the most. For no matter how I've ignored them or maybe forgotten to feed them on time, they steadfastly jump for joy when they'd see me. Not like dogs do when eyeing their masters, but as little faithful bundles of joy.

and they can well be on horseback,

but th*i*s gallant **C**uriouser and curiouser
person crystallizes them
as animate beasts.
and men will not stop,

but will wor**k**
into finer particulars
and geometrical questions
pro*Vid E* the treatment.

45

Subscriptions

thus, tHo Ught alice,

aND the flesh of all meN,

the appOinteD and the unappoInted day,

can be made to play

satIsfactoRily thE part

of the imitation GamE.

1965

Sometime during my career as graduate student in music at USC and living alone on Lime Street in Inglewood, California, I made the mistake of answering my doorbell. I opened the door and found a smiling and vivacious young woman who began talking before I could even say hello. She was, she said, working her way through school and needed just one more person to buy a subscription at great savings to earn her first year's tuition.

I tried to speak, but before I could she'd inched her way through my doorway and continued her spiel. It seemed she could offer me subscriptions to incredible magazines at one-tenth their newsstand cost, and wasn't this amazing. And she rattled off several names of magazines I recognized.

By then she'd found a chair and sat down while politely waving me to join her. All the while continuing to talk. An amazing feat. As I watched her rattle her mouth away, I was taken by her sheer determination. She was indeed an alpha in the world of salespersons, and I was witnessing one of the best in the business. And at such a young age.

Before I knew it, she was asking me which of the forty or so magazines I wished to select for four long years at nearly no cost. And, believe it or not, I was letting her help me choose.

When she finally said goodbye and good luck to me, I realized I'd been had. Four years of ten magazines arriving in the mail each month, none of which I would ever read. I was too busy to actually look at *any* magazine, no less the ones she'd pedaled me. All at the amazing price of thirty-some dollars per month. For four years. And here I was barely able to pay rent and buy food. What had just happened?

A few days later, and much to my relief, someone called me from the company the young lady worked for. I assumed it was for my delinquency of first payment or some other offer I couldn't refuse. Instead, it was a person asking if I really wanted all the magazines I'd signed up for. I told him no, and he revoked my bill then and there.

This seemed impossible to imagine, so I asked him why he was doing this. And he told me. Apparently, this young lady had walked through my neighborhood creating a wide swath of successful sales in a single afternoon leading to several complaints about her techniques. This man was in charge of checking to ensure more complaints were not forthcoming. I asked him how many people he'd called opted out as I had. All of them, he said.

Oh, he said, and by the way, he'd fired her.

that i can keep you**r** coun**S**el al**ive**

an*D* no*T* mine own,
be*Si***d**es t*O* be that
by all o*F* these wor*D*s
anywhere take up*O*n me
to define a*LL* of the kind
he left f*AR* behind u*S*.

46

George Perle

and

whi*C*h

t**e**ll**s** him

to c**a**ll fo*R*

th*E* **S**hoes was

ma*D*e an objec**t** of

der*I*sion and did no *T*

COntin**u**e his co**mme**nt**ar**y.

1965

I studied with George Perle during the summers, while I did my graduate work at USC. This meant fewer but longer sessions with him than with my composition teachers during the regular school year.

My style of composing at the time was quite different from his, and I contemplated long and hard as to whether such study would be useful. So, I stuck my toe in the water with a first lesson, knowing as I did that I could withdraw from the course without penalty. I needn't have worried.

George was a wonderful man, of good humor, strong insights, and clear explanations of his points of view. Never did he dwell on our musical differences, but simply regarded my music as it was and tried to help me make it better.

Given his later books on serial music, I'm sure he would have preferred a student more interested in those matters. But he never said so, and we spent our time together discussing serious musical issues laced with occasional stories of his eastern establishment colleagues.

What a pleasure. Especially when I showed up with my three-and-one-half octave Melodica that I blew into and played with both hands because I didn't otherwise have a piano available.

uP

to the

tenth book,

a new land waS

theRe but when the

bOy growS into a man

and is master oF thE houSe,

he pullS down that wall and buIlds

a new and bigger One. A question

of time, but faiLed to interpret the fluCtuating

appearances of the markings they mapped sO well.

One that was a woman, sir, but rest her soul, shes dead.

47

Discovery

the difficulty of the *S*ame **kin**d of fr**i**endliness occurrin**g** bet*WE*en **j**ust *A* m**a**n and **m**ac**h**in**e** a**s** be*T*ween **J**u*S*t a w*Hit***E** *O***R** green man.

1965

In my three years as a graduate student at USC, I found many interesting ways to make money. Playing piano in bars, ghost writing film scores, and, the shortest of my gigs, as copyist for a film studio in Hollywood.

This particular job requires some serious describing, since it entailed many different but related facets.

For the most part, Hollywood composers in the sixties created handwritten scores, often a collaborative effort since many composers in those days—and still today—required orchestrators, those people who take a rough piano part and turn it into a full orchestral score. After that, composers added or subtracted corrections as they saw fit.

By the time the score was ready for part copying, two or more people have had at it, and it's not particularly neat. Copyists, then, were the ones who ensure that members of the orchestra have only their part to perform when the time came. After all, the complete score was usually extremely long, and the players could not get through it without spending half their time turning pages, and the other half attempting to find the line each of them played.

Typically, copyists had plenty of time to create parts from scores. Even so, the pressure was high since one mistake could make the orchestra stop, often resulting in costs of a thousand dollars or more of studio time. This caused heads to roll, and one mistake at this level got you a warning, and two got you fired.

Then there were changes that composers and conductors made while the orchestra was rehearsing and performing. These were critical, since the music might not fit the scene properly—remember that orchestras play and record in front of screens where the film is showing—and needed cutting or addition of material. These situations often required immediate response from the person making the cut or addition, and the copyists to make changes in the parts.

This was where emergency copyists came into the picture. New hires, people like me just beginning as copyists, usually got stuck in a glass room just off the orchestra stage. We sat there ready for emergencies such as the one just described. Then, the parts were handed back to us, and we made changes faster than humanly possible. And without mistakes.

Of course, these situations were not without their perquisites. For example, we got to sit and watch most of the time because there weren't that many changes requiring our services. However, when the situation arose, we got one chance and one chance only. Usually a short break was called and we got busy.

Here—in this glassed off room—we couldn't make mistakes. Not one. Time was of the essence and the pressure enormous.

I worked in one of these sweat shops for a week and discovered it wasn't worth ten times the money paid. No matter the time spent doing nothing, it was not really doing nothing, for all we did was pray that no one would change anything besides a bowing or a couple of notes. But they most always did. If for no other reason than they didn't like a passage and wanted changes that required less time for us to make changes than it would for the conductor to read them off while the performers penciled them in.

When I began, I worked with several people and none lasted until the end of the week, when I decided to quit. I hadn't made a mistake. Yet. And, like many others in the room, had begun inhaling Tums, and thinking seriously about using any kind of illegal drugs I could get my hands on.

Times have seriously changed since then. Now scores are created and stored in computers where they can be altered quickly and then printed out anew in seconds. No reason for the sweatshop or anything but a single person skilled in whatever application used to create the score that will automatically produce new parts.

Ah, the good old days.

she tRied to fancY the fLamE of a candle, but failed to interPret the fluctuating appearances of the markings they mapped so Well In a chain or any ignominiouS baggage.

48

Knives and Toes

As we often see

AgaiNsT some storm,

the moon stiLl shown.

buT now thERE wEre

larGe ClOuds

in which the Great relative rest occurred.

1965

Many of my teachers in graduate school at the University of Southern California in the 1960s seemed to know everything. At least they thought so. They were smug, pretentious, and arrogant, no matter the narrowness of their field of study or lack of accomplishments.

Sometimes this was simply too much to take. But, not wanting to engage them in verbal debates since that might jeopardize the thing I was most eager to get—the paper with a degree printed on it—I hitched up my pants and took it. I felt then that their egos were like the penises of a motorcyclist's broken muffler; a sign that the louder the latter sounded the smaller the former actually was.

Unfortunately, this mental juggling didn't work long. My frustration had to have another avenue for escape. And so it was that, at age twenty-three or so, I took up a hobby. I called it "knife pegging 'tween my toes," for wont of a better description.

This expression, while prosaic and not very elegant, portrayed my actions completely. It went like this: come home, grab my pocketknife, open it, go into the backyard, take off my shoes and socks, spread my toes as far apart as I could, and then plant twenty-five consecutive knife tosses between those toes without, hopefully, sticking my pocketknife into a one of them.

Of course, I was safety conscious as I began, so many of the tosses did not land as they should have but further out in the lawn. These I did not count. So, before my exercise had been completed, I'd probably tossed the knife many hundreds of times.

Interestingly, I never grazed even one of my tiny foot digits. And I threw pretty hard.

Even more interestingly, my little game worked extremely well. By the time I'd finished throwing, I couldn't remember a thing that had happened that day without working hellishly hard on it.

I have not tried this since, even though I've attended many a conference and concert that paralleled if not surpassed my graduate schooling. Somehow, placing myself in danger of losing body parts had cured me of needing to do it anymore. I am grateful. For, as I look back on it, the perversion of what I was doing strikes me as clearly the mark of a man coming unhinged.

Or motion of this other body

gone incorrectly refuted by him.

in other words,

when he would call

the inhabitants to go to mars,
it was lit up by a row of lamps.

49

Buster

at relative re**S**t

         is the **c**ontinu**A**nce

   of t**h**e body

     *ke*pt in the s**a**me

      p**ar***t* **O**f the shi**p**.

1965

I discovered the film *Sunset Boulevard* during my graduate school days in Los Angeles. I'd heard of it many times previously, so was looking forward to seeing it even though my first showing was via television rather than on the big screen. Actually, it was premiered five nights in a row at eight in the evening by one of those TV stations in LA that took movies seriously enough to repeat them over and over again. And I took advantage of all five presentations. I loved the film. It was not until years later that I discovered that by not watching the credits closely enough, I'd missed the fact that my uncle John Cope had been soundman for the film, thus making it all that much more personal for me.

The film, for those that have not seen it, is about Hollywood in the forties, and particularly about a has-been silent film star called Norma Desmond—brilliantly played by Gloria Swanson, herself a somewhat washed up actor at the time the picture was made—and an out of work screenwriter named Joe Gillis—played by William Holden. The film captures the underbelly of Hollywood in true *noir* style. Black and white with shadows and strange camera angles to die for. Written and directed by Billy Wilder, this picture should be on everyone's top-ten list of movie greats.

What was and still is of special interest for me were the many subtle and not so subtle layers of real and unreal characters that appear here and there in the film. For example, Desmond's butler and former husband is played by director Erich von Stroheim. Other characters play themselves, as is the case with Hedda Hopper—gossip columnist—and Cecil B. DeMille—director. H. B. Warner and Anna Q. Nisson also play bit parts as themselves. This gives the film the surreal quality of being both real and not real simultaneously.

One of the smallest roles, however, goes to Buster Keaton, who characteristically recalls his silent film days by being, well, silent. He's the fourth in a hand of Bridge as Desmond's partner and the scene plays in counterpoint to Gillis losing his car.

I could go on for hours about *Sunset Boulevard*, but won't. My reason for bringing it up is that some fifty years after first seeing the film, and now having seen it several hundred times, I decided to take it one step further. In a short story of mine called Norma, I mix the soup begun with *Sunset Boulevard* a few steps further. For example, in this short story—which, by the way is published in a book of short stories of mine called *Of Blood and Tears*—the two men who attempt to repossess Joe Gillis' car near the beginning of the film are played by my Uncle John (the soundman for the film in reality) and my Uncle Gordon (a painter) who remark about how closely Gillis reminds them of William Holden, but just couldn't be him.

As things proceed in my story, the two brothers witness the burial of Desmond's chimpanzee, the swimming pool full of weeds and rats, and thus much of the full beginning of the film. Then the short story ends with my uncles going their separate ways, Gordon to his studio in San Francisco—true— and John to do the sound work on the actual film portrayed as a realization of the supposedly true story. William Holden then plays the part he was destined to play, that of Joe Gillis.

In short, that which was a wonderfully convoluted situation in the film itself for anyone that has any knowledge of the history of Hollywood becomes convoluted squared. And, of course, Buster Keaton has his silent walk-on in my short story as well. He had to. For Keaton was the most interesting actor in the film. His patented deadpan look represents a perfect cameo for what the silent films of early Hollywood represented.

has your audie*n*ce been most free
and bounteous?

the idea**l** arrangement **i**s to have

a te**L**epri**n**T**er keep

c**O**mmu**N**icating bet*W*een

the two room**S** at corn**E**rs.

*I*t spins sidew**A**ys,
rubber whee*LS* whining in the night
at the c*OrN*er of the street.

50

Bars

tommy do**B**kin**s** is dead, a*n*d said g**O**
and **T** ake **T** he li**t**tle b**O**ok whi*c*h is
op*en* in the hand of the ange. she will
kneel down and look along the passage,
and she he**r**self was sa**i**d to have been
born fro**M** the o*c*ean s**p**ray of broad
stret**C**hes of **p**opu**L**ous country.

1965

As a graduate student at USC in the mid-1960s, a fad developed in the neighborhood where I then lived. It seemed that Los Angeles County had no laws against public nudity, and many small areas in and around the city were therefore exempt from LAs restrictions. Partial nudity then became popular—not so much outside but in clubs—by parading barmaids around without shirts and bras. These businesses became known as topless, and what had hitherto been half-empty establishments suddenly drew large crowds. Mostly men, of course, but customers of such places had been primarily male anyway.

Once, when I was visiting my aunt and uncle in North Hollywood, the question rose as to whether or not, being of age by that time, I visited such clubs. Not wanting to lie about it, I told them I had. Not regularly, of course, but occasionally.

My uncle took issue with this. He told me that I was wasting my time. "You've seen one pair, you've seen them all," he told me.

I thought about this for a moment, and then said, "No, you haven't."

And narrow navy-crowd*E* d S*e*a**S**

out of this subject, and we he*r*e

di**S**patch the machine. it might, for

instance, type out mathematica*l*

equati*o*n*s* or sen*t*ences in eng**L**ish to

Me.

51

Cage

i**f** you P**r**e**ss** *A* ston**E**

with your *f* ing**e**r

to see if it will shrink any further,

the b*L*ack around you would stretch back

to the white mountain now mi*L*es away.

1965

Composer Paul Palumbo once—most likely in 1976 sometime—told me a story about John Cage and the semester he taught at the University of Cincinnati in 1965. Cage had been appointed composer-in-residence during that fall, and apparently had been expected to teach classes like any other academician. Of course, the words 'Cage' and 'academician' were about as remote from one another as 'intelligent design' and 'logic.'

The mix was, according to Paul, strained at best, and chaotic beyond belief at worst. In short, whenever Cage arrived on campus and recognized, the word spread, and before he'd entered a classroom, he was pinned down by hundreds if not thousands of students and probably faculty asking questions that took a great deal of time to answer. Not because Cage's responses themselves were long in terms of words, but because he often spoke slowly and very carefully, creating perfectly complete sentences and forming credible responses. Besides that, he often spoke softly which no doubt added to the confusion, many people asking questions already answered, and so on.

Before long, according to Paul who was, I believe, not actually present for these tidbits but one of a no doubt long line of storytellers passing the rumor along, the university stopped insisting John teach, and simply left him to do whatever it was he wanted to do at the time.

Paul had no idea why the university had given Cage his position in the first place, even for just one semester. After all, no one in music was unaware of John's views and the impact and controversy they represented. His many pointed barbs at standard academic approaches to teaching music had been well documented and should have been known to those in charge of his selection. But appointed he was. Probably because someone in the upper administration of the school had the idea that hiring Cage, if only for a semester, would attract high visibility to the school and hopefully many new students to the university. Paul doubted that it had. In fact, he told me if Cage had any effect on enrollment, it had probably been for unqualified students to attempt to meet entrance requirements.

When I met Cage later on in 1980, I offhandedly mentioned the University of Cincinnati to him at which point he gave me one of his patented smiles and then giggled slightly with that off-putting look that told me not that the subject was off limits, but did I really want to speak about something that was that ridiculous.

I didn't.

the second the universe

s*l*ay nor was it genera*l***L**y

un*d*erstoo*d* can *Be* fo*rm**U***L*a*T*ed

a*S* s*ILENCE*, which ca**n** neither be proved

nor disproved within the syste**M** th**AN** not.

52

Coaster

an**D** he **S**hewed me **A** *P*u*rE*
river of wa*TE*r of life o**N** a level
instead of **p**ilin**G** it into
a mountain. th**e**y hav**E**
Cont*r*iv**e**d to make of h**i**s
te**RrO**r the most harmless and
ener**g**etic form of a state.

1966

I have always been fascinated by films, probably due in no small part to my summer residencies at my Aunt Lois and Uncle Frank's home in North Hollywood in the 1950s. As well, many members of families on my mother's and father's sides were heavily involved in the business at that time and since.

Thus, it was no surprise that, when one of my graduate student friends at the University of Southern California asked if I would participate with him in the production of a student film I accepted.

As it turned out, he had already shot most of his project and left the action for last. The most difficult of these, he felt, was one in which he wanted his character, in a dream sequence, to be a roller coaster—not just take a ride in one, mind you, but *be* a rollercoaster.

I was curious how he would film such a dream, and so accompanied him to an amusement park south of Los Angeles in Long Beach which, I believe, has since been torn down. The park remained open until at least midnight in those days, and it was his opinion that most of the crowds would be long gone by that point, and that we could, if luck prevailed and our choice of a Monday night proved wise, find and ride a car with no other people in it.

His choice was correct. We not only found one such ride, but many. And it was then I discovered what he had in mind; attaching a camera to the front end of a lead rollercoaster car with him and me in the front seat, me holding a large brace of lights focused on the tracks to give the impression for the dream he then filmed.

While strange, none of these things seemed particularly difficult, and I remember asking him why he'd needed me along.

"You'll see," he said, and on with the show we went.

The first few takes proved quite unsuccessful. Not due to our inability of immediately viewing the shots which was not possible since film in those days took at least twenty-four hours to develop, but because he could see the camera mounted on the front of the lead car wobbling no matter how tightly we attached it. After all, we'd had to tie it after the car was in motion, otherwise the ticket taker would have seen us do it and invalidated our ride. Filming from rollercoaster cars was apparently not legal in those days.

After these initial failures, my friend decided the only way to make this work was to have one of us take the camera over the front of the car and hold it steady during the ride. And, since I was the gofer and he the director, it was I who'd be the perfect sucker to do it.

This, I hadn't planned on.

But, after several attempts at getting familiar with the ride and with his assurance that he'd tie me there thus making it impossible for me to fall or otherwise get hurt, I stupidly agreed to make one attempt at it. No more than one. One only. After all, this was not a paid gig.

So, with the midnight closure looming as our deadline, we took off on our somethingth number of rides that evening and probably our last, and he roped me into position on the outside front of the lead car. Since we were moving, I didn't really have much time get sick or protest what was about to occur.

Once tied to the front of the car, my friend handed me the camera, pointed straight ahead, and took his position as lighting man for the film. And there we were. Him, standing in the car attempting to focus his lights on the tracks, and me attempting to hold the camera forward as steadily as possible and wondering, especially as the coaster took us nearly straight down toward the ground at ungodly speeds, what kind of idiot my parents had raised.

But we survived the event. Unfortunately for him, the ticket taker called the cops as we arrived back at our beginning point, and we had to run for our proverbial lives. Him carrying the lights and me the camera with various ropes trailing behind.

We both survived, never returned to the rollercoaster in Long Beach, and the film as it turned out blank. I'd forgotten to push the shutter button to begin filming.

He still passed his course for which the film was the final project, and I regained most of my senses and graduated on time.

yet must not we *p*ut t*h*e s*t*rong

law on *h*im t*O*gether with some others not yet discovered,

*b*ut somewhat s*i*mil*a*r, or were separated joined together again.

53

MJ

the greek play ex*p*re*S*sed the s*a*me se*N*se,

   and a*F*te*r* thr*e*e days a*n*d an half,

*t*he *s*pirit *O*f life,

f*RO*m absolu*T*e and relative

   b*Y* their propertie*S* of *ca*uses and effec*t*s.

1966

I was introduced to my wife to be, Mary Jane Stluka, by two mutual friends in 1966 as we drove to and from a restaurant along a small river west of Bentonville, Arkansas. Interestingly, Mary Jane, interestingly, was not with us at the time. My two friends in the car were married, with the husband a geographer on campus, and his relatively new wife a gifted pianist there. I was a newly hired composer, piano tuner, theorist, cellist, bassist, and erstwhile conductor. Mary Jane, MJ to them, was a pianist at Cottey College, located in Nevada—pronounced with a long 'A' before the 'D'—Missouri, some distance from Pittsburg, Kansas, where the three of us in the car were employed.

They described MJ as a gifted musician and pianist, attractive, unattached, and, they thought, lost in the wilds of a girls' school far from any town or culture. This, even though she lived at this point across the border in Fort Scott, Kansas. While this may seem confusing, forget about our trip to Arkansas (pronounced, by the way, as Ar-Kansas, as in Kansas the state), and concentrate only on the triangle that outlined fairly equidistant sides with Pittsburg to Fort Scott being one side, Fort Scott to Nevada another, and Nevada back to Pittsburg the third. If this doesn't confuse you more, then fine. If it does, remember, I had to drive the route between two of those towns—Pittsburg and Fort Scott— more times than even I could count.

To continue with the story, however, Marilyn and Ron, the two mutual friends I mentioned previously, invited me to dine at their home one evening several weeks later. I don't remember whether or not they told me of MJ coming, or if I found out when I arrived, but it was clearly a setup. To try and disguise it, though, they invited two other couples to round out the event.

I remember the food being good and that I talked a lot for some reason. I remember that MJ and I were seated next to one another, but that she didn't talk all that much. Maybe she just couldn't get a word in edgewise.

A week or so later, I got the idea to invite her—Mary Jane—out on a date, and called her with my invitation.

I think she was surprised at hearing from me, since it had been a while since we'd met, but she kindly agreed, and I got my first taste of driving to Fort Scott. I have long forgotten where we ate that evening, but I rather imagine it was a place called the Red Barn just south of Fort Scott and serving honest to goodness Ozark food. Chicken fried chicken with mashed potatoes and gravy seems to ring a bell.

We talked of mutual things. I tried to keep my motor mouth at bay, and then drove her home. On the way, I stopped at a gas station, and, after filling my tank, we kissed. This was not an ordinary kiss. By that I don't mean it was particularly erotic, only that, at least for me, things went kazoom. (I noted this down in a diary I kept at the time and later, on our twenty-fifth anniversary, gave her that diary and the page that recounted that kiss and my reaction.)

We continued to date after that and, as I believe I've stated elsewhere in these pages, I asked her to marry me fully three weeks after our first date by saying, "Oh that marriage thing? Please consider yourself asked."

I realize now that I could have phrased it better, but so could have she when, a few days later and out of the blue she said, 'Yes.' It took me several minutes to fully grasp her meaning.

Forty-six years later we still seem to be on the right track.

and *h*er face br**I**ghtened at the th*o*ught,
and vio*l*ently squ*i*rted out the planet

in the making of the *c*oming **W**orld

from pro**C**lus.

r**O**bots darted and sang for si**X**

<u>**YEARS**</u> co**MING**.

54

Holmes

OR that the everla**S**ti**n**g

had n**O**t fixed or indeed

Whatever la*M*es or paralyzes you

dra**W**s *i*n w*I*th it the divinity

in some *f* orm.

1966

During my first year of teaching at Pittsburg State College in 1966-7, I was a ringer in the orchestra, playing bass or cello depending on where the conductor needed me most. While I hadn't expected this duty, it fit with my general assignment of teaching, tuning harpsichords, and conducting small ensembles. I also taught a stray piano lesson here and there, and coached sections of the orchestra on particularly difficult sections of music. This included adding bowings to string parts whenever needed.

That year the orchestra had four concerts, and I played in them all. The first concert, as I recollect, had a single work, Arthur Honegger's *Joan of Arc at the Stake*, an extraordinary oratorio and a very difficult work for the orchestra, vocal soloists, and student choir. But what a joy to perform. Even with the quite competent but sometimes narcoleptic conductor (which meant that at times the orchestra and choir conducted him rather than vice versa).

The second concert was not really a concert, but a production of an opera by Giuseppe Verdi (Joe Green in translation). I can't remember the exact opera. This was by contrast to Honegger's work, a boring and tedious job simply due to the manner in which Verdi treated the cellos and basses— endless repetitions of short notes. The opera may have been a good one, but I was too busy trying not to fall asleep to know.

Our third concert, the first of the second semester, was another oratorio, this one by Markwood Holmes, my fellow composer on the staff of the music department at KSC. Holmes was an unassuming, serious, and quite gifted man, I thought, and his work proved it. I enjoyed every minute of the rehearsals, and our two concerts were a good representation of his music. Whenever asked how we were doing, Markwood would simply nod his head as if things were just fine.

The work was serial in nature, a composition process I personally enjoyed due to my love of Schoenberg's music, but the orchestra and audience were not in agreement. Markwood seemed used to this kind of treatment, as he'd been there for many years before I arrived and had previously composed works for local ensembles.

This performance represented a world premiere of the piece and, I imagine, it's only performance. Markwood in no way promoted his music, something I would try to rectify when I later moved to Los Angeles and published a number of his works, though unfortunately not the oratorio.

I no longer have any idea where Holmes's works may be. He retired a couple of years after I left Kansas and, according to the Internet, is best known for a book on violin techniques titled *Above the First Position*. Beyond that, there is not much information available. This saddens me. A gifted composer with a lifetime of works apparently performed once if at all.

The final concert of my first year at KSC included a new work of mine called *Contrasts for Orchestra* with the second half consisting of Richard Strauss's *Oboe Concerto in D Major* (the latter being a curious non sequitur since the work traverses so many keys that its literally impossible to guess where it's going next).

I wasn't sure exactly how my composition went given I had to play cello. It's sometimes difficult to hear the entire ensemble when performing in it. But the reviews went well and I felt good about it. In fact, much of it can be found in the first movement of my first symphony, "The Phoenix."

No matter, though, I still worried about Markwood Holmes. A man apparently incapable of advancing the performance of his music and who simply loved his lifetime Kansas experience of ignoring the rest of the world. He lived well into his nineties. Maybe my worries are not so much about Markwood, but at the loss to the world of hearing his music. And I wonder how many other composers out there have sealed their fate in the same way. I wish that someone—a musicologist per chance—would spend a little time saving what may remain of such music so we can appreciate it instead of reading yet another book on Beethoven.

to r**e**pay an ange*L*

des**C**ending from t**HE S**ky

projec**T**s beams o**R** r**A**ys of *L*igh**T**

to the ground wh**I**ch m*A*y c**ON**t*R*ibute

to my present un*D*ertaking

as if in an unknown wor*L*d

and m*A*y be co*N*sidered

as a wed*G*e between the two internal surfaces.

55

Breakdown

we will ne**ver** be able **t**o

unde**R**stand har*mo*ni**C**

rati**O**s wh**E**n we

are sear**C**hin**g** f**o**r a

s**OL***u*ti**O***n* of some

p**R**oblem.

1967

I suffered my first—and hopefully last—nervous breakdown
in early 1967. While I had no professional analysis of such at
the time, every sign pointed in that direction. Complete lack
of self-confidence, sudden inclination to cry without cause,
inability to find a reason to do much of anything, and a lack
of cause to create things. This latter indication being the most
severe, since I had before then and since, never been in that
state of mind. I am what I make, and thus I wasn't anything.

Reasons for this breakdown were many and obvious. I'd
just finished my first semester of teaching full time. It was

my first such position, and every class seemed like some kind of test—for me, not the class. It was my first time being out of California or Arizona and in a climate (Kansas) that was, to me at least, harsh and unforgiving. I may have seen snow before in the mountains, but I now really encountered it up close and personal. I'd met my wife to be, Mary Jane, and we'd gotten engaged and I'd met her parents. Not that tough, since they were quite nice people. She'd met my parents. Tough on her more than me, I suppose, but I was worried that my mother might unseal the deal by saying something she'd inevitably say. After all, I was marrying a Catholic and had been raised in a house with a token God at best. In short, I should have seen my breakdown coming, and not been surprised when it arrived.

It took several months to re-energize. Marriage, a honeymoon, and life as a college teacher for a second year sealed the deal. But I will never forget those months of alternating fear and despair, and still look on those that suffer mental illness with great respect that they are able, somehow, to live through it.

Of course, doing what I do, I occasionally arrive at the doorstep of the same malady and have to take a step back to avoid the collision again. It's a delicate balance, especially for someone with my energy, but it must be maintained or surely the results will take me asunder. I can find those moments of imbalance in my past easily by simply observing the amount of my creative output and seeing the dips that occur.

and when *T*he se*V*enå *t*hunders h*a*d uttered the*i*r <u>V</u>oic<u>E</u>s, glassed eyes sea**R**chi*n*g and finding regarded thi*s* earth with envious e<u>Y</u>es. this ascent of the water shows its endeavour to recede with time.

56

Brown

and

whi**C**h

tells him

to c**all** fo**R**

his *P***u**rple

sh*O*es for

co*L***d.**

1968

I met Earle Brown in the oddest of places—an art gallery opening in Beverly Hills. One of his works had been performed there, and the reception that followed was one I wouldn't have missed. While usually hating such things, the idea of seeing Brown in what I'd heard was his milieu was just too tempting.

Brown was then known as a member of the Cage group consisting of Cage himself, Morton Feldman, Brown, and Christian Wolff. I'd met Cage, later met Wolff, never had the pleasure of meeting Feldman though I'd heard a great deal about him, and had never met Brown before. Here was my chance.

As I roamed the gallery, full of what passed for contemporary art in those days, I encountered him quite by accident. I introduced myself, and queried him about his history with such a wonderful group of people. He looked at me, dressed as I was in street clothes and not the tuxedo style he wore, smiled, and strode off to meet the hostess or another important person that I obviously was not. He never said a word to me.

I didn't immediately hold this against him. After all, I was rather ordinary in terms of my looks and the way I kept myself in terms of neatness, and so on. Unkempt might be the appropriate word. And I didn't particularly mind him skipping past me quickly, since there were no doubt many other much more valuable assets to be had in other parts of the room. And I use the word 'assets' quite purposely here. However, I did mind him not even acknowledging me as a fellow human being. A tiny greeting like 'I'm glad to make your acquaintance, but I have some other people I have to meet,' would have sufficed. Or even something shorter. But nothing?

It was with interesting emotion then that I received a ranting note from him for publishing a score in my book *New Directions in Music* that preceded his own notorious novelty by at least a decade. This composer's score had preempted what Brown had clearly thought he alone had invented. I took my time reading Brown's nasty note, but did not respond.

and wi*L*l

br*A*ce yo*U*r

pale limb*S* an*d* brain

t*O* g*e*nius. and make you

fo*r*emost of men for all time.
from one of the shelves from the

white mountain at greater distan*C*es
from the body of the earth, first

at the li*CK* observatory and

from t*HE N*th

*BERG*er till
he died today.

57

Moon

when **s**he turned the **CO**rner,

th*A*t w**a**s when i heard i**t.**

the woman,

b**u**t **r**est her sou*L*

be**C**ause shes *D*ead and

n**O** one wou*l*d ha**v**e be*ll* eved it.

1969

On July 20, 1969, Apollo 11 landed the first men from earth
on the moon, and these men then walked on its surface. That
day, my wife Mary Jane and I visited my Aunt Lois and Uncle
Frank's house in North Hollywood for a family get-together.
His family. That meant Italian food and drink, and I was very
much in favor of that.

We arrived to a scene of rare magnitude with two
musicians, us, both somewhat shy of crowds without stages
involved, finding a house with a line actually descending the
lawn to the street.

When we finally got inside, we were introduced to uncle this, aunt that, cousin this, grandfather that, until it was impossible for either of us to tell whom from whom.

Tables and requisite chairs were set everywhere, inside and out, and large containers of pasta, meatballs, and tomato sauce were in evidence on almost every flat surface. The smell was outrageously wonderful. Be it known now, I think Italian food is the most wonderful in the world.

As time progressed, we ate and listened to stories told in the most extraordinary of accents by all manner of people, young and old alike. Everything with an Italian twist that I had grown to understand and appreciate in my youth.

When the time arrived, the three or four television sets placed strategically were turned up in volume, and the sounds of the party suddenly stopped. Then, Neil Armstrong stepped down on the surface of the moon and declared the famous, "One small step . . ." line most of us old-timers still remember so vividly. And a great cheer erupted from the crowd. No longer just Italians and friends, but members of the larger family of human beings everywhere.

It was a extraordinary moment.

wheRefore **Ma*n*y** ent*I*re a*N*d ab**S**olute **M**otions

c**AN** be running through the **D**ull nature
of having the everlasting gospel to preach

unto the**M** that dwell **O**n the mo**D**ern **U**sua**L** **E**arth.

58

Towers

they stay upon your pat**I**e**N**ce. i hope

they will re**m**e***M***b***E***r her saucer of

milk. an**D** **I** suppose **w**i**th** high

m**A**g**N**ifie**r**s A**n*D*** th**e** transpar**e**nt

water an*d* the earth drank th*I*s force.

1969

I composed *Towers* in 1969 while living in Redondo Beach, California. My rationale for creating this mostly graphic work was because I conducted a small new music ensemble in Los Angeles at the time, and had discovered that many of the volunteers for the group had less than desirable skills in reading traditional music notation. While the score to *Towers* may initially appear almost random with many of the choices are left to performers, the piece is far from that. It relies on the improvisatory skills of its performers in following the rather rigid formal plan of the work. And notating the piece in this way certainly paid off for the new music ensemble I conducted, for it soon became the most popular piece in our repertoire.

As well, other ensembles became interested—most notably the MW2 Ensemble of Poland who used it as one of their test works for performers expecting to graduate from the Warsaw Conservatory.

Lately, on Internet sites such as YouTube, I've found several performances recorded. One of these—by Aleksandra Lelek (cello) and Maciej Zimka (accordion)—recently caught my attention for its beauty and imagination.

Knowing in advance what the score does and does not instruct the performers to do may lead some to question who the composer of *Towers* actually is. Certainly the basic idea is mine. But the clever ways in which well-practiced performers develop ideas and counterpoint is surely theirs.

I have pointed many people toward this particular video, and found that the question of who's the author keeps popping up. My response is simple: Who the hell cares? There's obviously some sharing of responsibility here. But does it matter? How do you feel about the music? That's all that really should concern us in the end.

Do you question Bach when he gives performers the responsibility to improvise figured basses in his music?

Does it really matter who actually composes them?

No.

Only the music matters.

consisting of **A**ctions only, and this by the d**U**ll co**N**str*uc*t**I**on of the machine will mean that the pac*k*age *worthy*, must actually get stuck, and there fell a great star from the hea**VE**ns ve**R**a**SITY**.

(1970-1977)

59

Cayahuga

and h*I*s fa**C**e was as **I**t were
the su*N* a swor*D*.

un***BA***ted,

and *In A* pass of p***R***a**C**tice.

1970

I spent three years teaching in Cleveland, Ohio at the
Cleveland Institute of Music. I taught mostly second-year
music theory, studied electronic music with Donald Erb, and,
for a while at least, ran the well-funded Contemporary Music
Series. During my time there I met many a distinguished
composer from around the world—discussed elsewhere in
this series—and took part in a contemporary music ensemble.
I also listened to an enormous amount of new music. But
what I remember most about my time in Cleveland is water.
Not in the form of snow, of which there was plenty, but in the
form of rivers and lakes.

First, there are plenty of rivers in northern Ohio, most
notably the Cayahuga that divides Cleveland down the
middle, and around which are located many deviant factories

that deposit enormous amounts of chemicals into the slowly moving channel of water. These chemicals, of which oil was certainly one, created one of the most spectacular fires known in the Western World. This fire occurred just before we arrived and was known as 'the river that caught fire' in all the headlines in newspapers that covered the story. It took the city fire department almost three days to put the river out, so covered was it with an oily slick.

As new residents, we took no blame for the fire, and stayed around long enough to see the city outlive the embarrassing stories that it caused. And we enjoyed many other fine rivers without oily slicks that feed into the Cayahuga from the surrounding areas. Chagrin Falls, for example, on one fork of the Chagrin River, presented an extraordinary example of an eastern river at its primrose best. We took our then two young boys there often for picnics and to watch the falls, well, fall. We lived at the time on Strandhill Road in Shaker Heights, with easy access to the wonderful countryside not that far south and east of us.

It was not the Cayahuga or the Chagrin that caught our attention, though. While we had just missed the Cayahuga River fire, we did not miss the island that had begun growing in Lake Erie on whose shores Cleveland sits and the Cayahuga empties—or maybe belches—its contents. Apparently, islands of toxic algae had bloomed in the western basin of Lake Erie (especially off Maumee Bay) such that, among other things, it glowed at night and could be seen by aircraft and from space. Miles in diameter, this island—or a group of many islands—actually suffocates fish and other wildlife, and has been worsening by the year since it was first discovered. It now contributes to the famous (or infamous) Lake Erie Dead Zone, an area of no oxygen along the bottom of the lake.

I spent most of my time in Cleveland busy grading papers, helping raise my sons, and composing, with little enough spare time to study the water around Cleveland. Since then, however, I've noticed that what began in the seventies, or more likely far earlier than that, has become much worse rather than better. No matter the dangers posed, it seems, the people in this particular part of the world seem to feel that the environment, no matter how bad its temper becomes, will indefatigably survive.

there was *N*ot a cloud **iN** th**E** *S*ky,

but there wa**S** nothing else to do

as **m**ost terrestrial men

fancied there might be many men upon mars.

i have brought **f**orward at this time,

the **C**onceptual diffe**re**ntiations of **geO**metrical matters.

60

Mackenzie

shoRtens not his own life,

bUt iST his law.

the five fiqures have

nOt been Distributed

Among the elements

as aRIstotle believed.

1970

I am occasionally asked about my book *New Directions in Music*, with the question usually centering on someone whose work I describe there, Icabod Angus (I. A.) Mackenzie. Mackenzie was a composer/sculptor who lived, at least when I knew him, in or near the small town of Angels Camp, California, along legendary Highway 49 in gold mining country. Mackenzie created musical sculptures, variations of wind chimes but much larger and more elegant, and placed them in remote locations where humans would not ordinarily go. Like the adage, 'Does a tree falling in the forest with no one around actually make a sound?' his work begged the question of both existing and not existing at the same time, along the same general lines of quantum theory and Schrödinger's cat. Since no one else writes much about Mackenzie, the question usually posed is whether or not he actually existed or did I invent him.

My answer to that question typically relates the idea of how interesting Mackenzie would have found such a question. After all, the notion that he might not have existed puts him in the same status as the tree in the forest, Schrödinger's cat, and even his own instruments. If he didn't exist, how did his instruments get where they are? If we cannot find his instruments, did they exist in the first place? Or, if we cannot find his instruments, does it simply mean we haven't looked hard enough? And on, and on. He would have certainly enjoyed this circular conundrum, for I knew him as a man of infinite jest. His house, still standing alongside Highway 49, at least the last time I drove by there—on the left going northward—looked like the old and gnarled man himself, brimming with the curiosity of a thousand cats.

but if we observed the dis**CO**rd,

there was*N***t** even a shadow

on the curta**i**n**s**,

but t**h**e li*G*ht *R*ema*I*ned.

and from the throne *S*aying,

there may be encountered ris*KS*.

61

Meningitis

t**h**e *P*oor **l**itt**l**e thing
sat **d**own and cri**e**d
in th*E* gree*N* forest,

in the blue l**a**ke, bu**t**
never as herself, no.

1971

When I lived in Cleveland and taught at the Cleveland
Institute of Music in the early 1970s, I caught a serious
case of spinal meningitis, a disease usually beginning as
influenza and then, typically due to neglect, rampaging on
until either powerful medicine helps or you die. I remember
the terrible headaches and the extraordinary medicines
the doctor prescribed. Typically of me at the time, I just
kept plowing ahead, taking one day off from teaching and
generally ignoring the fact that I had a high temperature and
felt miserable. Then, as to some degree now, I felt I needed
my pain. Part of my job description as a composer. Suffering.

Eventually, of course, I recovered. I told my doctor
that I knew I would. He claimed that my arrogance would

eventually get the better of me. I argued that I was confident, not arrogant. He begged to differ, and, after a fairly long debate—he was a personal friend as well as my doctor—told me to find another doctor if I was going to take such diseases so marginally.

In the fall of the following year when my wife became pregnant with our third child and it became clear I would have to find another position in order to keep our enlarged family afloat, my concern over applying for jobs and traveling for interviews brought several maladies upon me. Mouth sores, depression, and most terrible among them a lack of self-confidence. After many different tests, my doctor could not explain their cause.

go forwar*D* into t**h***E* celestial s***PA***ces.

but i w*I*ll attempt to *RE*ply i**N** **T**heologi*C*al term**S**,

not as your daughter **M**ay conc**E** i**v**e, fr**i**end, just **L**oo*K*

at the u**s**e of the **i**nv*I*sib**L**e n**o**t less tha**n** me.

62

Roosevelt Lake

If t*he r*est of my fortunes turn bad
as in the unknown worl**D**,
the *be*st kn**O**w**N** of th**E**se
*j*ust *r*esul*t*s in the kn**O**wn
god**eIS** th**e**o**R**em.

1972

In August of 1972, my wife, I, and our then two sons visited Phoenix, Arizona, to take a vacation while simultaneously housesitting for my parents. During this time, we had use of their car and decided one day to take a trip toward the east of the state to visit the four lakes that provide the city with most of its water. These lakes in order from west to east are Saguaro, Canyon, Apache, and Theodore Roosevelt.

I had spent a good deal of time exploring the lower of these lakes on the Salt River—Saguaro—and we visited it first. We got out of the car there, and I told my family of my daring exploits in a boat alone when younger, with lightning and a thunderstorm raging about me. Of walking neck deep underwater along the shoreline for most of its circumference for no good reason except to do it. And, of course, catching all the fish I'd never caught. We then saw the other three lakes from the car windows, and finished our trip by circling around through the Tonto National Forest and eventually back home to Phoenix.

Somewhere along the way, which by the way mostly consisted of winding roads and daring views into canyons, my two kids decided to give up their lunches and maybe their breakfasts as well. Having not prepared for this eventuality, my wife and I had no alternative but to listen to their regurgitations and hope for the best. This meant we prayed they'd aimed for the floor rather than the seats, this being a relatively new car for my parents and their pride and joy.

When our trip ended, we discovered—by smell alone—that we'd indeed been lucky. The floor behind our seats was virtually swimming in vomit, but the seats seemed clean as far as we could tell.

So, we spent the rest of the day cleaning the beautifully carpeted floor of every bit of the smelly sauce my kids had left there. And, for what it was worth, we did a very good job. No one could have detected the problem visually or by touch.

Unfortunately, smell was a different matter.

Every day we left the car doors open in hopes that the wind and fresh air would return the car's interior smell to something resembling normal. And every day our efforts proved fruitless. The smell of puke is, apparently, a thing of special design, not to be overcome by simply letting it disappear of natural causes.

As a consequence, we visited car dealerships and stores to find sprays that might do the trick. We finally settled on one particular brand with the advice of many, and applied it properly to the back seat floor of my parent's car. And waited.

The good thing was, after several attempts, the back carpet of my parent's car no longer smelled like vomit. It

smelled like the spray we'd used. Not that bad a thing, and
certainly better than the previous odor, but, unfortunately,
noticeably different than the car's interior smell when my
parent's had left it in their driveway.

We crossed our fingers and awaited their return. When
they arrived, we didn't mention the problem in hopes they
would not discover that their grandchildren had added
something special to their four-wheeled 1972 Ford. And,
when one or both of them drove it, at least while we were
there, neither mentioned the new smell that had been added.

However, on one of our routine phone calls about a
month later with us back in Cleveland, my mother asked me
if their car had run okay during our visit there. I responded
in the affirmative. She told me then that they had discovered
a strange smell as they drove, and had taken the car in for
servicing. Nothing had been found amiss, but the stench, as
she called it, would simply not go away.

I played dumb.

Not that it took much trouble.

And no more mention of it took place again.

they have not *b*een dist*ri*Buted

amo*n*g the elements as *k*ind

arist**O**tle believed, a**n**d the
farther they go the slower
seasons **C**hange, and huge
snowcaps gathered and showed
Me that great **C**ity of the holy
jerusalem.

63

Sal Martirano

progress of **a**bsolute time is liable to not **ch**a**nge with bloo**D** of the f**A**the**r**s, **m**others, *Da***u**ghter**s**, or so**N**s as *ThEy* passed the hayscaLes.

1971

When Sal Martirano arrived at the Cleveland Institute of Music where I taught at the time during the early 1970s, I was quite taken with the audacity of his work. He taught composition at the University of Illinois and was well known for his electronic instrument called the Sal-Mar Construction, which he built and modified over several decades.

I arrived to teach my first class one morning knowing that he would be there preparing his instrument for that night's performance. And indeed he was. What I had not prepared myself for was the elegance of his system. For this particular presentation, he had dangled several hundred small loudspeakers from the ceiling. I introduced myself, not that he would have heard of me but he had, and offered to help. He graciously accepted.

It was a pleasure to meet someone as well known as he in the midst of 'composing.' For his construction or re-construction of his instrument for each performance was broadly known at the time, and I was smitten with the whole idea of a traveling electronic instrument/piece combination. A kind of electrical Harry Partch.

We discussed several people we knew in common, the speakers burped a few sounds as tests, and I then excused myself to teach the intricacies of Bach chorales to a group of uninterested students.

That evening's performance proved to be one of the more convincing of my new music experiences since beginning my work on the various editions of *New Directions in Music*. The audience was allowed free reign of the instrument, and to hear the resulting work from an almost limitless number of points of view. It was magical. And I told him so when the evening concluded.

Don Erb, who had brought the show to the Institute, was quite pleased as well, and even though it must have cost an arm and a leg, it had been worth it.

you could predict with certainty which party would carry it burning as it fell upon the first part of the numbers, and not by algebra. whether this is possible in principle or not is a stimulating and exciting question.

64

Other Worlds

an**d** every entire motion

i**S CO**mposed *of the* motion

of the body o**U**t of its first p*la*ce.

AN*d* **T**h*e* co**M**mon so*r*t attribut**E**

Rest to earth make mad the guilty

and a**PP**al th**E** free

fr**O**m the forest.

1973

When our family of five moved from Cleveland to Oxford, Ohio, in 1973, and after we'd settled in and before school began, I regularly visited Acton Lake, north of town and the university. This small but quite engaging reservoir had plenty of fish and I wasn't going to let any of them rest in peace. Try as I might, though, they caught me more than I them and, after tiring of my bites but no success catch-and-release approach, I decided to head down to what I'd heard was a quite interesting place just below the dam. What I found there confuses me to this day.

The dam, placed there more for recreational purposes than flood control or drinking water storage, barely fed the small unmoving cement lined creek that eventually ended about fifty yards out. The stagnant water was so opaque that it looked nearly solid rather than liquid. And, as I tossed my line hesitantly into the water that first time, I had no idea what might be lurking within. But I soon found out.

Apparently, fish from above had somehow found there way here and, as I quickly discovered, had been fruitful and multiplied. And not only with their own species. My first real catch was a real catch indeed. The thing was a true fighter, and as I stared at its multicolored strangeness, I thought I saw it staring back at me. This fish had fins where fins should not be, more than two eyes, and a lack of symmetry that boggled the mind. I let it wiggle itself free, having no idea what it might do to me if I touched it.

After several hours of this, with each fish I caught being of different parents and apparently the result of several evolutionary mutations significantly different than the last, I couldn't imagine what this soup might look like if the water were clear enough to see these creatures swimming. Something no doubt far more interesting than the wildest imaginings of an Hawaiian pet-store owner. And that's when it hit.

The pull on my line was more than heroic, it felt like a great white in heat. The fisherman in me immediately went to work trying to haul the thing in. My semi-logical brain, however, kept asking me if I really wanted to see what it was. Or what it might do to me.

After several minutes of underwater gymnastics, the fish—at least that's what I think it was—finally surfaced in one amazing leap in the air. At least two feet long, battleship gray all over, large white teeth gleaming in the afternoon sunlight, and twisting in air like some kind of jaguar after a reluctant parrot, it finally splashed back into the water to begin again its contortions. The only way to describe this thing as I remember it now, is like an immense eel without eyes. How it got here was beyond my speculation. But I would not have any of it. I grabbed my fishing kit scissors and quickly cut bait. Then, without hesitation, ran back to my car and got the hell out of Dodge.

I occasionally visited this place after that, long enough to ply my fishing talents and prove that what I had seen that day hadn't been an illusion. It hadn't. The aquatic zoo was real and potentially deadly. The tables would turn on any fisherman unlucky enough to attempt to fill his catch tank with these members of a different world. And I certainly wasn't mindless enough to be that fisherman.

aboVe hIm crack.

It NecessariLy foLlows

That it is not only More distANt

from times beginning. but nearer its end.

it is a very useful assumption
under any circumstance.

a little door about
two inches high.

65

Studio

she turns the gigantic pagesleaf a*f* te*r* never return*i*ng *O*ne.

it had occurred toward*s* *m*idnig*h*t of t*he* twelfth.

Blue g*i*ve**S** its **O**w*n* life.

tw**A**s of some es**T**ate the dune**S** of freshly laid
sand covered it.

1973

From 1973 until 1977, I taught music theory and composition
at Miami University of Ohio. When I arrived, it quickly
became apparent that the department was woefully lacking in
technology on almost all fronts. And so, with encouragement
from the department chair and dean, I applied for funding to
purchase high-level recording equipment, a Moog synthesizer,
and other top-line equipment of the day.

For some strange reason, the funding I'd requested was
granted, and before long the various pieces of the puzzle I'd
imagined began to arrive. It was great fun. No one knew
how to use these gizmos except me—even though, truth be
known, I wasn't all that confident about my own skills—and

the Miami University Electronic Music Facilities came into being.

Compared to contemporary standards, this equipment was nearly barbaric. Razor blade splicing, half-inch recording tape, and plug and play modular electronic sound equipment was the period's best technology available. But I set about to teach my students how to use it, all the while teaching myself how to do it before class.

With the equipment came the need for space, and within several months I moved from a regular office to a combined office, recording studio, and classroom, all in one. One room. A thirty or so feet wide, one-hundred fifty feet long, and two-story high room with video setup necessary for recording recitals in the attached concert hall with no window and no one willing to create one through the brick wall separating the studio and that hall.

For several years after that, my office was visited by undergraduate students for classes, graduate students for lessons and recording sessions, electronic music composition for everyone who could sign up for time, and me trying to grade papers and prepare for classes ranging from sixteenth-century counterpoint to twentieth-century avant-garde music composition.

But this combination worked, and while it often seemed crowded, I missed it from the first day I left in 1977.

One of my last duties for this studio was to clean out my stuff so I could move it to Santa Cruz, California, for my new job at UCSC. While doing this cleanup, my assistants and I found something quite interesting.

I am fond of bananas. Always have been. Always will be. At least one a day.

And that's what we found. Buried behind one of the wastebaskets in the studio and partially under a filing cabinet, we discovered a petrified banana peel, so hardened by time that it could literally stand on its open end without collapsing. It must have lain there for the entire three years of the studio's existence.

after three days, the spirit of life will **B**e another part of the

s**ky**.

and so abso**LU**t**E**ly understood it will be perpetually mutable.

let it be your lot to slander what you do not understand.

the *g*reat **GILL** dersleave.

66

Indian Creek

To harp yoU, will mean pounding on each StRing. and eaTen Up by wiLd bEaSts, aNd so bliNded by vAnity and Formed as one.

1973

Indian Creek lies about three miles west of Oxford, Ohio, where I taught for four years at Miami University. The creek is about ten feet wide most of the time, and is usually no more than a foot or so deep. I often took my boys there to fish or just wander and see nature work its wondrous magic.

One afternoon, I left campus early and took my older sons to a special place near a concrete dam of sorts that created a nice but small waterfall. Thinking I'd get them closer to nature, I took off my shoes and socks, curled my pants' legs up, and wandered out into the creek, all the while inviting them to follow suit. After all, the rocks were small here, and there was very little if any chance to slip.

To a one, however, they refused, citing their mother's advice to stay clear of wading for such streams were full of dangers. Not wanting to contradict my lovely wife, I simply let the issue go and continued my stroll through the pre-dam puddle. It was a nice warm day, probably mid-spring, and the water felt wonderful.

That night, however, while taking a shower, I looked down in the collected water at my feet and to my horror saw it was red, not clear as it should have been. I hiked up first one foot and then the other, and on my second try discovered I'd picked up a hitchhiker on my little journey through the creek. A leech, though at the time I didn't actually know what a leech was. It looked like a small plump snail without a shell. I'd been born and raised in the west where, at least as far as I knew, no such animals existed.

After we'd disposed of the little bastard, and cleaned my toes and wound with rubbing alcohol, I turned to my wife and asked how she knew such things.

And then she reminded me she'd been born and raised in Ohio.

and the**I**r wor**ks** do *f*ollow

t**He**m as *i* look, and in the making of the world from

proclu**s** impul*s*es t*h*ose in motion.

67

Organ

we may <u>NO</u>w consi*DE*R
<u>TH</u>e ground to have been c*lea*red.
and <u>WE</u> are ready to *ki*ll th*e* debate
on our que<u>ST</u>ion that sh<u>E</u> was now
the **R**ight size for goi**N**g though
the little door into that lovely garden.

1974

During the mid-1970s while on tour in Chicago with a new music ensemble, I performed my work *Arena* for cello and electronic sounds on tape. I did so at my peril, for it seemed that the electronic music studio of the university where we gave our concert had not planned for a work requiring speakers as well as live performers, and scheduled the event for a church on campus. Normally this would not have been much of a problem, but these folks then placed the two speakers for my performance in with the organ pipes.

Now, for those unfamiliar with basic acoustic principles, organ pipes resonate on not only their fundamental pitches, but on the harmonics of those pitches. This resonation occurs whether or not the organ is being played at the time or not. In other words, with the speakers placed as they were, each sound emanating from them—and there were many—was picked up by most of the pipes and carried throughout the hall along with the actual sounds imprisoned on the tape I'd brought.

Thus, the audience that night was presented not with my work, but a completely different work created by a composite of the sounds I made and those of the huge pipe organ that basically obliterated my piece.

Quite incidentally, the audience did not recognize this was occurring. Thus, the enormous sounds they heard were no doubt spectacular. No organist playing, just a cello. What a show.

My work was the hit of the evening. Or rather what the audience took as my work was the hit of the evening.

I have never since performed or had my works deliberately performed in Chicago.

just as *m*u**C**h *i*ntelle*c*t

as you add,

so muc*h* or**ga**n*i*c ***P*o**wer.
he who sees throug*h* the design
presides over it,

*an*d must will th***A***t

which m**U**st be.

and yet as morta***L***
as his own all motions.

68

Ronson

of **C**ourse ele**C**tricity usu**A**lly comes in

where f**a**st si**G**nallin**g** is conc**E**rn**e**d.

*j*ust as milli**O**ns *o*f ac**R**es

*h*ere o*n* us *t*ill our **G**round.

1974

When I lived in Ohio, closer to the east coast, I traveled to
New York City more often than I do now. On one of my trips
there, I visited Raoul Ronson, then the president of Seesaw
Music one of the publishers of my music. We'd had many long
snail-mail conversations, and this was an opportunity to get
to meet him directly and understand why, of all things, he
preferred to publish the music of living American composers
rather than dead European ones.

When I arrived at Raoul's apartment on schedule, I didn't
quite know what to expect. He was known in new music
circles as an unusual individual of strong points of view and
often cruel opinions.

When he answered his door, I was quietly surprised at
the diminutive man standing there inviting me to enter and

would I like some tea. I agreed to both, and made my way to the nearest chair I could find. We engaged in conversation while he was in the kitchen, and I looked around to see walls covered with bookcases brimming with books and, strangely, with small piles of strange pebble-like things stacked here and there on the floor. That was when one of the sources of these stacks peeked slowly from behind a corner and stared at me. It was a turtle. Green. Moving in ultra-slow motion and quite free to roam as he wished around the apartment apparently. Or maybe an escapee from a glass aquarium where I'd previously seen turtles in captivity.

When Raoul returned with two cups of tea on a platter with sugar and cream, I asked him about the creature I'd seen, who was then plodding toward me.

"That's George," he said. "He's quite harmless. Pay him no mind."

I did as instructed, and George, uninterested in me, wandered slowly across the room to find a perfect spot to lie—if that's the proper word—in the sun.

By that time, however, George was not the only turtle in the room. Out from under couches, chairs, and corners, came all manner and sizes of turtles, maybe twenty in all. Every one of them on a separate course, and apparently unconcerned about me, Raoul, or any of the rest of the turtles moving around.

"Do you know all their names?" I asked.

"Yes. You want to hear them?"

And Raoul then recited the name of each turtle while pointing the named individual out to me. As if I would remember. Maybe from knowing their names I would be more reluctant to step on one or more of them.

Otherwise, we simply sat in the turtle-infested room and spoke about things musical, publishing, and otherwise. It turned out he was a kind man as far as I could see, completely undeserving of the reputation he'd somehow earned, and probably a vegetarian given his clear love of animals that I'd seen more often in green soups than walking around underfoot.

this is th**E** origin of r*a*mees

most co*n*fide*n*t c*o*nviction
that the five solids ought to be removed

and have no regard in this **P**lace

to a medium that no man kne**W**

but he himself th**A**t for the moment
she quite forgot how to speak.

it was then that i saw the ha**L**f of the **K**ill**ER**.

69

Iowa

speaking **wi**th a great harsh**neS**s
    and a great rashness,

      a <u>MA</u>n led

        f**RO***M* insi<u>G</u>ht and

        *Aff***lr**ms of himself

    what is true of the mi**N**d.

1977

I last saw Donald Erb for the last time in Iowa City, Iowa, in 1977 at a conference. Don and I had worked together at the Cleveland Institute of Music for three years in the early 70s. He was an earthy giant of a man and composer, with more orchestra performances than I'd ever hope to have in my lifetime. The conference—held at the University of Iowa campus—was another edition of the American Society of University Composers, known affectionately by many of its members as ASUCers.

After our meeting in Iowa, Don went on to teach at Indiana University in Bloomington and Southern Methodist

University in Dallas before returning to the Institute taking a distinguished professorship there. All this time, he continued his stellar career as composer and wonderfully opinionated composer—a former student notes that he never attended any of the Darius Milhaud concerts in Cleveland because 'Milhaud was a terrible, terrible composer.' Don suffered a debilitating stroke later in 1996 and eventually died in 2008.

At our meeting in Iowa, however, Don congratulated me for my just-performed chamber piece and asked if it was true that I had taken a position in California. I told him it was true, but that it was—at that time anyway—only for a year; it later turned into thirty-six years. Don looked at me carefully, and said something to the effect that I should be careful. Composers, he told me, tend to go to that left coast, and simply fall off the earth, never to be heard of again.

the janitor typed **S**heets,
  and as he left,
      he turned out the lights

          and *CLosE*s in the **c**onseq**u**ence.
              *A*y marry, or i*N*deed
          the key wa*S* too small
        under the name of viva voce
      to discover whether someone

really understands somethin**g**.

              or h**a**s learnt it in the **p**arrot fas**hion** th**e**re.

70

Johnson

are they any the
wOrSE for that? there
are aLso the nobLe
creative ForceS, for It
May be that there Is
no body reaLly At
Rest. the intellectual
side of Man alrEady
admits that Life is an
incessant struggle fOr
existence.

1977

When I first met Tom Johnson in the late 1970s in New York City, he wrote reviews for the Village Voice. I rarely read reviews at that time—never do now—but I read his reviews because they were intelligent and because he always wrote good reviews of my music. I had just had a couple of pieces performed in a new music concert called the Composers

Forum, and somehow we got shoved in a taxi together on our way to a post-concert celebration where I was to meet several luminaries including Elliott Carter. Along the way, Tom spoke so eloquently of the music he'd heard that night, that it hardly seemed possible he was a music critic. I believe I even mentioned that to him. He thanked me for what he apparently agreed was a compliment.

I remember him asking me several questions regarding my own compositions that gave me pause. Not in a negative way, but in a way that got me thinking. At the after-concert party, we went our separate ways and I've never seen or communicated with him since. I have, however, kept up with his activities at long distance. It seems that not long after that concert, he met a young Spanish woman—Esther Ferrer, one of the most well-known performance artists of her time— retired from the Village Voice, and moved to Paris. Since then, he has been composing music that I find extremely interesting. I use one set of his works—*Formulas for String Quartet* (1994)—commonly in my courses. He has a way of treating various algorithmic ideas musically that I find refreshing and unique.

an*D*   the   f*I*rst

v<u>O</u>ic*E* which i hea**r**d

wa*S* as <u>**it**</u> were of a

trum*PE*t

tal**kin**g wit**h m**e,

an**d** he looked at
the white mountain

fo**R**m,   ***A***nd
proportion   are   the

characteri**S**tics   of
quantities.

71

New Yorker

as i*F I*n an unkn**O**w**N** wor*L*d,
once he **f**ound hi*M*self

among **T** oys.

so now **HE**
plays a

pa*R***T**

1977

I remember seeing a cartoon in *New Yorker* once, with a man sitting in front of a fireplace with a pipe in his mouth. Above his head was the usual balloon showing what was going on in his head at that moment. This balloon contained the drawing of an attractive young woman who, in turn, had a balloon above her head with a drawing of the same man sitting in front of the same fireplace. I cut the cartoon out of the magazine and kept it for a while since it seemed to me it represented what all of us go through in our lives at one time or another. The pleasure of imagining someone imagining us.

After all, who wouldn't be smitten with a person who was smitten with us? Or so I thought.

That must have been the case when, as a freshman in college, I dated another student for the first—and last—time. After the concert we attended, I walked her back to her house, both to keep her company, and to be polite. Somewhere along the way, she pushed me into some bushes, and began to smooch, as they called it in those days. Before too much time passed, she began turning away from me doing everything possible, I realized later, to make me notice the single zipper that held her body within the bounds of her dress, and that she'd partially unzipped it. I was far too naïve at the time to make anything of it except confusion, and I eventually took her home.

The next time I spoke with her—which wasn't easy, as she wouldn't take my calls—she told me that I'd had my chance and refused it. Being still a bit unfocused as to whether I had interpreted her actions that night correctly, she made it abundantly clear. I tried to explain my confusion, but she couldn't believe my innocence. She hung up on me. After all, she said, she was still a virgin, and who was I to refuse to be the first with her, even in the bushes at night.

A week or so later, she called me from the bedroom of her one of her teachers who, she claimed, had not refused her offer. I wasn't sure whether to believe her or not, but as she continued I found it difficult to not believe the detail in which she described their intimacy. I wanted to hang up on her, but somehow couldn't bring myself to do so. Like the man in the New Yorker cartoon, I couldn't help dreaming of someone dreaming of me. Or at least talking to me about such a private matter. She, of course, thought all this talk of intimacy was driving me crazy. That I'd had the opportunity and had passed it up. She was getting even.

I tried to explain to her that I didn't feel that way about her. That I thought love must be a part of the equation. And that I didn't, or couldn't, take such things as lightly as she apparently did. She laughed at me. I was a mere boy, she said. But I could tell that she had imagined her teacher as me during that afternoon of rolling around in the hay. Or at least I considered it so.

After that, I never heard from her again.

in c**O**lossal syst*E*ms, and h**i**s gro**W**th

is declared i**N** his am**b**iti**O**n,

with his c**O**mpanions and

fire in immo*V*able space,

and from the relat*IvE*

motions must be

stuffed a*W*ay

in archive*S*

so no one

knows

when

the

race

i**S**

over.

72

Niblock

all the More So IN that besIDes euclId ANd his commeNtAtor proclus, he follows through on all her ascendIng changes and all kINdreds of the earth shall wall.

1977

During my first year teaching at UCSC in 1977-8, I brought as many composers as I possibly could to the campus to help educate students interested in the music of the day. To do this on a small budget, I connected with colleagues in the bay area at the colleges and universities there such as Stanford, UC Berkeley, San Francisco State, and San Jose State and extended their visiting composers' stay a day or two to avoid having to pick up full travel expenses. One of these composers was Phill Niblock, a minimalist of extremes from New York City, and an interesting person.

We used local performers for his concert, and thus we needed rehearsals. However, since Phill's works were relatively easy to perform in terms of pitches and rhythms, this still worked with only one afternoon's preparation.

I had the advantage over my colleagues who attended the evening concert of having attended the rehearsal and knew that Phill's music took a great deal of patience on both the part of the performers and the audience. In fact, it was difficult to ascertain when his works actually began and when they ended. And the audience was allowed to get up and walk around as they saw fit during the performance of his music.

This was all well and good, since most of our students were well aware of some of the extravagances that avant-garde music took. But one of the faculty didn't seem appreciative of the process. In fact, unaware that the concert had actually begun and misinterpreting the fact that the audience was up and about, he began speaking to me about all manner of faculty issues, classes, and who was this Niblock character anyway.

Finally having had enough of this, Phill walked over to this faculty and in no uncertain terms told him to shut the fuck up, as we would say in those days.

Since the music was still so soft as to be nearly inaudible at this point, Phill's voice carried far louder than the faculty member's had. Thus, for many in the audience, all to be heard was Phill's outburst. So everyone turned to see to whom Phill had spoken.

Without doubt, the color of this faculty member's face told the entire story.

he would be **g**iven away at once by slowness and inaccuracy in arith**m**etic which he had resorted to

composing fugues and three part *quartets*. i do not know where greater **ma**r**ke**t M̲inim**ALISM** a**r**e.

73

On the Road

*T*h*I*s argument is seld*O*m expressed

quite s*O* openly as in the for*M*

*A*bove. fi*N*all*Y*,

*T*his advi*C*e t*O* a*N*y pe*O*ple

who might be

*C*omp*L*etely unf*A*milia*R*

with m*A*themati*ca*l que*ST*ions.

1978

As any composer or author tends to do, I've spent many of my days on the road giving presentations, performing my music, attending performances of my works, and listening to reactions. I've tried to space these out over time so as not to miss too much of the experiences with my family. However, during the 1970s I traveled extensively and, after so many years passing since then, the trials and travails of the trips have bled together in ways that now amuse and entertain me no end.

I begin with a trip to Towson State College just north of Baltimore in the spring of 1973. My invitation for this visit was based on my book *New Directions in Music*, then still in its first edition—now in its seventh after forty-plus years in print. It seems that the music department at Towson thought many of the chapters in my book would wake up some of their napping students. Chapters that discussed such topics as 'danger music,' 'biomusic,' 'antimusic,' and so on, can fire up one's imagination apparently, and I was hired to give a two-hour lecture to what appeared to be a large selection of the entire student body of the campus. I had never to that point in my life seen so many people interested in anything I had to say about anything. And they asked plenty of questions, with one repeated in various guises many times: 'Is this music?' I could understand such questions in regard to some of the topics mentioned above, but toward 'minimalism' I could not understand.

No one seemed interested in my own music. This was all about Penderecki, Reich, Cage, Riley, Ligeti, Moran, Feldman, and so on. To them, I was a twentieth-century musicologist, not a composer. Thank God, it turned out that Bob Levy, trumpeter extraordinaire and a nicer person you couldn't find, had visited the lecture and watched the goings on with interest. Especially since I had just completed a work for him that involved him recording himself multiple times playing trumpet and various percussion instruments. Since he'd brought his sleeping bag along, we spent the late hours that night discussing my composition and his eventual performance and recording. So, aside from the fact that I may have seriously confused many young minds—my job as a teacher after all—I was able to get some real musical work done as well.

No doubt because of our friendship, Bob then invited me to be a guest of his summer music camp at St. Mary's College of Maryland located on one of the peninsulas on a inlet off Chesapeake Bay. Here I was, a young composer teaching classes during the day and at night recording the various tracks for *Extensions*, the work I created for Bob. Our recording sessions lasted well into the wee hours, with me standing on the armrests of a seat in an otherwise empty concert hall conducting Bob on stage playing his various instruments. We would then listen to the playback with each new track added to the others and critique the results and then repeat this process over and over again. The recording still, after these many decades, has not reached distribution.

After many days of this exhausting night and day endeavor, I remember standing on the shore looking across the bay and wondering if these road stops were useful to me. The quiet lapping of the waves and the occasional honk of an unseen buoy helped not in the least. Bob's dedication to my work and his attempts to promote my music were inspirational. At the same time, could I have been better served spending the time composing another work or writing another book?

Having come to no conclusion regarding my question, I eagerly joined a group organized by Bart and Priscilla McLean who'd I'd previously met on several occasions at various concerts. We were called the McLean Mix at the time, and the group consisted of Bart, Priscilla, myself, with Burton Beerman added later on. Our purpose was simple; perform our own music in as many places as we could to get reviews—positive ones if possible—and entertain audiences with our brand of new music. Aside from acting as a composer, I performed on cello and occasionally contrabass—if one were available. Since Burt came from northwest Ohio (Bowling Green State University), I from southwest Ohio (Miami University of Ohio), and Bart and Priscilla from northern Indiana (Indiana University at South Bend), we usually traveled to our concert dates separately and by car. The McLeans, being heavily involved with live electronic performance at the time, usually travelled by truck.

I don't remember all of the locations of our concerts, but they certainly included our three home institutions and several others of like kind in the general area. One in particular stands out in my mind; Akron, Ohio. Our venue was a newly constructed concert hall of large capacity in the downtown area of the city. In fact, if memory serves, we were one of the inaugural performances in that hall.

As Priscilla's book—*Hanging Off the Edge: Revelations of a Modern Troubadour*—states, we ended up beginning that concert late due to an incredible wiring snafu caused by the requirements of one of Bart's works and the electrical layout of the hall which was not at all prepared for our type of musical performance. I remember—especially since Priscilla has reminded me of it—spending time propelling myself around the stage in a loading truck singing some nonsensical tune while the audience sat quietly hoping, I presume, that they were not witnessing the opening work of the concert. I was clearly beginning to lose my confidence in balancing the workload entailed in such productions along with their ultimate worth.

Not long after that, I believe, Bart invited me as a guest composer to the University of Texas where he had just landed a new position. While there, I taught a couple of composition classes, helped with rehearsals of my works, and finally attended a full concert of my music. I was, at last, a composer, not a musicologist, teacher, or performer. I sat in the hall that night and watched and listened to some of my more radical works performed by people interested in giving them their best shot. One of the works on the program that night was *Deadliest Angel Revision*, a piece for solo violinist cum actor with projections. This work had had its premiere in Cleveland a couple of years previous and had not been received with the wild enthusiasm I'd expected when I composed it. Unfortunately, the same was true that night. My anti-war and pro-Cage piece—the work was dedicated to John—was not what the more conservative audience expected to hear. By this time, however, I was all too familiar with the aloof responses that academics tended to give me and my music, so it wasn't the least bit disturbing to me. Again, however, was the effort worth my time?

I do remember strolling around the beautiful Austin campus and surroundings and learning the incredible role that football, particularly in the form of the University of Texas and the Dallas Cowboys, played in the area's aesthetics. Thus, I worried even less about the responses to my music and even more about the worthiness of my efforts. Later on, Bart and Priscilla went their own way by touring, and continuing to perform their own music all over the world, something I find amazing in this day and age.

There was something about that concert that caught somebody's eye, however, and for the next couple of years I could not blink without receiving an invitation to one school or another. The first university I remember asking me to visit—not necessarily the real first one—was Sam Houston State University in Huntsville, Texas. Again, they wanted me as composer and over three days I taught, listened, and critiqued rehearsals, and gave public presentations. This visit again concluded with a complete concert of my music. And not just chamber works or me playing cello or bass, but large works for major ensembles. Heady stuff this, and I now felt that the effort was worth it. Regardless of the somewhat remote location—northeast of Houston—and the more or less scanty audience. Sitting in an audience and listening to my music played well was more than a treat, it was an educational experience like no other.

No more than a couple of months later I found myself in Corpus Christie, Texas, at Del Mar College. While the performances were less professional—it was a junior college if memory serves—my narcissism was well served. It was then that two events caught my attention. First, that the scrimp in that area of the world are as big as horses, and second, an administrator, the one who had driven me around and introduced me to the scrimp, told me I had made some kind of list of good guest composers to have for collegiate new music festivals. I'd never heard of such a thing. Yet he was so sure of its existence and my presence on it, that he guaranteed I would be hearing from other schools in the very near future.

And so it was that I ended up at Louisiana State University's New Music Festival as guest composer. That is where my memory begins to fail me, as one school begins to blend into another, one hall looks pretty much the same as another, and my works performed begin to tire me with the vicissitudes of their performances.

A couple of situations stand out, of course, due to their strikingly negative effects on me. The first of these I've written about earlier in this volume and took place in Chicago. Another situation I remember is Arizona State University—my alma mater, though no one knew it at the time except me—where I was at the end of a multiple stop tour. I presented a workshop of how to prepare pianos a la John Cage. I had become so tired and confused by my constant travel that I literally had forgotten where I was. Thus, I broke down and had a cigarette, something I'd tried once before and liked, but figured it couldn't be good for me so had quit. This time I liked it so much that I chained smoked for an hour or two, eventually giving myself nicotine poisoning. So much so, that I had to lie down for several hours without smoking to even attend the evening concert that night.

And yet another guest appearance involved me presenting electronic instruments to a large collection of young women at a Catholic College to the northeast of Cincinnati. I had driven there with a car full of synthesizers for demonstration only to find a gaggle of giggly young women prepared to hear nothing of the sort. I don't remember the name of the town or the college, and well that I don't. I do remember, however, thinking that it was not a good idea to send your daughters to a women's school, especially in the middle of nowhere, as the glandular swell of off color jokes and innuendos nearly put me off my game. My presentation was required for every student to attend, and it was all I could do to get my car packed and out of there before being accosted by young women in heat searching for anything wearing pants at the moment. Any woman who resents my saying these things wasn't there to witness it. Don't kill the messenger.

At Middle Tennessee State University in Murfreesboro, I was invited because a group involved with electronic music had performed my *Arena* for cello and tape the previous year and liked it. So they asked me to give a lecture on new music notation—another of my books at the time—and listen to a performance of my *Bright Angel* for trumpet and trumpet on tape delay. Performance of this work involves live performance with the trumpeter playing into a microphone being recorded on a tape that is then linked to another tape recorder playing back the same thing but seconds later.

Visually interesting, but beyond that, the work stinks and I knew it then. Today, such mechanical marvels are handled routinely by computers. Then, it was novelty. I had, however, become so fond of the device, I'd forgotten to actually compose a good work. Listening to it in performance after knowing many of the audience had heard *Arena*—a good work—the year before was indeed painful.

A second trip to Chicago—against my wishes—put me in the program of some piano teacher's association and, with an audience of several hundred such teachers, I once again demonstrated for all to see how to safely prepare a piano and the wonders of the sounds that can be thusly made. I avoided cigarettes and nicotine this time.

Hamilton College in Clinton, New York, reunited me with one of my former students, Sam Pellman and his wife, and he kept me busy judging electronic music tapes entered in a local contest for such. I then performed a one-man show beginning with a piece for cello, bass drum, wind chimes, and voice called *Rituals*. I had hoped my friend, composer Bill Duckworth, would be in attendance that night. Then I saw him come in late and, so that he would get a chance to hear the whole work, feigned to the audience that I'd made a mistake and played the work a second time. A lot of these kind of things began happening at this point. I was becoming a bit shell shocked from the onslaught of my various trips.

The University of the Pacific in Stockton, California witnessed a fracturing of my left kneecap when one of my self-built instruments fell on it. At Ball State University in Muncie, Indiana, I locked horns with a new music hater and nearly got myself into a fistfight with someone too large for me to have done anything but hurt myself. Two problematic visits to Terre Haute, Indiana, which I detail in the first two volumes of these remembrances, kept me from that part of the state, though my eldest son, his wife, and two beautiful grandgirls currently live not too far from that city. A performance in Cleveland that forced me to drive from there across the state in two-foot deep snow in the middle of the night, a couple of performances in the big Apple and one at the Kennedy Center in Washington, D.C., are chronicled in the first two books of these series. Two trips to California State University Dominquez Hills proved eminently forgettable. Two performances at Cornell University held great promise but turned out only relatively successful. Tours with my own group called Ensemble Nova to UC Davis, California Institute of the Arts, California State University at Chico, and Linfield College in McMinnville, Oregon were well performed but ill attended.

And on and on. I don't remember most of the rest of them. No one now mentions them or remembers anything memorable about them. Around 1980, I decided to curtail my road activities to one or two visits per year. Interestingly, that's about as many requests as I now get.

the wei*g*ht of th*e* wall remains adamant.

li**ke** unto b**r**ass, as if t**o** make o**u**t

wh**a**t a mar**VEL**ou**S** **c**ast it is.

(1978-1987)

74

Musical Saw

*t*here wa**S** n**O** one li**S**tening that expressed **A**ny ide**A** that i**NT**elligent life *m*ight h**A**ve developed there. for **W**ho **S**aid he did not know any greater good o**F** g**E**ometry than the art**S** whi**C**h a**r** e ne**C**essa**R**y **T**o l**i**fe?

1978

During my first year teaching at UCSC, Gordon Mumma and I teamed up for a duet of musical saws.

Before I continue this story, I should mention that, while I was a complete novice on this instrument, Gordon was not. His abilities with the 'saw' were quite amazing, and he attended musical saw festivals whenever he could. I told him of my being a novice, but he said it wouldn't matter.

I went along with it.

That is, until I realized that no rehearsals were planned. This took me by surprise to say the least, and I asked him about it. He told me that if I wanted a rehearsal we could have one and asked when did I want to get together. I gave him a time, he gave me a place, and set up it was.

When I arrived and sat down sans musical saw, I asked Gordon if I didn't need a saw and bow. He answered in the affirmative and handed me one of both. Extras he'd brought along just in case, he told me.

Then he just began playing. No music stands. No music. He simply sat down and played.

I had performed in many experimental concerts before, though most not this loose. But, I held my curiosity back, sat down across from him, and attempted to play. By 'attempted' here, I mean that at first I could barely make a sound, and only with practice did I get to the point of scratching out a version of the first seven or eight notes of *America the Beautiful*.

At that point, Gordon stood up and told me things would be fine. Rehearsal over. I looked at him to make sure this was indeed serious business. It was. So I asked him what had just happened. He told me we had just rehearsed his piece. I argued that we hadn't even improvised, we'd just been playing our versions of musical saw in the same room at the same time. He told me, wasn't that great. I didn't know what to say. While I'd written much about contemporary music, heard many concerts, knew that Gordon had worked with Cage for many years, and was prepared for almost anything, this still seemed, as Gordon would often put it, 'far fucking out.'

All this was in preparation for a full house concert the next evening.

For this concert I was strangely nervous. After all, I had no idea what I was doing. And that, apparently, was exactly how I should have felt.

When our performance time came, Gordon and I took our seats at center stage and spent a while—not sure how long in retrospect, but not too long I guess—playing our saws and then, for whatever reason, stopped playing them, put them aside, stood up, and bowed.

And the audience went wild. We were a hit. I had no idea why, but we were. I still couldn't play the musical saw. Probably had done better in rehearsal. Didn't matter. We were a hit.

And, by the way, many people congratulated me on my successful performance.

who then **I**nterpret these words for the meas**U**red quantities

who unto him who suffers himself to ***b***e *bet*rayed by the

fate *o*f a **Z**ebra. i could ***n***ot s***e***e him, a*n*d the fi***r*** st **V**oice

which i he**A**rd was a trumpet ta**L**king with me with *ze*n.

75

Presidential

or **b**etter still,

ty**p**ew*ri*tte**N**,

A k**I**nd **O**f wick
or snuff,

that wi*LL* a**b**a*T*e it in a c*H*ain
or a**X**,

Or a**N**y igno**m**inious **ba**ggag*E*.

1978

As I mentioned briefly in Tinman Too, I met Eugene
McCarthy during his 1968 presidential campaign at the Sky
Harbor Airport in Phoenix, Arizona. McCarthy had risen to
fame by opposing the Viet Nam War and eventually forced
then president Lyndon Baines Johnson to withdraw from
the race. Robert Kennedy—the leading candidate for the
democratic nomination—had been recently assassinated in
Los Angeles and McCarthy was trying his best to fend off the
late run of Hubert H. Humphrey.

McCarthy was a poet-politician which endeared him to me, but gave him little clout against the real politicians that the American public seem to want in the White House. So I didn't give him much of a chance. However, shaking his hand while standing in a relatively short line of well-wishers seemed like the right thing to do. And so I did. I think I may have mentioned that I hoped he'd win, even though I knew he wouldn't. And, of course, he didn't. And neither did Humphrey. Nixon did, and we all know how that turned out.

My next meeting with a presidential candidate was many years later when I was a Dean and Provost in California. George McGovern had run as the democratic nominee in the 1972 presidential race and been beaten by Nixon, too. This time, I had the opportunity to actually spend some one-on-one time with the man and enjoyed it immensely. For he was a true intellectual in the best sense of the word, a charismatic individual, and would have made, in my estimation, an excellent president. But that was all water under the bridge by the time I met him, and we spoke about more relevant and timely issues.

I came away from both meetings with similar feelings. America seems to want hard-core politicians for the most part as their presidents. And I would characterize the same as true for their judgments regarding senators and congressmen. The kind, the poets, the intellectuals, need not apply.

Maybe the public is right. Wars require hard decisions, dealing with the house and senate a sturdy backbone, and even arguing treaties needs tough men so they can return home with the larger of piece of the pie.

Poets and intellects need not apply.

*Author's note: This was written prior to the election of Barack Obama.

and all that the primary power
or Spasm opera$T$es

in still vesi**C**les.

vesi**C**les AND thus

a **r**easona**b**le ti**m**e,

s**a**y a thousand yea**r**s,

and **C**aked on t**H**e**i**r wet skin
might scrutinise the transient creatures

that swarm an**d** multiply

in a single dr**O**p oF**W**ater.

76

GM

but a stuPendous antagonIsm,

a dr aggI ng togetheR of thE poleS

of the univerSe,

and a throne was set In heaven.

anD the onE that sat oN The throne

was the great diSillusionMENt.

1978

I have known composer Gordon Mumma for well over thirty years. He was, and still is, a major force in the world of new music, and with several others a veteran of the Once Festival, a 1960s Michigan new music venue that tauted that music would be played but once. Hence its name. Gordon was one of the two people responsible for getting me to come to Santa Cruz, where we became fast friends and colleagues.

They say that opposites attract and that was surely true with Gordon and me. He loves to hug people. I, on the other hand, am loathe to even touch people, feeling insecure about it, and generally convinced my doing so would prompt a misinterpretation of motives. Gordon is an archivalist exemplar. He photographs nearly everything he sees, and takes notes of when, where, and who. His small, extremely neat handwriting is unmistakable, and found on any item he deems important, which is nearly everything. I, on the other hand, tend to toss things on the floor without giving them a second thought, scatter things everywhere without name or date, and generally don't give a damn about what someone someday might think of what they've discovered.

Gordon and I, however, had one thing in common, though he had it more than I. Far more. Gordon, as effusive as he appeared when with people, loved his privacy. Likewise, while amiable in public, I adored mine.

One day, during the early summer of 1978, composer Roger Reynolds and I decided to pay Gordon an unexpected visit. Roger was in Santa Cruz staying with me while we both attended the Stanford CCRMA (Computer Center for Research in Music and Acoustics) summer workshop on computer music. Roger and I had driven the few miles between my house and Gordon's, and parked across the street just as the sun set. As we did so, we saw the silhouette of a figure, resembling Gordon, reading a book under a lamp in his front window. Very good luck. He was home.

Roger, who had known Gordon for much longer than I, having participated with him at the Once Festival, took the lead as we headed for Gordon's front door. The window being closed, he did not move on our approach. When we arrived, Roger knocked and as he did so we took turns announcing ourselves by name. As we did, I noticed the figure get up from the chair, turn out the lamp, and, I presumed, come around to open the door to welcome us.

I was mistaken. No one answered the door. The house was now dark. We waited for a half minute or so and then repeated our knocks and calls, hoping and even expecting that Gordon might have misheard our original introductions. And we waited. And we waited some more. But the door remained shut, and the house remained dark. No Gordon. No nobody.

I mentioned to Roger that it could have been Narrye Caldwell, Gordon's significant other at the time, but Roger said she would certainly have opened the door. And I agreed, knowing her. It couldn't have been a babysitter, since they didn't have children then.

We waited some more, and discussed whether we should knock again. We decided against it. Finally we made our way back across the street and drove to my house. Along the way, I asked Roger what he thought of what had just happened, or, what had in fact not just happened. Roger said something to the effect that Gordon was Gordon. No one had any idea what to expect of him. I argued that with two of his closer friends coming to visit, wouldn't he have wanted to see us.

Obviously not, Roger said. And he was right.

a**N**d he carr**I**ed me away

        i**N** the spirit

              t**O** a **G**R eat an**D** hi**g**h mountain

        b**e**cause i would understand the truth.

77

Meetings

and **H**e*L*d **A**t rest together
w*I*th th*E* water,

and in the ***m***aking of th**e** wor_l_d,

*BrE*ak you*R* own n**e**ck

down **t**he **a**nalytical engine.

1978

Academic faculty meetings are the worst such events I can imagine. It's not that I don't like the people involved for, with few exceptions, I do. It's not that the matters discussed are not important, although most of the time they aren't. It's that academics seem to leave their normal personalities at the door and take on demonic ones when they sit down at the table. The reason for this particular transition seems simple enough. They have to protect their sub-sub-sub-disciplines against their friends—now enemies—grabbing the small available funds for their own sub-sub-sub-disciplines. These meetings, initially scheduled for an hour or two, often last twice that long, with most of the agenda items tabled for further discussion to avoid out and out brutality.

One pundit described such occurrences as 'important to the participants because the stakes are so low.' And this very much seems to be the case.

When issues become particularly byzantine, like whether the department should move the drinking fountain a foot to the left to give the bulletin board more space to advertize concerts that few will attend anyway, I've tried every possible way to lighten our spirits, but to no avail. Aware of my proclivity towards attempting humor, I'm simply looked at and then ignored. The battle then rages on.

At one particular faculty meeting in Ohio, I remember an hour meeting having gone too long without a break and the chair announcing such before another two hours elapsed. During that break, I went to the men's room. There, while drinking a Diet Coke and peeing at the same time, the department chair came in and looked at what he must have thought quite a spectacle. To amuse him, I lowered the Coke from my lips and announced, "In one end, out the other, what does it all mean?"

I thought this a quite sage comment on the afternoon's administrative session, but he did not. For several weeks after that he avoided me in hallways and looked away from me during subsequent meetings.

I guess he already knew 'what it all meant.'

it was **J**ust a universal **D**igital co*M*p**U**ter
so th*A*t if its storage capacity a*N*d speed
were adequate.
the strongest idea incarnates itself

in **m**ajor**i**ties and nations

in the hea**l**thiest and strongest.

the b**l**ack charr**e**d **r**uins remained behind
to carry warfare sunward, their only escape from the
destruction.

78

Anniversary

wi*T*h   the   **GR**and
pro**b**ab*l*iti**ES** of *te*n and
eleven when she had ti*r*ed
herself out w*i*th tryin**G**, the
gre**a**t walls, the fur**n**iture, the
fl**O**o**R**s, and the *P*eople.

1979

My wife and I celebrated one of our wedding anniversaries—
most likely between years fifteen and twenty—at Nepenthe,
just south of Big Sur, California on Highway 1. The
restaurant and gift shop have been stalwarts of visitors along
the lonely highway there for some sixty-plus years. One story
of its origins suggest that Orson Welles created the place
on the north end of Big Sur for Ava Gardner when they
were married sometime after *Citizen Kane* was released,
and represented his answer to William Randolph Hurst for
building his monstrosity on the south end of Big Sur. But
that's just rumor. It was actually built by Bill and Lolly

Fassett in 1949. The restaurant was designed and built by Frank Lloyd Wright for twenty-two thousand dollars.

Nepenthe was a hotbed for notables in the 1950s and beyond, with writer Henry Miller, actress Kim Novak, and singer Joan Baez often visited during those and later years. Richard Burton and Elizabeth Taylor also ate there in the 1960s when filming *The Sandpiper.*

But all this does not cover what happened the night my wife and I held our private anniversary there. This was one of those special nights when after dark they lit the bonfire in the cage to the east of the restaurant, and anyone and everyone sat around it on benches and stared into the great fire, sang songs, and simply enjoyed the scenery we couldn't see. Nepenthe stands over a thousand feet above the Pacific, and that night we could actually hear the waves crashing far below us.

In any event, as the evening wore on, someone got the idea that two of its younger members were celebrating their wedding anniversary of something-something years. Not wanting to engage ourselves in whatever inebriated method our colleagues of the fire might have for congratulating us, we attempted to slip silently away. And we thought we had when we finally reached the parking lot below the restaurant and bonfire.

We were wrong.

The entire crowd, or at least it seemed so, had followed us down the hill quietly, and as we stepped into our car, the voices from out of the darkness sang happy anniversary to us. All as one. One as all. My first reaction was to get in the car and get going as quickly as possible, as it was clear some of the participating group were quite drunk. But we stayed. Glued to our stances aside the car. Something special was happening. We just didn't know quite what.

When the song finally ended, a huge round of applause erupted and someone lit some kind of lantern they'd happened to bring along.

And a merry time was had by all.

Particularly by Mary Jane and I, as we drove home along the once lonely road that was lonely no more.

all covered wit*h* dust, th*e* *M*artia*n*s seem t*O* have calcula*T*ed t*H*eir descent whose sore task does not to divide sunda*Y* from the week whose face the earth and the heaven fled awa**Y**.

79

The Bee and Big Sur

and sHoWs thAt

In any Sufficiently

Powerful loGical system,

statements will write upon Him

my neW nAme.

1979

In the fall of 1979, my family and I drove to Big Sur south of Monterrey, California, and camped for two nights in the regional park there. On the afternoon of the second day, we drove out Sycamore Road to Pfeiffer Beach and parked. This is a little known area that boasts extraordinary vistas of the Pacific and the cliffs of Big Sur itself.

While standing around the car waiting for my wife and kids to relieve themselves in the park's restrooms, a bee came buzzing by and decided to sting my left hand between my thumb and forefinger. For no good reason I could figure. After all, I wasn't its enemy. We hadn't even been properly introduced.

Ordinarily, such an event would not be worthy of inclusion in a book such as this. However, I am incredibly allergic to the toxic chemistry of bee stings and, like composer Alban Berg who died from complications from just such a sting, I was immediately in fear of losing my life.

I quickly rushed to the first aid kit we'd brought along and, using an alcohol dipped cloth, attempted to wring out as much of the poisonous crap as I could.

By the time my family returned from doing their business, I informed them that we should be getting back to civilization as soon as we could. I then showed them my hand that had by then, even in so short a time, swelled to twice its usual size. By the time we'd reached our campsite and our large tent—after all we had four young sons at the time—I felt woozy and faint.

As I lay down on the tent floor, I remember taking little solace in the fact that the bee, too, had died from the experience. And then I passed out.

Sometime later, I woke in the same spot with my wife rubbing my thumb and forefinger softly and the pain having subsided somewhat.

I obviously lived through this experience and, thank God, have not been so bitten since. It's interesting, though, to live alongside bees in this world. They mean no harm. Yet I am, when outside at least, at their mercy and always on the move in hopes they won't suddenly get the idea I'm honing in on their territory and about to attack them.

i ha*v*e never read

anYthing mOre CoNfusEd

and involuted.

                            and i Suppose *w*ith high
magnifiers,
mr frauenhofer and the man left,
and then dipped suddenly down,

and yet less ad*van*tage
as shall hereafter be shown.

80

Gug

Seal up those thin Gs which the seven

thundeRs utte red. outsIde, the LAst

of the red cards had Been exchanged for

silver coins taken Up. for mE who hunts

for the cAuses of things, no other path
will lead to them apart.

1980

During my years as an administrator at UCSC, I grew tired
of the drudgery with which my colleagues and myself took
our jobs. True, much of our work was tiring, maddening, and
repetitive. At the same time, I felt then and still feel now that
one can be of good humor and enjoy almost anything in life.

So, on a beautiful Sunday afternoon I decided to spend
my time indoors creating a marionette, a puppet with jointed
limbs that moved by strings attached to them from above.
My marionette turned out to be a large, gangly bird that I
built from various found items in my garage. This colorful,
duck-like being had a silly grin and long strings so I could

walk it alongside me while standing up straight. I could also control its mouth so it would appear to talk. Of course, I provided the words, and by using a high-pitched voice gave the impression of the bird itself speaking. Effective, since it was difficult for onlookers to watch my mouth and the bird's mouth at the same time.

Once a week or so I took Gug—the name I gave it and having no particular meaning—on a tour of the administration building. It spoke to each person it met on a first-name basis, and before long smiles appeared and, at least on the days I paraded Gug through the halls, people seemed happier after Gug and I appeared than before.

I still keep Gug hidden away. I pull it out of its hiding place whenever life gets me down. While I can't parade it through the halls of administration buildings any longer, I find it works great with grandkids, visitors, and even when I'm alone. Just looking at its homely face and weird skeleton-like body gives me back my humor, and the knowledge that life is no fun without a natural sense of play.

that not enough remain**S** for the animal

functions. hardly enough it is **B**y its gravity

that it is drawn aside. s**O** alice ve**N**tured to
taste it, but then in what remains we find a
further skin to be stripped off, and so on.

81

Memories

who indicated that

he himSelf Had knOwledge

Of these sPecific diffeRenTiaTions

of gEometRical Matters wHO

confound real quanTities themselves,

with their relatiOns and vulGaR

meAsures do seem to mean

something at least to the

People wHo deal

wIth all of it.

1980

I believe there are times in one's life when a chance set of connections in one's brain creates memories of events that never occurred. This may be one source of *déjà vous* and similar experiences. I have one of these memories that I cannot place in my reality, nor can anyone involved remember a time when it occurred.

I am sitting in the passenger seat of a car I don't recognize, with my father driving down a long road with desert on either side of us. We eventually approach a farm or ranch, I don't know which. My father drives into a large flat area in front of a barn, gets out, and immediately meets a tall, lanky farmer who seems to know him. They begin a discussion, while at the same time my father points me towards a barn, as if asking me to investigate.

The smell of the place is overwhelming. Mostly dung from chickens, cows, horses, and so on, I imagined, not actually having been on a farm or ranch before.

I walk into the barn and, when my eyes adjust to the darkness, see the stalls of large animals, and the nesting places for smaller ones. Everything is neat and tidy, and the animals seem more like those found in dioramas than real. They don't move. Just stand there as if trying to please me. Not even seeming to breathe.

I step outside again under the blazing hot sun. My father, his car, and the tall farmer are no longer there.

At first I'm shocked and even a bit frightening. But then I assume I've somehow walked through the barn to the other side, and am now standing behind the barn and cannot see them.

In the far distance, low mountains with small clouds nestled around them crowd the horizon. But no trees anywhere. As if this barn and animals are the only things that exist beside my father, myself, and his friend.

When I return through the barn and back outside again, the car is back in place. My father and the farmer, however, are still missing. Since there's no house, just the barn, I have to assume they've gone in there. And since my father is an accountant, I assume he has followed the farmer into the barn to count the animals or something.

Not wishing to see the diorama again, or even fearing my father and his friend may have turned into stuffed humans, I go to the car, get inside, and wait for them to return. All the while, I cannot get the smell out of my mind. It's overwhelming, and even as I remember the memory now I can smell it.

My father eventually returns to the car. I'm not sure from where, because I'm not paying attention, and he turns us around and we drive back the same way we came. I cannot see the farmer.

And that's it.

A meaningless memory so vivid that I can, with little effort, place myself back in that car and barn whenever I wish to.

But, I'm told, it never happened. My father never drove me to a barn in the desert. He told me that several times when I brought up the subject.

A dream?

Someone else's memory?

So real and so lacking in meaning.

Lacking in everything, really, except for the sense that it really happened.

and in finer skies
and earths does the

appearan**C**e of some

*z*inc dante or columbus
apprise you, and i will write upon

*h*im my n*e*w name, wet *f*ingers
opened, flipped out into the
air, and early in the
twentieth century

ca*m*e the g*r*eat
disillusionment.

82

I Remember Him

*a*t

fi*r*st,

i thought

Mor**N**ing

h**A**d **c**ome

and must h*A*V̲e

ACcel̲er*A*ted its coo*L*ing

to t**H***E* temperature at which

life c**O**ul**D** begin, and thi*S* ver**y**

Accou**N***T* must *E*ve*R* remain unmoved.

1981

During the early 1980s, I began building musical instruments in my garage and eventually in my in-garage studio that I built for them. This was an exciting time for me. It was also a schizophrenic time in that my music for these self-made instruments seemed diametrically opposed to the work I was doing with computers and algorithmic music. But, somehow, that didn't bother me. I also had no idea that I would eventually have to dismantle my studio for legal reasons dictated by the expansion of our house, and that would lead to curtailing my instrument-building career. For the time being, however, all was well. Except, that with four growing sons eager to get into just about anything they could—for justifiable reasons, I might add, since I'd preached to them about the glories of creativity and curiosity—I needed to protect my tools, resources, and finished instruments for fear they would otherwise find their way into family use.

One of the works I created for my protected instruments was called *I Remember Him* for voice, inverted resonator with long springs attached, a bass bow, and wind chimes. While performance was made difficult by the need to transport this instrument and to perform the piece myself, all my instruments could be played simultaneously.

I recorded the piece several times, but was never happy with my performance and these recordings never made their way to vinyl or CD. Not really a problem, since the score to my piece never made it to a printable version either.

At least two decades later, and after I'd given up my instrument building career, a Korean performer commissioned a new work from me. She played the gayageum, a twelve-string zither-like instrument usually performed in a seated position and sounding incredible with someone using the right skills. Like her. A colleague of mine, Hi-Kyung Kim, arranged the rehearsals and final concert.

So busy at the time with other events in my life, I ended up killing two birds with one stone. The first bird was to accurately notate *I Remember Him*. The second bird involved rewriting it for the Korean instrumentation that involved, at this point, a Korean drum, wind chimes, and the aforementioned gayageum, not unlike the spring resonator I'd used twenty years prior.

As it turned out, the performer was quite taken by the work, as was I. Of course, she had to sing as well as play, but practiced carefully to make this happen successfully. And it worked, if you'll pardon the expression, swell. So swell, that she performed this new version of *I Remember Him* several times in the US as well as Asia. And eventually recorded it for a Korean CD company of which I have no further knowledge. Just that she did.

Before she began rehearsing the piece, she had her voice, her drum, her gayageum, but no wind chimes. So I loaned her a set from my ceiling at home. The set that had begun my collection originally when it was given me by the owner of a wind-chime store in Cambria many years before.

As she traveled from performance to performance, it slowly became clear to me, and certainly her, that these particular chimes had become a definitive part of the piece. As if no other chimes could be used.

And so, with some regret and sorrow, I finally gave the chimes to her as a gift for her many performances. And so those chimes are somewhere out there even now, actively—I hope—engaged in remembering him, based on a poem created in English by a young Navajo girl for a high school writing assignment.

the foils young osri**C** cousin haml**E**t.
for them the water drowns ship
and sailor like grains of dust,
but learn to swim and wave

Zeal**O**usly drow**n**ed.
it will be cloven by it

and carry it like a
plume and a
power from
one of the
shelves.

83

Andre

and *l*ooked at *it* and **S**aid, <u>**G**</u>o and *t*ake
He *little* book which is o*p*en in the h**A**nd
o**f** the glassed eyes of bu**i**ldi**n**gs, but close**d**
to t**h**e ai**R** <u>**O**</u>f **T**he city and natu*r*e and
pass*i*<u>**O**</u>*n*.

1981

One of the best films I've ever seen is, interestingly, barely a film. It is, rather, a dinner held between two fascinating people with very different slants on life. This film is called *My Dinner with Andre*, and its script is based on actual conversations—over dinner and not—between playwrights Wallace Shawn and Andre Gregory playing themselves in the movie.

I suppose my intense interest in this picture is based partly on the fact that I still can't believe that most of the action—if one can call it that—takes place in a restaurant with just two people talking. The film score consists of background music of inconsequential muzak. Inconsequential

characters, such as the waiter and busboys, are simply that—
inconsequential—and the camera angles, while not arbitrary,
seem almost ruthlessly bound to who's talking at any given
moment, with an occasional reaction from the listening party.
How can a film so uninteresting visually be so completely
mesmerizing? Obviously, the conversation is spectacular, with
Andre—the title character—as the primary focus.

That said, an important descriptive passages that Andre
relates to Wally consists of an important visit to the hospital
that I couldn't paraphrase nearly as well as the actual
monolog,

> You know, we'd gone to the hospital to see my
> mother, and I went in to see her. And I saw this
> woman who looked as bad as any survivor of
> Auschwitz or Dachau. And I was out in the hall,
> sort of comforting my father, when a doctor who is
> a specialist in a problem that she had with her arm,
> went into her room and came out just beaming. And
> he said: "Boy! Don't we have a lot of reason to feel
> great! Isn't it wonderful how she's coming along!"
> Now, all he saw was the arm, that's all he saw. Now,
> here's another person who's existing in a dream. Who
> on top of that is a kind of butcher, who's committing
> a kind of familial murder, because when he comes
> out of that room he psychically kills us by taking
> us into a dream world, where we become confused
> and frightened. Because the moment before we saw
> somebody who already looked dead and now here
> comes a specialist who tells us they're in wonderful
> shape! I mean, you know, they were literally driving
> my father crazy.

This simple and presumably accurate recollection—these conversations represent transcriptions of actual conversations between the two characters that occurred without any knowledge at the time that they might become a screenplay—describes a type of specialization that has become rampant in the past century, and fits with so many similar situations in my own life that the word 'countless' comes easily to mind.

The reason I'm quoting from this wonderful film and making such a big deal of it may be self-evident to some, especially those familiar with my work. But try as I might, I cannot help but once again relate my feelings on such matters. And, of course, the importance that, as a civilization, humankind cannot continue to operate in this way. Henry Ford's assembly line may produce more cars, better cars, and cheaper cars, but it also produces less knowledgeable people, people with less feelings of self worth, and people who are less adaptable to new challenges. Thus, high unemployment and poor economy. But worse, of course, is the problem of no one knowing what the hell's really going on.

Apparently, we must give titles to things. He's a lawyer, she's a doctor, and so on. And, of course, present day society doesn't stop there. She's an oculist, he's a trial lawyer, or he specializes in contract disputes, and she in surgery, not diagnosis.

Somewhere in these pages I describe a meeting I once had with a well-known astronomer who, I came to find out, didn't know where in the sky the star he was currently studying was, had never had an interest in telescopes or optics, and, in fact, had no real interest in astronomy. He worked with computers only, spectroscopy only, and probably had more in common with chemistry than astronomy excepting his degrees were in the latter. But, even in chemistry he would be considered someone with a high level of specialization. I didn't want to embarrass him, but before I understood these points, I asked him question and after question about things astronomical basic to an amateur astronomer's knowledge. He couldn't respond. His tack was simple: "What has any of this to do with my work?" Like asking a jockey what his horse that day might have eaten for breakfast and getting the reply, "Hey, I just ride 'em, I don't feed 'em."

I believe that most young people are a lot like I was at their age. Interested in everything. I wrote my first epic poem before the age of ten. Amazing? No. After all, it wasn't any good. I also wrote short stories, drew bad comics, built small telescopes and powerless radios, studied rocks, practiced piano, went to art school, composed, and on and on. Impressive? No. Not in the least. Most young people are interested in everything. As they should be. 'Specialization,' as Robert Heinlien put it, 'is for insects.'

And then along comes school, and we begin to see the world as divided into specializations. Our teachers tell us that if we are to survive in this world, we must center our studies on one small area. The reason given; there is simply too much knowledge to be had out there, and our minds too small to understand it all. We must become small cogs in a very large machine. In other words, know what the cog must do to keep the overall machine running, and be happy knowing that, like ants, we should believe that there is a queen ant keeping the whole thing moving in the right direction, even though the queen ant has no idea either. That we aren't just eating, sleeping, working, and so on, until we retire and then get bored and die. That there's something more to life than that, even though, given most such situations, there really isn't.

When I'm asked what I do, I tell the truth as well as I can. I compose, write books both fiction and non-fiction, author plays, design board games, program computers, create visual art, teach college, and on and on. As a response, I usually get something like, "Oh, I mean for a living." Luckily, now I can answer, "I'm retired." Before that, I typically said that I teach music and artificial intelligence, narrowing the field down to two areas, usually finding that enough. But some still need more refinement and so I tell them music theory and composition, or just music composition. Whatever makes them happy.

A friend of mine who is equally if not more concerned about the state of the world's specialization terms himself 'an unrepentant dilatant.' This then brings up the notion that those who do not specialize are, in fact, nothing more than dabblers. Or, worse yet, people who 'know a little about a lot, and a therefore, 'a lot about nothing.' A convenient and expedient way to dismiss those who tend to embarrass themselves with their ability to relate things across disciplines in ways that connect rather than separate.

In my own life, the ability to cross-fertilize between disciplines has given me enormous challenges and extraordinary opportunities. As example, I am, by education, degrees, and life-long dedication, a musician who, I suppose, could be described as a specialist in theory and composition—even though I teach other subjects in music as well. I am also a novelist, for no other reason than I have written novels that people have read and liked. And these novels are published. Over the years, composing music and writing novels—and short stories—have been extraordinary bedfellows for me, each area feeding the other with questions and answers. This is not to say that one individual composition is particularly related to one particular novel. Such is not the case. This means that a problem encountered in a particular piece of music, say continuity without boredom, can be solved by writing a novel and discovering the same type of situation there and solving it, learning the process, and applying it in my music.

Let me give examples, and begin with writing since most everyone reading this will have had experiences with writing and the associated skills necessary to that subject, and not so much with music and its associated skills. To begin, a novel requires three overarching elements that I call, plot (P), character (C), and description (D), the latter of these including such things as description of location, circumstance, weather, personal conditions at a particular time, and so on. Every novel I've read has all three of these elements, but in much different proportions to one another depending on the author's style. For example, popular novels that take a legal point of view are often more plot, some character, and little description. I'm reading such a novel as I write this. This book is a legal thriller where the plot is dominant, a little character thrown in for effect, and almost no description whatsoever. I never seem to know whether it's rainy, sunny, foggy, what the characters are eating, and so on. Everything is centered on plot with occasional explanations of how the legal process works. This book was number one on the New York Times bestseller list and is clearly well written. I shall label it is Pcd with upper case used to emphasize plot. The book I read before that one was pCD, where character development and the extraordinary winter of Wyoming were the major forces in the book, and the plot almost secondary. For some people, plot-centered books belong to the pop fiction category, and character-centered books more to the literary category. To some, such categories mean that the former gets tossed or passed around, and the latter gets placed in libraries and checked out. I tend to ignore all that crap, and try for PCD, with emphasis being as equal as I can make them.

In music, the P, or plot, typically relates to form—where idea(s) gets the most attention, C, or character, typically equates to the manner in which ideas in the plot are examined or varied, and D, or description, involves orchestration, dynamics, articulations, associated with P and C.

While the emphasis of each of these areas will change slightly during the course of a work or novel, they rarely suddenly change and remain that way for long without a dislocation in the reader's mind occurring. This I call continuity. Continuity in writing and music simply means that characters and themes cannot suddenly shift their moods or dialects, and so on, without some kind of explanation. Musical ideas can't suddenly disappear without occurring again or something to suggest their necessity in occurring in the first place.

Both language and music require rules, though they are often quite different in usage. Language has definite syntax and semantics, and to vary these requires some kind of explanation no matter how subtle. The same is true in music, where major triads appearing among more challenging harmonies provide shock, but one occurring among many similar types can provide consistency and, without variation, boredom.

All relations and complexities can exist given the right circumstances in both mediums. It's how one deals with these relations and complexities that make the difference between success and failure. As example, I like to begin my novels with a demonstration of the problem that needs fixing in terms of plot. Hit the ground running as it were, and not let up until there's an opportune moment to do so, if at all. My music tends to take the same tack. But both these tendencies repeated over time can make novels and music predictable and formulaic. Even highly problematic, as is the case with slow movements in music, where hitting the ground running can work contrary to the basic concept. Or having the protagonist always as the center of attention in novels. Variety is not just the spice of life, but most of the meal as well.

Every time I encounter a problem when composing, I sit back and review what the parallel is in writing. I've never been disappointed, and have never been unable to solve my problem in this manner. And, of course, vice versa as well.

One of my greatest personal successes has been discovering that I'm a better sculptor than painter. I've mentioned this many times before but it bears repeating. Sculptors consider the block of wood, marble, clay, whatever, as already containing the finished work, and the sculptor's job is to find that work by removing, not adding, material. I find by creating in whatever my medium may be as a rough first draft as quickly as possible—thus maintaining the true essence of my initial imaginings—and then slowly peeling away material, separating what I then have into what I want, a perfect way to achieve my goals. Without my art school experience in my youth, I would never have imagined this process.

Another example of how a broader approach can help one achieve a successful end result is by actually blending two or more different mediums into one. For example, I always read my novels aloud, word by word, as a musician might sing them, to see if the rhythm works, the sentence—or phrase in music—doesn't get monotonous, and whether my breath will hold as I do. These and other indicators produce many corrections per page, corrections that would never have taken place were I to have simply read the material in my mind as many writers do. Likewise, as I compose, I always include at least one sing-through—even in instrumental passages—in which I listen for a sense of stress and non-stress so clear in writing. All of these tricks occur only when having similar experiences in more than one medium. This makes, I believe, for much better results, at least from the creator's point of view. By which I mean that the results more exactly reflect what the creator wants, not that the work or novel will be better in the eyes and ears of the public—even though I think that true as well.

While teaching, I firmly believe in telling my composition students to study other forms of art in order to better understand music composition. My words often fall on deaf ears, but I keep at it nonetheless. My favorite advice is to tell them to watch the standup comedy of Bill Cosby and Garrison Keillor, incredible storytellers who reveal the secrets of the narrative of any time-sensitive art form. Plays. Novels. Films. Music. Ballet. And so on.

For example, Cosby can—and typically does—build a complete show around a single innocent fact of daily life, captivating audiences for hours without a single joke in sight. Stories about his kids, for example, that stood for many years as a model for me of how to raise my own children while maintaining a sense of humor, gave me hope that my fatherhood stood a small chance of succeeding. He also taught me how to take a simple fragment or motive in my music and see it from every point of view I could and still lead it to an inevitable ending. That should have been obvious to me but wasn't. An important lesson for composers to learn. The subtleties and nuances to keep one's attention, while not seeming to do so. The humor may not transfer so easily to music, but that's hardly the point. What does transfer is the timing. And timing is what music is all about.

Garrison Keillor's magic comes from his ability to spin his stories from a make believe place called Lake Wobegon, Minnesota. Of the ordinary and not so ordinary people who live there. Again, his timing is extraordinary just as Cosby's. He can circle around a single focus for an hour or two, never quite getting there, but approaching it ever so closely. He produces diversions, yet somehow brings them back to the subject so that everything, in the end, weaves together in a strange but logical way.

What I have written so far in this diatribe is not a story, but more of a position paper. So I will end with a story, both relevant and, I hope, purposeful. This story, interestingly, has little to do with my integrated creative processes as discussed above, but more to do with how multi-disciplinary work is perceived in the real world.

I have just completed signing two contracts, one for the use of my music in a film, and the other for the use of my non-fiction writing contribution to a non-fiction book. Both have been accepted, and are in no jeopardy of being revoked given the following.

Interestingly, the same publicity person had been hired for both projects. How that occurred, I have no idea. I discovered this potentially useful collision over a two-day period. On the first day, the woman involved in the publicity for the film had received my bio as she'd requested, called me, and asked me for a revision. I had, of course, listed myself not as a specialist, but as a generalist, with several of my fields of study and creativity listed. She argued that this would only confuse anyone reading it, and could I re-write it such that only the music part remained. I argued, of course, that I was active in all these areas, and that this was an opportunity to publicize my other activities as well as the one I was representing in the current film. Her response went something like this, "Sure. Well. We're all writing novels, poems, reading books on astronomy, and so on, but I'm talking about what you do for a living here." I responded,

"I teach for a living, along with administrating, advising students, and so on." She then said, "No. I'm talking about your creative life." And the conversation continued for some time before I finally gave up, told her to rewrite my bio for her publicity anyway she wanted, and promptly forgot about the whole matter.

That is, until the next day, when she called me back and made the same comments about my bio for the book. It was clear from the beginning of our conversation that she made many such calls each day and had forgotten my contribution to the film. Thus, our conversation seemed funny to me. Where the previous day she'd argued for me to be a composer, today she argued for me to be a writer and, in this case, a scientist. She even included a repeat of her comment about how we all did the things I'd mentioned.

I listened to her and agreed she should rewrite it to her needed specifications. Then, I told her of the similar conversation we'd had the previous day and about how she'd then argued for me as being a composer. She was quiet for a moment, and then said, as I sort of imagined she would, "Oh, that's interesting. Well good for you." And hung up on me.

Neither of these story-teller comedians ever tells a stock joke. They take simple ideas and people, and join them in ways both odd and commonplace. Exactly what composers should do.

For me, the great composers and their works depend on this kind of timing. Whether they come by it naturally or by studying the works of other non-musical artists, I don't know. Not so much what you do, but when, exactly, you do it.

the g**O**ds, for the ne*ce*ssity fo**r** their five-fold **n**umber *W*as k*N*o<u>W</u>n, if the nebular hypothe<u>S</u>is has any truth, if the meaning of the word thin**K** is to be found by exam**I**nation.

84

Panetta

overwhe**L**me**D**   by   th**E**

MOCkery   of   ramu*s*   by

t*h*e   oergrowth   of   some

Complex*i*o*n,* *a*ndh**e**ca**R**r̲ed

me **A**way in *t*he spiri**T** t*o* a

g*r*eat and high mountain.

1981

During one of my tenures as Dean and Provost on the campus of UC Santa Cruz in the 1980s, I had the good fortune to meet Leon Panetta, who has at one time been US Secretary of Defense, Director of the Central Intelligence Agency (CIA), President Bill Clinton's Chief of Staff, Director of the Office of Management and Development, and far too many other distinguished posts to mention here. When I met him, most of these positions lay in the future and he was then still a US Congressman from California.

The occasion for our meeting was his being invited to my college's graduation ceremony as distinguished guest speaker. An excellent choice, I thought.

As provost, it was my job to greet Panetta, accompany him in a long procession to the outdoor stage, sit with him next to the dais, and then introduce him to the two or three thousand anxious parents awaiting their sons or daughters to get their diplomas and graduate. Finally.

Luckily, Panetta's politics and my own jelled quite nicely, and so we fell into conversation quickly. And not just about politics, but about education, conservation, and terrorism—yes, it had been prominent then nearly as much as today.

Unlike some other guests of the college at this time each year, I did not argue my own views or dominate the conversation as I am wont to do occasionally, but spent most of my time listening. I found him almost exactly the same person that his political ads made him out to be. A rare commodity for a lawyer/politician.

I quickly revised my introduction in my mind to make it more personal and less an iteration of his accomplishments, and all went swimmingly. Until that is, some idiot with different politics shouted something unintelligible but obviously disagreeable from the large crowd.

Uncertain whether Panetta understood the comment, I watched him as he waited the man out, and then told the audience that disagreeing was not only an American right, but the first sign of a democratic society. Had he left it there, the man may have continued. Instead, however, Panetta added something along the lines of "for all, that is, except those of us who have to take the brunt of free speech." This brought two things; laughter, and a round of applause that silenced the man who'd spoken without being recognized.

The rest of graduation went smoothly.

I thanked Panetta for taking the time from his busy schedule to speak to the graduating class. We then spoke briefly about our shared political views, and off he went. On to far bigger and better things than I.

> and as its slow seasons
> changed huge snowcaps
> gathered, and the man
>
> le*f*t, and the ***O***thers
> proportionally relieved
>
> and thus the *f*orce of
>
> the **S**crew may <u>**BE**</u>
>
> deduced f<u>**R**</u>om <u>**A**</u> <u>**L**</u>ike
>
> resolu***t***ion of st***aff***
> forces.

85

Doe Doe

and

in t**he**

*r*ight **O**rder,

an eye **LI**ke

mar**S** t**O** thr**e**ate**N**

an**d** *CO*mmand come to an end.

1987

We live on the edge of a canyon about two miles from the
Pacific Ocean. While not completely wild, this canyon is
home to many different species of animals such as coyotes,
skunks, possums, deer, and so on. My wife Mary Jane loves
flowers, and so is happy that our land rises enough above
the canyon, that the deer there—which love to eat roses,
for example—cannot easily leap our fence. On the other
hand, I have much more affection for animals than plants,
and secretly built a small ramp—using biodegradable grass
clippings—so deer could leap our fence and enjoy our yard
while I then enjoyed watching them. To make a long story

shorter, the deer finally made it over our fence, and one evening we discovered a left-behind doe in our yard. We named this deer "Doe-Doe," since it did not seem very bright.

When we first encountered Doe-Doe, I attempted to speak to it. All the doe did, or course, was leap back over the fence in terror. However, as I continued to speak to it on its subsequent visits, I noticed that this doe responded to certain sounds quite differently than other sounds. For example, when I raised my voice two octaves into falsetto and "cooed," much as I do when speaking to human babies, Doe-Doe would pause and listen, and not run for safety. After a few more visits and some experimentation, I selected certain sounds that Doe-Doe seemed to prefer and, even though neighbors often stared at me as though I'd recently been lobotomized, Doe-Doe seemed perfectly content to listen to me and calmly chew its evening dinner. Whether the doe considered me a harmless idiot, or a non-formidable but interesting onlooker, I don't know.

By this time, my wife had discovered a way to discourage the deer from munching on her roses and other plants—a non-toxic and biodegradable spray. She applied this spray according to the instructions provided and, sure enough, Doe-Doe stopped feeding on her garden. Unfortunately for me, Doe-Doe then crossed our yard off her dessert menu and, except for a few scant glimpses of her in the distance, we never saw Doe-Doe again.

Several weeks later, while I looked through various containers in our garage for lawn food, I encountered an unlabeled can of liquid and asked my wife about its contents. She explained that this spray had convinced the deer to leave her plants alone. She then told me its name: "Not Tonight Deer."

and

lowl*Y*

a**S** are the

m*O*nkey**S** and

lemurs, *T*o us b*E*low

and w*i*thin, and from without,

revolvin**g** below t**h**e *S*phere of

the most fixed **S**tars carrying the planets.

86

Marmots

i may be considered as a wed*G*e

between t*h*e tw*O* *i*nterna*l* sur*F*aces

*O*f a body s*P*lit by it.
and *HE*nce, the fo*R*ce*S*

of the wed*g*e

and t*h*e m*all*e*t* may be dete*RmInE*d

as may d*i*sho*NoU*r him.

1987

Marmots look like elongated fat prairie dogs, but generally like to sit on their butts rather than on their hind legs. Unlike prairie dogs, marmots also tend to eat almost anything. As example, smart campers on the western side of the Sierra Nevada Mountains of eastern California bring along a long coil of aluminum screening to wind around the bottom of their cars or trucks at night to keep the damn things from eating the rubber hoses off their engines and anything else up to and including tires. Like cats, many of them know they are cute, and will use that to their advantage whenever a crisis looms.

Once, a marmot stored himself in the wheel well of my Toyota Tacoma truck and went for a ride for five hours there on my way back from the mountains. How he survived in there without wheeling his legs on the spinning tire for four hundred miles was beyond me. But, when he staggered out and wandered into my backyard that late night in August, it was clear he'd done it. And survived. At least for the moment. I was too tired to follow him, and haven't seen him since.

take heeD of that.

yoU may as weLl ask a loom
which weaves huckaback

whY it does not make cashmere,
as expect poetry from this engineer.

let it be your lot to slander what you do not understand.

(1987-2000)

87

Yosemite Redux

on t*h*e h***orse***s b***a***ck were two riders. i***n*** short, then, there might be men c*L*everer than any given machine. b**U**t the**N** again, there might be *O*ther machines c*l*everer a*G*ain. an*d* s**o** on till at last one per**FOR**min*G* *I*ts revolutio*N*s in the same times **w**ith the vessel.

1986

On another of our yearly trips to Yosemite National Park, my wife and our four young sons decided—or maybe it was me who did—to pack a picnic lunch and head out toward Old Yosemite Road, the one that heads up the north side of the canyon to the high crest of the valley. Never paved, this somewhat harrowing ride was a switch-backing thrill or nightmare, depending on your point of view, and, unfortunately, historic or not, had never been maintained.

We knew that our hike would be short due to a large rock fall about two miles up, but had heard that the view of Bridlevail Fall was spectacular from that point. Both of these pieces of information proved true.

After lunch, the kids and their mother decided to investigate other views and various animals they'd seen on our way in. I, on the other hand, had much more devious plans. For the rock fall that prevented us from going further was enormous. Not only did the fall begin so high above us on the slope that I couldn't see its origins, but it consisted of extremely large boulders that just begged to be walked on.

So, without giving it much thought, I took a tentative step to the first boulder and arrived just fine. Then another. And another. Then a fourth. I should have stopped at three, for the fourth—maybe ten by fifteen feet in all—wobbled as if it had not yet settled in for the duration. And I began slipping. I reached back for some kind of leverage with my back foot and suddenly found myself spread eagle between two unstable rocks over the slide dropping quickly to the canyon floor maybe two-thousand feet below me.

When the two rocks finally settled their chaotic teetering, I discovered I was equally balanced on both simultaneously. Step forward or backward, and face the distinct possibility of toppling headfirst into the canyon below. I thought long and hard about it. Mom and her four boys initially finding Dad missing and then sprawled dead, or wishing he was dead, several stories below on a plateau of scree was not a pleasant picture.

My position was also jeopardized by the wind, which at this point in the afternoon was blowing up the face of the canyon wall toward the sky, but liable to shift at any moment to the opposite direction, aiding in my imminent demise.

My only hope for survival was to make a decision and without hesitation do what was required. If I failed, so be it. But to remain in my current position, I was bound to tire and lose whatever chance I had to escape.

So I stepped backward toward our picnic spot and hoped for the best. I took a deep breath, thanked God for having at least lived this long, and pulled my right foot from the rock more in front of me backwards toward the one slightly in back of me.

And it worked. For the first time since I'd been so stupid as to get myself into this mess, I was out of it. As if to guarantee my safety, the wind grew stronger, pushing me yet further back on my safety rock.

A couple of more steps on the remaining boulders, and I was back at the place where just a few minutes ago I'd been standing with my family. Now, thank God, I was alone with no one but me to account for my miserable one-digit IQ.

*G*o seek him the*R*e. he will stay till y*O*u come, *A*n*D* say **G**o and take the l*i*ttle ***b***ook which is open in the hand of the angel, and scr*U*tinise the transient creatures that swarm. finally i ***g***i*V*e th*i*s advice to a**N**y people who mi***g***ht be completel*y* unfamiliar with lon*G* mathematical questions.

88

Administration

aNd thence aΓ*I*se ce*R*tain
prejudices f**O**r the remo *VIN*g
of which it will *b**E** conv**e**nient.
a problem an**D** theorem **I**s disco**VER**ed
for all th**e** *d*ifferent kind**S** and quant**IT**ies
Of the arts **b**ound up with them.

1987

In the late 1980s, after having served nearly ten years in various aspects of administration at UCSC including a deanship and provostship, and having resigned due to my whistle-blowing activities because I could not in good conscience both serve and bring to justice simultaneously, I decided to apply for another job in the UC system, that of Dean. At the time, I figured the experience I'd gained over the years as an administrator should not go to waste if I could help it. While I'd been a reluctant victim initially, I'd apparently become fairly good at doing it. The money was much better than a faculty salary, and there was the apparent adulation of those below you in rank that was difficult to pass up even though, of course, I knew such adulation was fickle and not real.

With some hesitation, I got interviewed for the one job available that year. Since being drafted was more my style, I decided to prep myself for this interview so as to not waste my time. Thus, I carefully studied the documents the school sent me in advance, and even had a friend go over them and advise me carefully on what he felt they indicated. I had also been asked to give a forty-minute presentation and that I should take this invitation seriously. So I did that as well, writing a speech I felt would provide them with a good indication of the type of administrator I'd be. I even took time to review the previous dean and why he'd left his post. So much as I could ascertain, he'd been a minority highly interested in diversifying his faculty, students, and staff, something that I would find extremely important as well. Whether or not that played a role in his resigning his post or not, I had no idea except by rumor. I did know that the city and county where this school resided was well known for its lack of diversity, so I knew this might be a sticking point for me as well.

With all this preparation behind me, I flew to my interview, was picked up at the airport by an important member of the search committee, and did, I felt, a good job of representing myself to him. I then slept as peacefully as any insomniac can under the circumstances.

The next morning, my first interview was lunch with twelve members of the division I would lead given the job were to become mine. They had prepped themselves well, and didn't waste time getting down to details. I remember the first question they asked: Did I think their division was funded properly, and why or why not?

This was a good question, but almost impossible to answer. I had researched their budget, and my friend and I decided that, push come to shove, they were doing fine. At the same time, no group of twelve people interviewing a candidate for the position of dean wants to hear that they're doing just fine. After all, they were hiring a new dean to get more resources. So I answered as I thought they wanted me to. No, they weren't adequately funded, and the reasons were obvious; the arts never get funded properly in comparison to the divisions of science, social science, and humanities.

They asked for specifics. Having my sheet of salaries and budgets for various items of worth in front of me, I picked out several line items almost at random and simply added another person or a larger budget at will. The committee was good at not providing me with a 'tell,' signals of nodding heads, smiles, and glances among one another that give away that you've struck gold. So, when the grueling meeting concluded, I had no idea how weak or well I'd done.

So be it. I was by now used to speaking to dead audiences that, once they fully understood what I had to say, would agree and give me what I wanted. In this case a job as dean.

I then met with a series of individuals in different departments in an attempt to find weak spots in my understanding of fields different than my own. This meant meeting with visual artists, theater people, film directors and historians, and so on. I listened to their pleas for more equipment, more classrooms, more faculty, less students, and so on, and nodded vigorously when necessary indicating I agreed with them. I pointed out their lack of a foundry, appropriate green rooms, lack of practice rooms, and so forth, attempting again to read them for signs of disagreement but got none.

My final meeting of this sort was the most confusing of all; the vice-chancellor of the campus, a high-powered and quick talking woman who'd invited me for drinks at her campus home. I took a pass on the liquor and had water instead, expecting hard questions for which I needed a clear head. And a hard question I got. Immediately. How did I get along with her counterpart on my campus? This was a problem for me for two reasons. First, I didn't get along with her counterpart on my campus, since she was very much a party to the activities I felt strongly about in terms of conflict of interest and to which I was whistle blowing. But second, and more interestingly, my vice chancellor was also a high-powered woman much like the one to whom I was then speaking. I couldn't duck the question, though I figured I had to equivocate in some way. But how? My response then went something along the lines that while I occasionally disagreed with my vice-chancellor, I respected and admired her work ethic. The best I could do under the circumstances. Little did I know then, but the vice chancellor to whom I was speaking disliked my current vice-chancellor in the extreme. Had I responded correctly or not? Given that I was the only candidate that had such a situation, or at least presumed so, it seemed somewhat unfair of her to put me in this position. But there it was.

At day's end, I had dinner with the department heads that reported to the dean and immediately found myself knee deep in a fundamental contradiction. They asked me about my views on affirmative action. On this subject, I couldn't be evasive. I knew it was, at least to them, my Achilles' heel. I had by then been made acutely aware that the previous dean's views on this subject had done him in.

So, I measured my words carefully and explained that, for me at least, affirmative action was a situation in which all things considered equal, a minority candidate should be hired over a majority candidate whenever possible. Of course, the 'all things considered equal' part was the sticky wicket. And so, before the first course had even been served, I was in it up to my ears. Questions like, 'Doesn't my Irish blood make me a minority? After all, Irish blooded people were not in the majority at the moment.' I countered with 'race is the consideration, not politics or country allegiance.' And similar questions emerged that seemed equally volatile. Obviously, this group had been placed in a position where they'd had to hire a minority no matter what. I told them that unless the position had been advertised in that way, affirmative action was not that type of issue. And on and on we went, into the good night.

By the time I reached my hotel room and headed for bed, I felt like I'd been the victim of a tribunal, a kind of trial by fire. At the same time, I also felt like I'd held my own and was ready for the next round of hot questions.

My first agenda item the next day was my presentation to a large aggregation of students, faculty, and staff for which I'd written my speech. I'd taken their written statement that this be taken seriously, seriously.

When I finished, there were a few innocent questions and I was shepherded on to my next assignment. On my way there, one of the department chairs with whom I'd had dinner the previous night stopped me and told me she'd liked my speech. I thanked her, but she resolutely stood her ground. I remember her exact words then, "No, really I did." She said this as if I would find that hard to believe in some way. I let it go, and continued on to an afternoon of show and tell. Seeing concert halls, painting studios, and particularly the surrounding community including residences that were for sale. While I knew this latter opportunity was no doubt given to all applicants, it did give me the sense that my interview had been taken seriously.

My final duty was to meet for dinner with the head of the faculty senate. This, for me at least, was an easy one. I believed in the rights of faculty to express themselves not only on issues of importance in their areas of research, but also on issues of concern for the entire campus. Even though I was tired, the meeting went well and ended on a high note.

When I returned to Santa Cruz, fresh from my interview, I was confused at best, and worried as well. While I felt positive of my responses to the questions posed, and that I presented myself well, I feared that my current situation in whistle blowing had ultimately undermined my possibility for getting this position. At the same time, though, I could worry about these things uselessly forever and not be given the answer. That would arrive with either an invitation or a rejection.

When neither of these appeared over the next six weeks, I was not surprised. My guess was that they'd offered the position to someone else, and were simply bogged down in negotiations.

During this time, however, I took stock of my chances. I placed myself mentally in the position of those charged with hiring or not hiring me. As I did, I began to realize that I'd done just about everything wrong. Whether by subconscious design—down deep I didn't really want the job—or by reading the situation incorrectly. But 'wrong' was the 'right' word to describe the situation.

First, to assume that the committee that first interviewed me wanted nothing but more was incorrect. Each member wanted something for themselves, not for the others. By answering as I had, I'd created a situation in which it seemed I just wanted a larger budget. By inference, by making a random selection of where weaknesses lay, I'd put off those departments I hadn't mentioned.

Second, by not researching how the vice-chancellor felt about her counterpart, I'd missed an enormous opportunity to tell the truth rather than obfuscating.

Third, my responses to questions regarding affirmative action didn't suit those who felt strongly in their own rights of being granted special treatment, at least in their minds, for their nonconformist backgrounds.

Finally, by simply reading a speech, I'd bungled my opportunity to get the students, faculty, and staff behind me. I'd have been better off comfortably stating a few basic facts and spent the rest of my time responding to questions from the floor.

All in all, my evaluation of my own interview was that it had been a disaster. From the beginning onward.

I consoled myself with the fact that this was my first administrative interview. That I didn't realize how different it was from a faculty interview (although it was that as well since, when hiring administrators, the UC system required that each successful candidate be granted tenure as a faculty in their respective departments).

At the same time, I realized something more important. This was not only my first such interview, but my last as well. It had been an interesting experience, one I certainly wouldn't forget, but I should not have taken my previous positions as dean and provost as lost time just because I wouldn't continue along that path. In short, I decided that no matter the outcome of my interview, I'd had it as far as administration was concerned. My life was meant to be in teaching, research, writing, and composing, and not in running administrations.

Ultimately I did not get an offer, and for that I was truly thankful. For I knew that the temptation of good money and fake adulation would have been hard to pass up, no matter my previously stated position.

A dip in the water was good enough for me. I'd swim in other pools, thank you very much.

i saw a sta**r** fall from heaven
unto the earth, and moved

*i*t to *a* more barre**n**

spot sa**Y**ing
i have noticed
a man likes
to be complimented.

89

Breakfast in La Jolla

fo**r** this was *Ce*rtainl**y no**t
the first time f*O*r the
positio*N*s an**d** distan*CE*s
of thin**G**s f**R**om any body
cons**I**d**e***R*ed a**S** immovab*l*e
*T***H**e intelle**c**tu**A**l si***d***e of **M**an.

1987

At some point in the 1980s, I was asked to be a member of a three-man team to review the graduate music department at the University of California at San Diego, hereafter referred to as UCSD. Participating in such reviews in the UC system is an ordeal I had previously left to others. However, since I'd never served before I felt I could at least participate in one. So I accepted.

The actual review was not particularly interesting, even though the music department at UCSD was unusual in that it centered almost exclusively on contemporary music. What interested me most, however, was that my room in a posh

La Jolla hotel overlooked an outside dining room that served breakfast all day long.

So, on my first day there, the Sunday before the actual review process began, I looked out my window to see none other than Nameless sitting at the head of a long table of maybe twenty people having what some might call breakfast. I say some, here, because this breakfast included wine. It seemed to me that even though this wine was being sipped slowly and with the greatest of care, it seemed a bit early for drinking.

Nameless was—and still is—an extremely well known author of several New York Times best-selling novels. Not caring much about such things myself at the time, I was shocked that I even recognized him. No doubt from television interviews, photographs in newspapers, and so on.

With not much else to do at that point, I decided to take my time and watch what happened. I had a bird's eye view of what well-known novelists do when their time permitted it.

The first thing I noticed was that I recognized none of the other guests. Not a big deal, except that since I'd recognized the head of the group, I thought he would have garnered a more well-known audience.

The second thing I noticed was that Nameless talked very little. He listened, smiled at a small joke or two, nodded to someone who'd made an interesting point, and nibbled at his breakfast to ensure it wouldn't be taken away by an overzealous waiter before he'd finished.

Whenever he did speak, however, his minions stopped what they were doing to hear his pearls of wisdom.

Of course, with my room window permanently shut, I could hear none of this conversation, only watch as it took place.

I sat there for hours. Nameless never took leave of his seat. Never had need to use the porcelain convenience. Nor speak to the waiters. He just listened, chatted occasionally, and pecked at his food. It was an amazing sight to behold.

In our unspoken battle to see who had the greatest staying power, he won. I left my seat first. And before he'd dismissed his admiring public, I had to see some of La Jolla before my dreary days of administration began.

I had, nor have, any idea if this kind of behavior is typical of successful writers. Was he gathering material for a new book? Looking for an unusual tidbit to describe a character in his manuscript? Or just having breakfast with friends?

I have since read one of Nameless's novels and found no answer to my questions there. His characters did not resemble any of those I found fawning over him at breakfast that day. Nor did the plot reflect any of what I saw, though certainly I'd not heard anything and thus could not be sure.

Maybe he was just hungry for some company and having fun. His kind of fun. Intellectual fun. Nothing to do with writing. Nothing to do with his craft, and thus my eyedropping on his breakfast meant nothing at all.

But it was curious.

he already admitS

that life is an incessant
struggle for existence.

90

Ghetto

an**d** r**e**moter from t*H*e s**U**n,

*O*n **a** level in**St**ead of piling it into a mountain,

t**h**ey *H*ave c**O**nt*R*ived to m**a**ke of his te*RrOR*

the **m**ost harm**L**ess and energeti**C** f**O**rm of a state.

1988

During one of my first visits to Germany in the late 1980s, I presented a paper on my work in algorithmic music. That was followed by a meal with a self-selected group of presenters. This free lunch took place at a favorite restaurant of one of the organizers of the conference, and chosen because it particularly reflected what he felt was Germany's finest food. Since I didn't consider food one of Germany's most important contributions to the world's cuisine, I couldn't wait to discover how wrong I was.

As it turned out, I would still be left in the dark about this finest food, for the culinary tastes of our host was ham, and nothing but ham. Now, I must point out something here before continuing. While I know some aspects of my ancestry, others are more opaque. For example, my grandfather on my mother's side was named Schleicher, a German-Jewish name. However, my grandfather did not wish to discuss religion at any time. He also did not, as far as I could ascertain at least, attend any kind of church, temple, mosque, and so on. His words on the subject actually suggested that he held no regard for religion of any kind. In fact, he was equally biased toward all religions, backgrounds, races, and so on. Including Jews, who he held in equal contempt with other religious groups. Thus, I do not believe he was Jewish by birth, nor do I believe I am in part Jewish. At the same time, I will not eat pork. No how. No way. I'm not exactly sure why this is, but it is what it is.

So, as we sat down to lunch, and I realized that the menu contained nothing but pork dishes, it was clear I wouldn't be having any food other than bread and water. Unless, of course, since the rest of the menu was pork, they hadn't snuck some pork into the bread dough and water.

When it came my turn for ordering, I asked for my requisite bread and water as well as a desert that surely could not have contained pork. As I did so, I immediately became the center of everyone's attention. No one else had refused a meal, even those whose last names I presumed were Jewish.

In their minds I was Jewish. Simple as that.

Having no immediate way to set them straight without making things worse by denying what had become obvious, I let things be.

When we'd finished eating that afternoon, our host gathered us together for what he called a slight change of plans. We were to visit a very special place not too distant from the restaurant.

So we set out on foot to discover our host's special place.

When we arrived, I was shocked to discover that he'd brought us to a Jewish ghetto, the place in the city where Jews were kept separate from the rest of the city. My first reaction was that he would then explain that this was not one of those places set aside as a prelude to the extermination camps of WWII, but a place that Jews themselves had selected to gather together for reasons of common grounds and beliefs. But, this was not the case. He'd brought us there so that I, as the apparent serious Jew, could see the prelude to what had occurred not so many years ago.

I was dumbfounded. This was an incredible act as far as I was concerned. What would he imagine I would make of all this? What would the others, along for the ride, think I would make of all of this?

And so I watched the others in the group watch me. And together we looked at the ramshackle housing created by the Nazis to house the Jews of this city in preparation for their eventual murders in concentration camps.

It occurred to me then that I must be misinterpreting what was happening. That it wasn't some extremely callous act of cruelty. For none of my colleagues seemed to be of that mind.

So I searched my thoughts for some kind of rationale that would make this excusable. For example, was the group supposed to feel angry and sad at seeing this? Had our host felt that his unspoken guilt for his country would swell over and affect us all?

After this inspection of the unspeakable, we had coffee in a place reserved for coffee only, and headed back to the hotel where all of us were housed for the conference.

On arriving, one member of the group, possibly Jewish by the nature of both his names, asked if he could talk with me. I told him I was going for a walk. He asked if he could come along and walk with me. I told him I wanted to be alone. He told me he understood.

And that was that.

and t**h**ere **p**ut on him

and **s**ho**W** that

In any suffi**C**ien**t**ly powerful logic**A**l system,

statements later look o**U**t

would **S**how **T** he reasons
why some members were omitted

by the centripetal force of **Z**ero.

91

Dead Man

can you make

    a forest-ran**ge***r*,

      P~olicem~**an**,

        or *t*imber merch**A**nt

      out of the a**R**chitect

by thin**K**in**G** of **E**ucl*id*?

1990

Just north of Mammoth Lakes, California, is a campground on Deadman Creek. Dusty and dry in late August, this is one of the most downscale campsites in the eastern Sierras, surprisingly close to Mammoth Lakes, one of the most upscale towns in the eastern Sierras.

One particular day, two of my sons and I awoke wanting nothing more than to hike up to the high country and cool off.

Our first visit was the town of June Lake, about twenty or so miles north by car. We needed breakfast in someone else's place, not over a campfire that would put the forest around us at extreme risk. June Lake, just like Mammoth down south, has its own ski resort. Unlike Mammoth, though, it doesn't make its slopes available for bikers and motorcyclists, and thus the town during summer is fairly baron of people and the streets relatively free of cars. We stopped in a small breakfast and bar, if you can believe it, because it was the only place open at that hour.

At roughly nine in the morning, therefore, three campers entered the place that, yes, was a real tavern with several people belly up to the bar and drinking beers. We took seats in a booth at a window overlooking the main street, and ordered our pancakes over easy.

Looking around, I was immediately impressed by the dress of the other visitors. All women. And all looking at me. What a treat. Of course, I was the only male of age in the bar, and apparently the women had free access to the liquor and had served themselves as their needs demanded.

It was then that I began to get the idea of the lay of the land, with an accent on the principle modifier to 'land.' It was not that I was handsome, for I was a mess that only several days without cleaning myself, changing clothes, and getting stung by mosquitoes the size of eagles could provide. I was red meat. Not that I thought these women were prostitutes. Not in this town. Not at this hour. They were most likely middle-aged divorced and still active females looking for a desperate male to lasso. And I was it. For the moment.

I checked my sons for signs that they, too, had noticed this strange but silent charade. But they weren't the slightest concerned. Obsessed as they were with the morning's blueberry pancakes with a heavy dose of syrup from Maine.

Since this was not the way I wanted to begin my day of hiking, and I happened to be quite happily married, I got the three of us out of there as quickly as possible, leaving the women to tend to their makeup and other morning ablutions.

I should have taken this beginning to our day as the omen it was, but didn't. After all, how was I to know that the next eighteen hours would turn out like they did?

After parking my car in the lot provided across from Silver Lake, we then packed our gear and struck out for the country in which the predators were less dangerous than the women in the bar—black bears, mountain lions, skunks, and God knew what else.

The first hour or so was hardly roughing it. The trail we took was conveniently wide to accommodate the trucks that at one time had helped build the dam at the reservoir some thousand feet above us. Views of June Lake Valley were plentiful and quite lovely. Lots of green forests, various blue lakes, and several hundred white clapboard houses only partially hidden by the trees.

After reaching the first crest, the lake we encountered, the one behind the dam, was clear and quiet, with a hint of glacier melt—the whitish blue color that such lakes demonstrate. We hiked around its northern shore and watched the few fisherman trying their luck. Almost immediately we found ourselves lost in the forest. By lost, I don't mean that any of us was concerned. After all, we'd just seen a large lake accessible in both directions by a broad access road. I do mean, however, that the trail stopped. Or rather it branched out in several directions at once, with none of the branches indicating something like a true trail that would guide us toward our ultimate destination—Thousand Island Lake, one of the most beautiful, I'd been told, lakes in the Northern Sierras.

Hoping that these unsigned trails would somehow combine once again into a single signed trail, we stayed together and continued on. Down one side of a forested hill, and up another. Across dry creeks, over dead trees, and all the while kicking up our share of dust that even up here in the high country gave one pause. What kind of insect eggs were we inhaling into our lungs? Valley fever? Who knew?

Now beginning to feel that even my inner compass that I always kept for such occasions was not going to help us any, we stopped to reconnoiter. However, and mostly due to my oldest son's desire to constantly move forward, we hiked on again quickly. Toward where, exactly, I wasn't all that sure.

When we finally found a sign, it didn't indicate a pass or upcoming mountain any of us had ever heard of or could find on our maps.

Now we *were* lost.

While I encouraged us to head back eastward toward our parked car, the environment blocked us at every turn, as if guiding us toward its destination, rather than ours. And, of course, that's exactly what high country environments do; guide hikers downward toward watersheds and lakes via creeks, brooks, riverlets, and whatever the hell else you like to call them. Gravity will have it way.

Before long, I looked at my watch and it was near three in the afternoon, with no mountain I saw looking like any mountain I should have recognized. But we still followed my oldest son, for he had once created a four-foot by four-foot topological three-dimensional frieze of the area, and seemed to know what he was doing and where he was going.

When I finally begged for a respite, carefully measuring my words so as not to indicate my growing fears of our taking a wrong turn someplace, we came upon a sign that vaguely indicated the direction in which our destination lay.

Happy, I sat down in what seemed like a soft place but turned out otherwise, and told my two sons to go down to the lake and enjoy themselves. That I'd be along in short order.

After they left, I lay back on the dry pinecones, and ate some of their seeds—not bad for that time of the season. Hard to get comfortable, but the suddenly cloudy sky was rife with suggestions of cooling storms on the way, and the view of another lake, not Thousand Island, was extraordinary, lying a thousand feet below me. I then felt that sense of freedom in my bones that so often accompanies visits to the very high country.

Too quickly, however, my reverie was interrupted by the sound of voices approaching. And then, right in front of me, several other hikers, all of them female in gender I now noticed, appeared. Worse yet, I recognized some of them from that morning's breakfast in June Lake.

They stared at me.

And I them.

Awkward didn't cover it. Especially since, as they watched me, they began shedding their backpacks. It was my small meadow, damn it, and they had interrupted my reverie, not I theirs.

But here we were, some three or more thousand feet up from our meeting that morning, all alone, no more sons to shield their advances.

I realize that, at this point at least, my memory may sound a bit arrogant. But put yourself in my place. Outnumbered by ten to one. Alone in a high mountain meadow. Sans my kids for protection. I in my mid-forties, they about the same. None of them wore wedding rings, but I did. Though it didn't seem to make a difference to them.

What to do?

Once again, as embarrassing as it may have been, I stood, gathered up my backpack, and headed down the trail toward

Thousand Island Lake to find my two young sons. Leaving my un-introduced friends behind.

Were they really following us?

Or did they think I was following them?

Had I imagined the whole thing, confused by the high altitude?

Had I insulted them by being so quick to judge?

What would my wife say when I told her?

How could they be interested in me in the first place, no matter how lonely they might be?

All these thoughts and many more flooded my addled brain as I hustled down the trail, looking back over my shoulder for the women who had obviously, at least to my mind, followed us into the forest.

But, as I walked, I began to realize how stupid this was. The women did exist. They even might have been lonely. But our meeting was happenstance. Purely accidental. Coincidental. Random. Jeez, why are there so many words for the same thing.

In any event, I decided I was being foolish, and turned and walked back in the direction I'd come.

As I did, I realized it was nearing five in the afternoon and my kids had not returned from Thousand Island Lake. Had they taken another way back and I'd missed them along the trail? Had they come upon the bevy of females in my place, misjudged their own calculations, and headed off further into the wilderness?

I hurried my pace, and finally found the meadow in which I'd laid so innocently an hour before. No one there. No sons. No women. Just me.

What to do?

Was I now lost?

Was this a different meadow?

Forget about the women, where were my kids?

Where was I?

I decided the best thing to do was to remain stationary. Let them find me. If we were both moving, we might miss meeting. Lost here for the night without tents, matches, anything to eat, or sleeping bags in which to sleep.

What a mess.

That's when one of the women arrived. And smiled at me.

Good God, I thought, did they know I'd return, draw straws, with the winner getting her shot in first when I returned?

As I smiled back but withdrew at the same time, it occurred to me that once again, all these thoughts were crazy. This was the twentieth century. Civilization. Not the Stone Age.

So I gathered my wits about me, and asked my guest a simple question, "By any chance do you know where we are?"

She looked at me for a second, and then answered. "Why yes," she said, with a slightly southern accent, "we're in the John Muir National Forest."

And she smiled again.

"What I meant was," I said, "do you know *exactly* where we are?"

"Why yes," she said again, "we're on the trail to Thousand Island Lake."

That was not much more helpful, but it meant that maybe, just maybe, I might find my sons before dark that night.

"Have you seen two boys along the trail here by chance?"

"Why no," she said. Why she began all her sentences with the word 'Why' escaped me, but I didn't argue the point.

I wasn't sure that 'no' did me any good, except that it might mean they still hadn't arrived and that I hadn't missed them.

Then she smiled again.

'Jeez,' I thought, what a hell of a mess.

"Do you know the way to San Jose?" I asked her, before I'd really thought about what I was saying.

"Why no," she said, "I'm from back east."

"Actually, I meant 'Do you know the way to June Lake?'"

"Why yes, I do, it's back that way."

And she pointed eastward, as I knew she would. Of course, I already knew that. But I smiled and nodded my head anyway.

And she smiled back.

"Where did your friends go?" I asked her.

"We spilt up," she said, her first sentence without 'Why' beginning it.

"Oh," I said.

And that's when, thank God, my two young sons wandered into the small meadow, clearing, whatever it was.

"You should have come with us, Dad," my oldest said, "it was beautiful. And it actually looked like there were about a thousand islands."

I nodded to them as they then turned and looked at the woman standing there in her shorts and backpack. And some other things, too.

Then they looked back at their Dad.

"We've got to get back to June Lake before dark," I said, nodded toward the lone woman, gathered my sons, and took off toward the east.

Before long, we'd left the meadow far behind and had begun climbing. Something I didn't want to do, but what passed for a trail led only in that direction.

"Who was that?" my oldest asked me as we hiked along.

"Just another hiker," I said. "Someone who happened along."

"Do you know her name?" my youngest asked me.

"No," I said. "Just met her when you guys appeared."

My oldest turned and looked at me. He was sixteen or so, and the complexities of the situation were not lost on him.

"Really," I said.

"Sure, Dad," he said.

"Really," I repeated, "that's all there was to it."

He smiled, and I realized then that the more I protested, the more guilty I looked. Of what, I wasn't sure. But I didn't want to take a chance, so I shut up and concentrated on the trail. By now it had become quite narrow, with occasional views over a very deep chasm to our left. But, we were still heading east. At least there was that.

"Why did you guys take so long?" I asked, attempting to change the subject.

"Beautiful scenery, Dad," my youngest son said, and then actually winked at me. He *actually* winked. Jeez.

We finally stopped around six thirty, and drank water from a stream that blocked the trail and then slid over a fall several hundred feet down to a lake below that I now recognized. We were on the other side of the reservoir we'd hiked past that morning.

The trail then vanished into an enormous mile-wide pile of boulders that separated us from the dam that held back the waters of the lake.

So, we began our trip across, boulder hopping, while simultaneously hoping that the fence we could see on top of the dam would not prevent us from crossing. Else wise we would surely be stuck on the boulders for the night.

Then, if we didn't get some disease from our drinking untreated water from the creek, we'd most likely die from hunger, exposure, and loneliness because of our blocked passage.

As we prayed for the trip across the dam to be open, my oldest pointed across the lake to a group of women hikers walking serenely along the trial we'd traversed earlier and now waving at us. Or, more likely, at me.

My sons waved back.

I didn't dare.

When we reached the damn as the sun began to set, we found it open—thank God—and traversable.

We then walked across it and began the final leg of our journey. As we did, I noticed the outlet creek from the dam spilling into a forest and immediately over a fall there. This reminded me of the still looming stretch of road ahead of us. In twilight. With many switchbacks. And taking an hour or more, though going down would be faster than coming up.

As we began our last stretch, my oldest son noticed railroad tracks heading straight down from the road with an old single-person rusted car at the top no more than twenty yards from us. He decided to push the envelope.

He ran to the car, jumped in, pulled the noticeable brake back, and began heading down the near vertical tracks that no one with any sanity had taken in fifty years or more.

I screamed at him.

He smiled from ear to ear.

And straight down he went.

For maybe three more feet. Then the car abruptly stopped and he jumped free. With the brake set again.

By this time, I expected the ten ladies to jump out of the car in their birthday suits. But we made it back to the parking lot without further incident.

The car, of course, was extremely hot from the day's sun and being locked up tight during that time. The sun had set long ago, but a faint light remained, just enough to illuminate the exploding can of diet cola in the glove compartment that had clearly waited until this precise moment to drench all of us in its warm, sticky, caffeinated, bubbly, and sickening rain.

We arrived home in Santa Cruz sometime after two in the morning. Safe and demented from a single day of fun and excitement.

th**E**y we**R**e **a**ll loc**ke**d.

there *w*as*n*t even a *s*hadow,

but the light re*m*ained.

it is d*o*ne and there were voices

and th*un*ders.

bu*t*, however well
these deficiencies

Might be overcome

by c**L**ever engineering,

one could not send the cre**A**ture
to school without the other children

ma**K**ing **E**xcessive fun of it.

92

Bristlecone

but sO much to the PoInt
we have left.
we woUld make
as of ThE liBerty and glory
of the way.

1991

On one of our visits to the eastern Sierra to hike in the
high country, my oldest and youngest of four sons decided
to revisit one of the strangest places on earth—the Ancient
Bristlecone National Forest in the White Mountains, east
of the Sierras and just southeast of Mono Lake. Here, some
of the oldest living things on earth reside, some of them
reportedly over four thousand years old, having weathered
some of the foulest weather known to man. Standing over
fourteen thousand feet above sea level but not quite the
elevation of Mount Whitney down south, these trees literally
devour themselves for food and water during lean times, and
look like gnarled versions of Joshua Trees turned into pines.

This particular year, probably sometime in the early 1990s, the snow had been particularly deep, and even in August we could find shade from snow banks.

By the time we reached the end of the road that, by the way, led to a weather observatory higher up, we abandoned the car and hiked our way up the southern slope of the mountain.

For those that have not taken this journey, it comes highly recommended. The trail is steep but well kept. The altitude is very high, but quite survivable. And the views are incredible, mostly of the Sierras beyond the city of Bishop, which lies in the deep valley between the two ranges.

When we reached the first crest, we could see the trail ahead for four or five miles as it first dog-ears to the right into the mountains, and then reverses itself up the backside of White Mountain to the very top. Most likely a four to five hour journey that the kids did and I not wish to attempt given that it was already two in the afternoon.

So we investigated as far as possible the observatory manned year around, and then, after resting and having a granola and tuna fish snack, began to retrace our steps back toward the car.

As we walked, the mid to late afternoon sunlight lit the Sierras across the way from us in an angelic way, impossible to describe. Suffice it to say, the sight literally ascended into the sky.

At some point along the trail, I decided to use that sight to attempt to convince my oldest son, who was approaching his late twenties and still working at a copy shop in Santa Cruz on the midnight to dawn shift, to see the error of his ways and return to school and get a degree. Or more than one.

Try as I might, however, he wouldn't budge. He continued to argue in favor of his current job, and the strange creatures that helped him through the night, ranting and raving about the state of the world or some other world, and how much seeing these people was reality and not the infantile—his word—unimaginative world of higher education.

Having sat through many a faculty meaning, it was hard for me to argue with him, but I did. After all, I was Dad. Teaching at a university. Carrying the title of full professor. And so on. Ad infinitum.

I tried to convince him that if college was not his choice, he should use his job as a launching pad to express himself in his art. He countered that he had no use for his art.

His younger brother, having no patience for this conversation, had by now moved well ahead of us down toward the car.

With little ammunition left in my quiver, I finally gave up and changed the subject. In some ways, high school had been nothing more than way stations for my sons. While it may seem like a father proud of his kids, we brought them up in a house full of books and reason, and they found school boring beyond belief.

While I lost the battle, I or he—whichever you prefer—won the war, for he now has tenure in a respected university with a Ph.D. from Stanford in geology. My youngest son, on that same trip and bored, has a Ph.D. in biochemistry from Cal Tech and works for a genetic firm in northern California. My second son has a Ph.D. from UCSD in Literature, and my third is a professional surfer in Hawaii—Kauai, to be exact.

Every once in a while, like right now, I think back to that day when all seemed lost. That we'd raised four wonderful people who were essentially going to discard all they'd learned for a lifelong stay in mundane jobs far below their capabilities. I remember looking at the view across from White Mountain and the gargoyle Bristlecones, and figuring that I should thank who- or whatever changed their minds.

And I do so now.

So as the painteD tyrant pyrrhus stood,

so he carried benefit Away

iN the spirit into the wilderness

and the motion of this plaCe

out of its place, and so on,

and she jumped up on to her feet

and to carry out their preparations

the stream gurgled over wet rocks
moving down into unknown lakes

and amber pools benefit.

93

The Kid

she took the male **F**orm of that k**INd**
unt**i**l she **becА**me at last woman and
Godd**E**ss, and the veloc**it**y of it**S**
mo**t**ion may also **d**o his multi**P**lications
and additions on a d**E**sk machi**Ne**.

1991

About twenty-five years ago, my wife Mary Jane and I took
an evening walk after dinner to visit the house we'd lived in
for a year when we first arrived in Santa Cruz. This walk took
us around Nobel Drive—a strangely designed street that did
a near three hundred sixty degree circle through a compact
neighborhood—and onto McMillan Drive. Interestingly,
Nobel Drive was named for the famous prize, and each of the
side streets named for a winner who worked at the University
of California. McMillan Drive was therefore named after
Edwin Mattison McMillan for his 1951 prize in chemistry on
transuranium elements.

As we walked slowly down the slope from Nobel toward the 'Y' that McMillan makes at the base of a small hill, a car turned suddenly from Nobel down the hill behind us. As it did, a small child, hidden from the approaching car by a parked vehicle on the side of the road, moved toward the same space. Everything was wrong with this picture. First, visibility in most every direction was blocked by houses, trees, scrubs, parked cars, the median dividers both on Nobel and McMillan, and the sudden downward trajectory of the approaching car. Second, it was clear that the kid hidden alongside the street could neither see nor hear the oncoming car. And the same was true of that quickly moving vehicle's driver.

Suddenly, I couldn't allow what was about to happen happen, so, without thinking, I simply screamed "No!" as loud and as forcibly as I could, knowing as I did that neither the boy nor the driver could hear me.

I don't know what happened next exactly, except the boy stopped, the car moved onto the median divider slightly while simultaneously jamming on its brakes, and, in the slow motion that sometimes accompanies such events, no accident occurred at all. The car moved on without a problem and the boy looked back in my direction seemingly confused as to why I had yelled, though I was sure he couldn't have heard me.

My wife looked as startled as I must have. What had just happened?

The boy continued his game of hide and seek with himself. The car disappeared down McMillan Drive, and I wondered if I'd just gone nuts. Imagined the whole thing.

But my wife confirmed it. Something had occurred.

But what?

Could they have heard me after all?

Had I yelled that loud?

Was the boy going to stop anyway?

Had the driver somehow seen the boy and swerved?

None of these seemed remotely possible.

But the alternative seemed less possible than that.

Are humans capable of mentally causing things to occur? Or in this case, not to occur?

Or was this one of those times when, as some physicists suggest, we skipped to one of those alternate universes where the accident hadn't happened, while it had in another universe somewhere else?

I have no idea, except that I didn't want that accident to occur at that moment more than I wanted anything else in the world.

he felt a ha**R**d blow on h*I*s head, a*N*d the

*Spe***C*t*r**oscop**e** to which h**e** h**A**d a*t* o**N**ce

resorted,   thanked   rosencrantz   and   gentle

g*UiL*denstern. *And* an **YON**ewhoha**S** writtena commentary on Euclid.

94

Aunt Lois

i know not what the word S*ubl*I*m*e

me*an*S, if it be not the intimationS in this

instant of a terrifiC forCe. wHAt if tHe

pythagoReans did teach the same thing?

that i do as if in an *u*nknown worLd i*t is*

resistance in s**O** *f*ar as The body.

1995

On the occasion of my sister's second wedding, my Aunt Lois
took the opportunity to tell me she felt like I was her son.
This took me by surprise. On one hand, my sister and I had
spent a good deal of time with her during the summers when
my parents traveled, and she may have been referring to that.
On the other hand, though, she had three children of her
own and, by now, several grandchildren, and considering I
was in my sixties, declaring she had been—or now was—my
mother seemed strange to me. On the other hand, she could
have been referring to her being more mature than my real
mother, even though she was my mother's little sister. After

all, there were many times in which I most likely wished she were my mother, given the circumstances that surrounded my youth and my mother's participation in my upbringing.

I smiled when she told me that, not actually commenting on her statement one way or the other. And, as I did, I realized in one fell swoop that my mother, regardless of her foibles and deep-seated problems, had raised me as best she could. She'd given me, despite herself, many attributes that would serve me well later in life. For example, her almost constant criticism of what I did and didn't do prepared me for a life of difficult reviews, angry and dissenting attacks on my work, and, as a result, made me more resilient than I could imagine being otherwise. Her attitudes toward people that weren't like her in race, religion, beliefs, and sexual orientation, made me incredibly sensitive to why those people she so cruelly treated reacted the way they did. I not only survived her biases, I overcame them because they were so incredibly stupid. And, from her intense sense of survival, I gained a backbone that stood me erect through many a disaster that might have beaten me otherwise.

Compared to my mother, my Aunt Lois was a gem of a person. Almost faultlessly kind, gentle of humor, and wonderfully spirited in her own way. A woman who'd endured and survived breast cancer with a smile, worked full time when her children were young, and devoted her life to helping others. Nothing of the sort could in any way be said of my mother.

So, as she said the words "she felt like I was her son," I had mixed feelings. I envisioned a life with my Aunt Lois with fewer worries, more support, and kindness, the most important differences between the two sisters. And how different my life would have been.

Better?

I have no idea.

i**T** app**E**ars to me, that the arg*u*ment quoted above imp*lie*s a ser*iou*s re*st*riction of th*e* omnipotence of the a**L**mighty h**E**aven. make thee f*r*ee of *I*t. i follow thee to make a re*sp*e**C**table person of **HER**.

95

Islands

As put t**O** p**H**ase

a**n**d to th**e** *forc*__E__

w**I**th which it presses,

the outter **PL**a**n**e

has twenty **O**cta| pentahed**R**a**L**s

gl**i** mmering o**n** Th**e** b**R**acele**t**

as the tin**y** man
tied the metal ends

with b**O**ne fingers

on **A** yo*u*ng gi*r*ls wrist.

1996

It was early morning when my wife Mary Jane and I left Lone
Pine, California, towards Death Valley National Park. We'd
just spent a couple of days investigating the places along the
eastern Sierra Nevada range where her husband and sons had

hiked and camped many times, and had decided to explore new territory. Neither she nor I had ever visited the park of extremes, and figured it was time to see what the hubbub was all about.

Our trip on Highway 136 began innocently enough by circling the northern extremity of Owens Lake, a mostly dry and quite colorful lake bottom, now feeding its water to Los Angeles through an aqueduct beginning up river and tunneling many hundreds of miles under and over ground.

The mostly ghost towns of Dolomite and Swansea presented austere recollections of better times gone by, when Mississippi riverboats traversed the lake with tons of gold and silver culled from mines high up on neighboring Cerro Gordo Peak to the northeast. To the south was one of my favorite spots, Dirty Socks Hot Springs, where an entrepreneur once attempted to build a resort before the lake dried up, leaving but a pair of dirty socks and an empty swimming pool mostly filled with sand behind.

Highway 136 switches to 190 which passes a favorite haunt of mine, the town of Darwin and its falls, where I'd once fended off rattlesnakes, both real and imagined, and Rainbow Canyon, a much vaulted and colorful slash in the completely barren soils to the west of Panamint Springs.

Being only mid-March, we didn't expect that, before lunch, Stovepipe Wells would have temperatures above 95 degrees already, but it did, boding danger of boiling radiators and other noxious adventures in the valley below. But we eventually found our way to Furnace Creek that didn't, as far as I could see at least, even have a thermometer. But it was as hot as the name Death Valley suggests.

The lower-than-sea-level Badwater basin, with its cracked and parched earth, testified to what I imagined the temperature might be, and after overhearing story after story of pain and anguish, we returned to our car and headed for more humane climes. There are, of course, moments of grandeur here. Artists Drive with its other worldly landscapes, Telescope Peak across the valley with it cool altitude contrasting the lifeless desert below, and a stream called, unlikely enough, the Amargosa River, with its small nearly-extinct pupfish that can survive extraordinarily high temperatures.

So, we retraced our tracks to the less severe Panamint Valley, one of my favorite lonesome drives in California, on to Ridgecrest and back into the eastern Sierras, across Walker Pass, by Lake Isabella, and followed the Kern River into the San Joaquin Valley and Bakersfield.

The setting sun shown directly into our eyes as we headed west on Highway 46, the so-called Lost Hills Route, toward the Pacific coast. Once the sun set, however, the driving became more comfortable through Paso Robles and on toward Cambria, our final destination for the day. And it was here that I realized we'd taken a complete trip from hell to heaven. For, as we crested the un-named pass from where we could usually see Morro Rock to the south—the huge monolithic icon marking Morro Bay—that what had been an unusual day of temperature twists and almost every imaginable landscape, became surreal beyond belief. For there before us, were islands in the clouds. Literally, not figuratively. At least so it seemed.

The fog had arrived on the coast and found its way inland. For many miles. And it was here that we could see nothing but the barren tops of hills poking through that fog as if islands in a soupy ocean, brightly lit by a full moon behind us. I remember thinking that this unremarkable day had suddenly become truly remarkable. For now, rather than simply a living travelogue, we'd entered a twilight zone of fifty-degree temperatures as we entered and then exited, over and over again, first the fog reducing visibility to almost zero, and then what seemed like outer space, completely above the fray. And we stayed that way until we found the coast and our destination at the lower end of Big Sur, the magical highway. One testimony to humanity's inability to fully rule its planet.

twe*n*ty questions,
a technique not
t*a*king the form of a blow.

an**D** upon the seats
i saw four and twenty elders

sitting by ele*c*tricity

and standing on tipto*e*
threatening to hunt the eagle
in his own element.

96

Favorites

nAT uRE is No spendthrift,

but t**a**k**e**s the sho**r**test w**a**y

to he**R E** nd**S**.

As t**H** e genera**l** says t**O** his so**l**diers,

the re**a**der wi**L**l have la**X** anticipate**D**

th**A**t i have **N** o very convincing arguments

that will get her into the gar**D** en,

and so **bli**nded by his **V** an**I** ty

and immediately wa**S**

I n the spi**ri**t.

1996

I was once asked to name the four favorite pieces of music
I'd composed in my life. I immediately begged off by saying
I hadn't yet finished composing all my works, and that my

next four would probably compete heavily for those honors. My interviewer, however, didn't buy my excuse, and forced the issue. With my back to the proverbial wall, I answered the question to the best of my ability at that moment.

"Without including any of the thousands of works my numerous computer programs have created, my favorites would be *Triplum* (flute and piano), *Requiem for Bosque Redondo* (brass choir), *Concerto for Piano and Orchestra*, and *Symphony No. 4*," I told him.

My response, of course, was missing many other works that I very much enjoy hearing again and again—a good sign—but these I felt expressed the epitome of my overall work.

My interrogator, as I now began to think of him, asked me to elaborate on why, and to particularly note that all my choices were ancient (his choice of words) rather than new.

I answered the last of his questions first by pointing out that I'd had more opportunity for these earlier works to settle in, age, and understand, and felt I had more of a chance to fully appreciate their worth.

The answer to the first question was much more difficult. For those interested in such things, I here provide paraphrases of my responses.

For me, *Triplum* coalesces two mid-career aims in my music. First, to set constraints against which I could find my voice. In this piece, the constraint was to use a twelve-tone row of twelve half-steps downward (i.e., a chromatic scale) and make it interesting by using dynamics, register, timbre, rhythm, and other musical elements before resorting to variations of the row itself. Second, *Triplum* also includes elements of Navajo folk songs and text—as whispers—in ways I felt appropriate. The final modal/tonal statement, an actual quote, is a reflection of all the subtle variants that had gone before it but may not have been obvious to listeners. I very much like reverse variations in which the theme occurs last rather than first. Thus, the integration of the algorithmic serial elements and the folk idiom of the Navajo quotations grow from high to low, with the theme revealing itself only at the end. I still listen to this work with great interest, and find myself never quite able to predict what will come next even though I composed the piece.

The *Requiem for Bosque Redondo* is somewhat similar to *Triplum*, except that it's for brass ensemble and includes all members of the group performing on wine glasses near the end. Bosque Redondo is a place located it the eastern part of New Mexico, and represents the destination for the Long Walk of the Navajos following their defeat by Kit Carson. I felt then as I do now, the enormous weight of that walk, of its sadness, and the savagery of the American military treatment of Indians. Again, the music reflects a rather simple twelve-tone row in a wide variety of guises along with folk references. The music is extremely dissonant, loud, and wonderful.

I conducted the premiere of my *Concerto for Piano and Orchestra* with my wife as soloist. Unlike the two works I mention above, this concerto includes various kinds of notation including proportional techniques, where time is indicated by seconds rather than metric beats, and entrances are proportional to those seconds. Thus, while notes are accurately written, entrances can vary slightly from one performance to the next. By slightly here, I do not mean improvised or by chance, but simply differ my micro amounts, in most cases no more or less than would occur in a traditionally notated work. However, by using proportional notation, performers can perform the music much more easily. The constraints I imposed during creation of this work involve intervals explored, mostly seconds, sevenths, and ninths to give it consistency. The concerto is dramatic and romantic, even given its often highly dissonant textures and leaping melodic lines.

Finally, my *Symphony No. 4* of five movements is a special work for me. It consists of basically one downward motive varied in so many ways I cannot now find them all. Unlike most of my other symphonies, this audible coherence—of hearing an idea repeated in different movements—marks this as a unique work for me, and one I especially enjoy hearing. The final movement includes elements common with my previously—discussed concerto. That is, ostinatos occurring over and over again with variation reminding one of minimalism. However, this is really nothing like minimalism, being as it is limited to one movement and decidedly offset by long melodic lines that carry it to its conclusion. Again, I enjoy hearing this work when the opportunity arises.

When I finished my explanations, my 'interrogator' asked me one final question; who I thought had influenced my music the most.

"No *one* individual," I remember answering confidently. "I am influenced by everything I hear. Not the people, but the music. I cannot help it. For, like my computer programs, I, too, am an imitator of what I hear. Any composer who denies that is either ignorant of their composing process or lying."

With that said, he concluded our interview.

desert r*O*ads crumbled

i*N* to du*S*t

and w**h**ispered away
into the white hills of sand.

97

Pianissimo

natur**E** is no s**p**endthri*ft*, b**U**t t**a**kes the sh*orte*st **WA**y to her e**n**ds, as the **GEN**eral says t**o** his soldiers.

1996

As an erstwhile conductor, someone who's conducted a wide range of music with a wide range of ensembles and orchestras but never actually called myself a conductor, I've spent hours in rehearsals attempting to coerce groups to play softly. This would seem like an easy thing to do for those not familiar with the task at hand. But it's not. Ask a group to sight-read a passage they've never seen before on their instruments, and you'll understand what I mean. The more difficult the passage, the louder they'll play. It never seems to fail. It's completely counterintuitive. You'd think that making a fool of yourself would be better if you made yourself invisible. Visually and sonically. Doesn't matter. But the opposite is the case.

I think, however, I've figured out the source of the problem. Performers, even the twentieth-something violinist,

337

have trained for years on their instruments, and will be damned if they're not going to be heard. And each performer who plays louder requires the others to play louder as well. Thus, the ante keeps getting upped.

Once I asked a string section to play a passage softer. Over and over again they played it, while I conducted. My response each time was, simply, "Again, but softer." And, as predicted, the resultant sound was not even *piano*, no less *pianissimo*. I finally told them not to play at all, but simply lay their bows on the strings and think the passage rather than moving those bows. When they finished, I told them, "Still too loud."

I hoped from that experience, they'd get the idea. Not so. When they played, it was still too loud.

And yet, when I hear recordings, orchestras *do* play *pianissimo*. So, maybe it's me. Maybe I just can't get my ideas across. Maybe that's why I don't advertise myself as a conductor.

Once, when I had taped a work while conducting and heard the playback, I was amazed by the delicate and barely audible sounds that emanated from the orchestra during soft passages. I commented to the sound technician that it had hardly seemed that way to me while I conducted.

"Oh, it wasn't," he said, "we always follow the score and turn the volume down during the soft passages. After all, everyone knows orchestras can't play soft."

Since that time, I've noticed that no one can play *pianissimo*. Only sound engineers can.

What a revelation.

the reader will have a**N**ticipat**E**d

that i have n**O** ve**R**y convincin**G**

argu**M**ents of **A** positive **N**ature to
support my views. so either way ill get

into the gar**D**en and so be blinded b**Y**
his vanity.

98

Beautiful

one **MA**y **P**erh**A**ps dec**I**de
that it is safest to stop,
but some further difficulty
may *w*ell ar*i*se

from this decisio**N** la**TE**r.

1996

One of the most beautiful drives in the country doesn't have much of anything by way of special or unique features. It's a wide stretch of flat land that lacks trees and any other particularly distinguishing features. It resides on both sides of Interstate 40 between about thirty miles east of Flagstaff, Arizona, to just west of Gallup, New Mexico.

Reading maps can fool you, though. There you'll find Wupatki National Monument and Sunset Crater to the northeast of Flag, as the locals call Flagstaff, Meteor Crater to the south about halfway between Flag and Winslow, Petrified Forest National Park about halfway between Holbrook and Chambers, roads that go north to Canyon de Chelly National Monument and Chinle, the Navajo Nation that I-40 crosses, and the Zuni Rez to the south as you cross the border into New Mexico. All these provide wonderful side trips for intrepid travelers. But nothing surpasses the beauty that surrounds the Interstate from between about thirty miles east of Flagstaff, Arizona to just west of Gallup, New Mexico.

'Why?' you might ask. 'What's so special there?'

The answer to that question might confuse you, for almost nothing is there except wide-open spaces. No houses, few roads, and no unique features. Nothing, that is, except for the most amazing sky you can find on earth, the most beautiful real estate anywhere, and no mountains to mar your view of nothing much. It is lonely beyond belief.

And extraordinarily wonderful.

Unlike most of the great landmarks that dot the west and soon grow old once you've seen them, this stretch of road will remain with you for a lifetime. Nothing to get tired of, because there's nothing there in the first place. Just the feeling that you could lie in the dirt away from the Interstate for the rest of eternity. Listening to nothing much but the occasional wind and a stray thunderstorm. And see the same thing, day after day after day with the beauties of simple changes of light to keep you company. At night, the ribbons of stars that cross the sky have nothing to mar them but the distant almost unseeable lights of Flag or Winslow or Holbrook.

The smell of the sage, the occasional dot of a small bird in the sky who's most likely lost his way, or the sound of jet aircraft that sound so out of place you wish you could make them go away.

And yet, all of this nothing is the most extraordinary place on earth.

aND beholD,

a thronE waS sEt
in heaven,

and One sat

on the thRone,
and above all,

You need

aT tentiveness oF mind.

the streAm guRgled

over wet rocks Moving

down into unknown lakeS

aNd amber pools.

i mean my lord,
the opposition

of your person in trial
is very odious.

99

Boomerang

aNd *n*Ot to sPeAk *i*t

p*r*OfAn*e*ly,

THat n*e*itheR havIng the aCcent *of* chrIstians.

1997

A student of mine in the early twenty-first century introduced me to the wonders of boomerangs, the Australian version of the flying saucers we call frisbees. While these latter disks depend on the wind and accuracy of the one tossing, they do not return to the sender as a good boomerang will. Boomerangs can also be made from almost any substance, from plastic to wood to even glass. While weight does matter, especially for long-distance throws, it does not limit accuracy and eventually perfection—catching your 'boom' without moving from your original position.

Throwing boomerangs well depends on a number of factors, but the two most important are the boomerang itself and skill. Boomerangs are typically created as aerofoils that spin according to their line of flight. By design, they thus travel using aerodynamic forces that create elliptical paths, thus returning to their senders. The shape is extremely important to effective use, and good boomerangs compared to bad ones have incredibly different characteristics. A great thrower is as hampered by a bad boomerang as a bad thrower is. In certain areas of the world, hunters using boomerangs can bring down even the largest of prey.

My own experience with boomerangs is precisely the same as with juggling or playing chess. No matter my mood when I begin, I am soon lost in the art of them, forgetting all the pressures of life and living in the moment. Far better than liquor or other drugs that fight tension, these non-lethal activities relieve anxiety rather than covering it over. They teach as well as respond to one's skills, whatever those skills may be.

While my age prevents me from throwing boomerangs as often or as long as I used to, I still own many of them and attempt to explore their subtleties whenever I can. Even indoors with paper 'booms,' I'm able to recreate their bone fide effects on my temperament and soul, whatever that is.

and they were ful*l* **O**f *e*yes,
within which was an object of derision
that did not continue its commentary.

and in a gi*ven* time,
everything is so out-of-the-way down here.

100

Brian Ferneyhough

th**E** vis insita,

with hono*U***r**s at th**e** stake,
how stand thee,
or indeed, if at all?

1997

I met Brian Ferneyhough several years ago when we both presented our work at IRCAM—*Institut de Recherche et Coordination Acoustique/Musique*—in Paris. Ferneyhough is noted for his extremely complex and difficult to perform works, and for creating what is often called the New Complexity style of composition. We spoke briefly about the current state of contemporary music, and I was quite taken with his supportive attitude and wonderful British accent.

My presentation, for some reason, required a translator—his did not, though he spoke in English as I did. Mine was about my work with Experiments in Musical Intelligence. His was about the manner in which he composed using a program called PatchWork to algorithmically produce small segments of music, and then overlay them to create the extremely complicated passages that characterize his works.

My presentation raised the temperature of the room and the bodies in it several degrees, and the questions posed were either non-supportive or hostile depending on your point of view. His presentation caused his audience, more composers than mine I guessed, to compliment him on his approaches. All well and good.

Since our meeting, I have listened with great interest to his music, many times with score in hand. My only comment is that I have yet to hear any of his works performed correctly. The extraordinary demands he makes of performers, and the various methods by which he complicates things (e.g., nested tuplets—triplets within quintuplets, and so on), are at best approximations and much more accurately performed with less rigorous notation, regardless of how oxymoronic that may sound.

every**y**thi**n**g is **p**ush**er o**r pushed,
        and matter and mind

                        are in perpetua**l** tilt an**d**
                balan*C*e.
        *S*o everything really move**s** continuously,
                        an*D* everything is caused

        by the **f**inite and the infinite,
                        the limited and the
                unlimited.

        the e**X** tr**E** me ci**RC**umscr**I**pti**O**n

                        in **r**elation to a for**m**

                and voi**ce**

        came out of the throne **S**aying, let the

        Spac**ES** of life go.

101

Fire

a**N**d th**E**refore it**S** true

that *c*ircular **M**otion had not y**E**t b*e*gun.

Thus, he has many more of the same bevy that *i* kno**W**.

1997

In 1997, my wife and I decided to remodel our kitchen. Since I have no particular attachment to kitchens except to visit them for food every so often, she designed and oversaw the construction. I did the painting. Unlike the upstairs addition to our house that involved the contractor's son constantly putting his foot through our downstairs ceilings, our kitchen conversion went almost without a hitch. Unfortunately, the 'almost' part of that sentence was more than enough to convince me I never wanted to try such construction again.

Halfway through the process, the plumber assigned to reengineer the pipes to accommodate the various new connections, set our house afire. This was no mean feat for a plumber to do. He had been working on one of the nearby bathrooms and attempting to weld two sections of pipe together, when something in the wall left over from the original construction caught fire. And he couldn't put it out.

You'd think a plumber would have plenty of ways to put out errant flames, but this one didn't. Or, more likely, he thought he did, because he kept the fire a secret from us for at least ten minutes as he tried to turn the water back on, but somehow couldn't. His mind had gone blank, and I found him sitting at the front yard spigot staring blankly at the faucet trying to will water from its depths.

After several seconds of attempting to decipher his grunts and hand gestures, I finally found the source of the sudden heat in the bathroom, a blue glow from inside the wall under the sink. I immediately called 911 and turned the water to the house back on. By this time, however, even with the open pipe under the sink flooding the area there, the fire had grown so hot that the water had virtually no effect on it whatsoever. Attempts with the bucket sitting near the plumber—still comatose on my front lawn—didn't work either.

With all my wife's and my belongings at stake including computers, clothes, and so on, I convinced her there was nothing to do but join the plumber in the front yard and pray the fire engines arrived quickly. My wife then reminded me that our beloved cat—called Emmy after my computer program Experiments in Musical Intelligence and given me by one of my classes at the university for a birthday present— was still in the house. I ran inside, found her cowering in a corner, and picked her up against her will. Being as shocked as I by the goings on at this point, she decided she didn't want to be picked up and promptly sunk her teeth into my forearm and hung on for dear life.

I didn't have time to scream, but figured that leaving her attached would at least guarantee I'd save her from the danger she was in. Together we found our way through the smoke and back onto the front lawn that had by then become a staging area for neighbors and interested passersby. I screamed at my cat, who finally let go and ran under my car. And there we stood, all except the plumber, of course, who remained sitting in his place staring at the faucet that now ran water harmlessly into the street in front of our smoking house. I was too numb to feel the wound on my arm, which now bled fluently down to my hand and from there into the grass at my feet.

Some twenty minutes after I called them, the fire truck appeared with apologies from the captain who, as his minions ran with fire hoses in hand into my house, stood by me explaining that the group had been on a training mission to deal with burning houses. I didn't then have the tenacity to point out the irony of this to him. Maybe he'd figured it out on his own.

Ten minutes after they arrived and already worrying about the firemen suffering from smoke inhalation and burns from the raging fire, these men rushed from the front door and, speaking in quick syllables to the chief, told him about the firewall. He had, it seemed, never seen one work so well. The flames had not yet succeeded in getting more than an inch into what was a six-inch deep firewall separating the rest of the house from the flames. In other words, the fire had not damaged anything much beyond the immediate area under the bathroom sink. Smoke damage would prove less contained as time wore on, but for the most part we'd survived the worst of it.

A paramedic saw to one of the casualties, the plumber, and finally got him to sign some papers admitting his guilt and sent him on his way. As far as my arm was concerned, the medic told me to get to a hospital or 'doc in the box' as we call the local quick-serve medical staff in our neighborhood. I did, and, after receiving severe doses of antibiotics—cats are not known for clean mouths—sent me on my way home to heal.

We slept that night in the odor of the fire and with suspicion that the nascent fire fighters had missed a spark or two. But nothing happened after that except, aside from finishing our kitchen, we had several more months of new carpet installations, drywall replacements, and a cat who wouldn't come near me. Oh, I would be remiss if I didn't mention that the plumber decided to sue us for having flammable pipes. Or at least something to that effect.

We won.

the DrOssy age dOtes have
onLy got the tune,

an outWaRd habit of eNcounter.

everybody haS wOn,
and aLl must have prizes.

Whoever haS had experieNce
of the moral sentiment,
cannot choose but believe in unlimited power.

102

Rock and a Hard Place

a**n**d l**O**wly,

as a**R**e **th**e monkeys and lem**u**rs to us.

I saw a star fall fro**m** *HE*aven
unto the earth,

and the *L*abors of a*L*l men **i**n the world
for time be.

1998

The music department that I chaired had just moved into a new building overlooking Monterrey Bay when the complaints began pouring in. Not about the building or the view, mind you, but the resonant sounds of the local environment. It seemed that when those in charge of placing the new building where it now stood were either unconcerned about or ignorant of the fact that next door, in a rather innocent looking but acoustically unsound—pun intended— building, was the student union, or something akin to it. That meant that as soon as the sun went down, its main auditorium—read as a large room with nothing but wood planks between it and the outdoors—became a haven for all manner of loud sound-producing people and their electronic instruments.

Now, the music building had been well furnished with soundproof walls so that teachers in one classroom or studio or office could not hear those in neighboring classrooms or studios or offices. Unfortunately, like most such acoustically protected areas, windows still provided plenty of un-acoustically protected areas for the loud sound-producing people next door and their electronic instruments to pervade. Thus, those faculty who either taught or researched past dusk were constantly bombarded by the sounds of wannabe bands that pounded their innocent instruments and voices with enthusiasm. These faculty could only wish their own students would practice their more classically invented music as much.

To put this more simply, the music building was a riot of sound from sundown to the wee hours of the morning. Clearly this was not going to work. And just as clearly it was yours truly who would have to make it stop.

My first action was to gather the affected faculty together, listen to their complaints, and then ask for suggestions as to how to deal with the situation. On the first point—listening to their complaints—they told me that they could not do their research or prepare their classes with this God-awful noise going on. On the second point, they suggested that I make the offending noise stop. Clear enough, though I'd hoped for more imaginative solutions as to how to accomplish this.

My second action was to ask the student group in charge of the building next door to meet with me to see what we could work out.

And here was the rub. Not having the meeting, but what they said when the meeting began. I was completely surprised.

It seemed that the students had three main problems with my suggestion that they cease and desist.

First, the building they used was theirs. At least in principle. That is to say, their student fees had been used to build it, and thus it was clear, at least to them, that they could use it in any way they damn well pleased.

Second, it was in no way their fault that the powers that be had not used acoustically proper materials in the construction of their building.

Third, and maybe most important of all, the music they played, and the decibel level at which they played it, was part of their *culture*. To have me, or anyone else for that matter, force them to stop, would be chauvinism at best, and culturalism, even racism, at worst. If I or my faculty assumed their student rights were going to be abrogated easily along these lines, I was sadly mistaken. Any action I took would be met with the harshest reaction imaginable. In short, if we thought the student center was loud now, just wait until thousands of students gathered outside the music building and began chanting twenty-four seven that they wanted their civil rights returned to them.

In short, to hell with me.

When I politely pointed out that the primary function of the university was to teach, and that their arguments were curtailing that function in the extreme, they simply dug in their heels and stood their ground.

I returned to the music building where the chair's office awaited me, and began my own kind of chanting. Softly, but energetically. "Between the devil and the deep blue sea," and "Between a rock and a hard place," and "Fucked," came to mind.

A colleague of mine had once told me that no-win situations were the easiest to solve. You lose either way, so what the hell, choose whichever side you prefer or just flip a coin. It didn't matter. In this case, my mind's eye saw the music building, the one my office was in charge of, surrounded by chanting students or by chanting faculty. Those were my choices. And both stunk.

I decided to punt. At least for the time being. I did this by telling the students I was conferring with faculty, and the faculty I was conferring with students. All this, just to give me time to think things through.

That, of course, didn't help either. The faculty began speaking in terms of filing suits against the university for demanding they teach and research under these conditions. The students simply played louder than before, leaving all available doors and windows open to underscore their point, as if they needed to.

Interestingly, I had been asked to give what the university calls a Distinguished Faculty Lecture around this time. This lecture included a dinner with the university's chancellor in which I could invite fifteen or so of my colleagues—presumably other faculty and staff—to chat and eat well beyond our usual means. I, of course, took this opportunity to introduce the chancellor and friends to my problem. Or, what I called the 'university's problem' to ensure everyone got the point.

I waxed, I thought, eloquently on the issue and had my faculty and staff back me up. She—the chancellor—listened carefully, and then said something along the lines of 'problem solved.' Words that I could not have imagined hearing before my talk that evening.

Then, of course, I had to ruin it by asking her *how* it was solved.

She replied that there were plans in the works to build a new student center well away from its current location and having proper acoustic design.

I asked her what she meant by the word 'plans.'

She said that several years in the future, the current wood building would become university offices that made no sound except those of discussions between staff and the occasional typing on computer keyboards.

I asked her what 'several years' meant.

She said probably somewhere between five and ten years was a good estimate.

I then told her that the problem was indeed not solved. That there was a question of immediacy that went along with the problem.

By that time, of course, I had to give my lecture, which, thank God, had nothing whatsoever to do with loud sounds or marching groups of faculty or students threatening to disable teaching and research.

Later that evening, while basking in my having given what I thought was a good presentation, and having my name added to the legion of twenty or so other names that had given such talks onto the sides of coffee mugs, I got an idea.

The next morning, I revisited the chancellor to ask her to consider the possibility that the new student center might be built incrementally rather than all at once. In other words, could a soundproof auditorium be built first, while the other parts were still on the drawing table so to speak? That would solve our raging problem of sound and silence wars. And, in the meantime, while that building might take a year, could we find temporary housing for the students to blast their eardrums to hell and beyond if they wanted to?

And she agreed.

And the students agreed.

And the faculty agreed.
And I took several Tums to make it all go away.

he **S**hall l**e**n**GH**th en and shor**T** en

s**p**a**c**e. **T** he **O**n**L**y w**a**y we kn**O**w of

fo**r** finding s**U** ch laws
is scientific observation

an**D** we certai**N** ly know of no circumstanc**ES**

under which we could **S** ay

we may **p** leasure at the increase
in the distance.

n**O** w we must return

to the main **l** ine of discussion:

wou**l** dst tho**U** no**t** st**i** r in this n**O** w, **n** ear hamlet?

103

Stanford

i am SurE that the professor does not wish to adopt the soLipsist point of ViEw i have swornNT not to give waY, and would nEvEr have fouNd the same obscurity in human letters.

1998

My oldest son Tim asked me to help him move his belongings from a storage facility in Santa Rosa, California, to Palo Alto where he was about to begin graduate study for a Ph.D. in geology. I agreed, and on that day we drove together up to Palo Alto to get the key to his new place of residence, an apartment on the second floor of a building with a pizza joint just below it. Unfortunately, the woman who rented out the apartment but lived ten miles distant was not in, so we missed that first chance to get things straight. But, we drove to Santa Rosa, where we rented a truck to carry Tim's belongings to Palo Alto. Since he had not reserved such a truck, we had to wait while others in line got theirs first. But this worked out fine. We got the truck, drove to the storage unit where his things were kept, transferred them to the truck, and headed back down to Palo Alto.

I drove the truck, and he drove my car. It was fun. I hadn't moved in years, and taking part in one, even if it was not mine, gave me a real buzz. I remember particularly driving over the Golden Gate Bridge southward, with the radio playing a Schoenberg orchestration of a Bach fugue. I'd never heard this version before, and it was quite stirring.

We arrived in Palo Alto and drove to the woman's house just before dark. Luckily, she was home this time, and we got the key to his rented apartment. We then moved him in to his new home, while all the while smelling various kinds of pizza being cooked. Not a bad aroma, except when you don't have time to stop and eat anything. Then, it's damn annoying. We couldn't stop when finished since we were in a hurry to get the truck back to the rental agency to avoid extra fees. We did that, just in time, and drove together back to Santa Cruz.

I don't think Tim had any reservations about his studies at Stanford. He could handle that. It was his home above the pizza joint that bothered him I think. Right there on the curb of El Camino Real. Where I'd come to San Francisco for the first time after I'd been born with my parents to get sick on chow mein in Chinatown.

The two of us were painting the walls and ceiling of our newly redesigned kitchen at the time to save money, and so when we arrived we took that up again, while a friend described our cat being run over by a hit and run driver across the street from our house.

I suppose I miss those days when I just went with the flow, letting the insanity of a day's activities simply guide me in whatever direction it wanted. After all, what could I write about now had those things not occurred?

if they warred in the same **z**ero spirit, and his feet |iked fine

*B*rass as *If* they burned in *A* furnace, the rabbit vio|ently dropped the white kid gloves and the fan.

(1999-2013)

104

Aesthetics

to keep it from divulging, let it

feed on the next thing that was to

eat the Comfits.

1999

Understanding aesthetics has occupied much of my life during the more than seventy years I've spent on planet earth. After all, as someone devoted to creating works of music, visual art, and language, I must consider and reconsider my views on the subject.

Like you, probably, I hear people speaking about this great piece they've heard, this fine work of visual art they've seen, this incredible story they've read, and all spoken as if the speaker knew precisely what it is that makes great, fine, and incredible music, visual art, and literature. In a world where very little is really defined.

Well, I don't know these things. Not in the least bit.

I sort of know what doesn't make great art. For example, it's not how many people like it, or Macdonald's would be the world's greatest restaurant, rap would be the world's greatest music, and prostitution would be the world's greatest sport. If it's the world's most original thing, then John Cage would be the greatest everything.

Or is it just a matter of taste? You like that, and I like this.

I'm told that Beethoven is great. But to me, some Beethoven consists of scales and arpeggios just like Vivaldi but without the sequences. I do like some Beethoven, but I don't thrust my taste upon other people by claiming how great Beethoven is. I just tell them I like this or that piece. I'm sometimes curious if they like these pieces too, but never argue about it with them. I'd like them to keep their own opinions and not be saddled with mine. And vice versa.

But this is an important subject. If we don't know what makes one work of art better than another, then how is an artist to know what to do? After all, just like most composers, I'd like to create great music. Do I just follow my instincts? Or follow whatever bandwagon is currently hip?

I don't know the answer to these questions, and so I just keep pounding away, like a gerbil on a wheel in a cage, creating things I hope that someone else will appreciate my work as well as me.

Maybe we're all lying to ourselves and everyone else. I have this theory that most people have a virtual threshold above which they will never lie, and below which lying is an art form. Above the threshold are matters of importance like ethics, principles, honor, and so on. Below the threshold are things like how people look, was it as good for you as it was for me, and so on. Taste and greatness for most people are probably well below the threshold. In other words, we lie about them. Maybe we're so into the tribal thing, that we like things we really don't and not even know that we're lying. I'm doing a lot of rationalizing here. Maybe everyone really does like the stuff I find abhorrent.

I've resolved questions like this partially by separating the issues of whether I like something, and whether it's good or not. 'Good' I define as a work of art that develops ideas, has logical structural boundaries, and that successfully puts tension and resolution into some kind of balance. Obviously, 'bad' I define as the opposite of these. Then I let my taste run free. For example, I cannot listen to Beethoven's fifth symphony any longer. I've simply heard it too many times. I hate it. However, I have little doubt in my mind that it's a 'good' work of music. On the other hand, I love to listen to Shostakovich's tenth symphony, but I have serious doubts as to its fundamental worth. I have no idea whether this separative approach to aesthetics has value to anyone else, but it works for me.

I also often turn to Sisyphus at times like these. Camus's Sisyphus, that is. Sisyphus, as you may remember, has been sentenced to push a rock up a hill only to have it roll down the other side again. Over and over again for eternity. But Camus worked it out so that in his version of Sisyphus, he finds the rock interesting in itself, tenderly fondling its surface for the familiar and unfamiliar imperfections that then make his life bearable. And so, fooling myself or not, lying to myself or not, I use my double standard and get on with things.

I leave this subject with a review of Debussy's *La Mer* from 1907, a work I consider good if not great:

> *The Sea* of Debussy does not call for many words of comment. The three parts of which it is composed are entitled *From Dawn till Noon*, *Play of the Waves*, and *Dialogue of the Wind and the Sea*, but as far as any pictorial suggestiveness is concerned, they might

as well have been entitled *On the Flatiron Building, Slumming in the Bowery,* and *A Glimpse of Chinatown During a Raid.* Debussy's music is the dreariest kind of rubbish. Does anybody for a moment doubt that Debussy would not write such chaotic, meaningless, cacophonous, ungrammatical stuff if he could invent a melody?

But if the *A*nswe**R**s are **A**s satisfa**ct**o**ry** and sustained as in t**H**e above **p**assa *GE*, i do not think h**e** wou**l**d d**e**sc**r**ibe it as an easy contrivance. not in the velocities, but in the **M**otion**S** of bodies.

105

April

and i **b**elieved

that there i*s* no **u**se

for the reg*u*lar solids,

licking their te*n*der wounds

and blowing them at the moon.

2000

In Tinman Too, I wrote about my creating April in Santa Cruz in 1980, an annual event now in its thirty-fourth year. In that recollection, I described my meeting Lou Harrison and his partner Bill before a concert, both having spent the afternoon locked out of rehearsals of Lou's own work by the unknowing performers. Reading that account, I now realize that there are many other events that might be of interest in regards to April in Santa Cruz.

For example, composer Laurie Anderson was scheduled to be our main guest composer one year. She was, however, actually invited by the university arts council on their tab. We were but a pimple on their butts so to speak. Completely at their mercy. When Laurie landed in San Francisco expecting to be met by someone driving her down to Santa Cruz, she found no one there. She called the appropriate person who

367

informed her that she would have to get herself to the campus some ninety miles south. On her own dime. No exceptions. Instead, she decided, as I most likely would have, to fly right back to NYC and forget her performance in Santa Cruz. Score one for university administration.

On another occasion, this time with April in Santa Cruz funding, we invited Iannis Xenakis to headline our festival. We found the money to bring him, set aside the dates, prepared to perform his music, and then his agent backed out and we were left holding the bag. Same idea as with Laurie, except the other way around.

Then there was the time that I spent a great deal of my efforts to create a festival for new music instrument builders, something I was very interested in at the time. Then, at the last minute, something came up in my administrative schedule such that I couldn't make it. No big deal. After all, the instrument builders could make it, and did. But the fact that the festival's leader and instrument builder himself at the time had not seen fit to attend their presentations didn't make my colleagues in the field any too happy.

But I do not wish to give a bleak picture of our thirty-four year old festival. Most things go right. For example, Bertram Turetzky, bassist extraordinaire, came and delivered a wonderful concert. John Cage was an early visitor, as were many of his school including Christian Wolff, Alvin Lucier, and others. We dedicated a complete festival to Gordon Mumma and his music the year he retired, and presented many of his lesser known works. We invited composer Elliott Schwartz for a concert that included me conducting some of his works for chamber orchestra. Other composers honored include Roger Reynolds, Terry Riley, John Adams, Andrew Imbrie, Pauline Oliveros, Chinary Ung, Henry Brant, Benjamin Boretz, Paul Dresher, Ernst Krenek, Jim Tenney, Fred Lerdahl, Joan Tower, and many more that I have unfortunately forgotten.

We annually present top-notch performances of our

faculty composers as well including David Evan Jones, Paul Nauert, Larry Polansky, Hi Kyung Kim, Ben Carson, Karlton Hester, and others as well as our graduate students whom we treat as equals. We also invite ensembles including such luminaries as the New York Contemporary Music Ensemble, Borromeo String Quartet, composer/pianist Frederic Rzewski, and, again, many others too numerous to mention.

And, since the mid-1980s, the faculty has shifted responsibilities around so that each has a turn in charge. Thus, I am in no way responsible for all these visitors, performances, performers, and audiences thus brought to our stages.

May April in Santa Cruz continue for another thirty-four years.

from he**a**ven, and

From its orbit

towards th**E** earth,

i **F**ind th**E l**ike unity

in viru**L**ent an**D** pervasive

b**L**o**o** **D**.

d**E**a**R** **M**e, i sh**A**ll **N**ever get to twenty at this rate.

106

Shepherd Pass

a transcendent ta*l*ent

dra**W**s s*o* largely

***O**n* **HI**s forc*e*s

as **T**o la**m**e him.

a defect *p*aying h*i*m reve**N**u**E**s.

2001

In August of 2001, my youngest son Gregory and I went camping in the eastern Sierras of California. On our last day, we took a washboard dirt road to a little known parking spot that begins the trail to Shepherd Pass where he wanted to scope out his next conquering of passes on that side of the great mountains of the west. We hiked over several lower passes and I finally fell behind and found a good place and sit and look down on Owens Valley some six or so thousand feet below.

It was a beautiful summer's day, and at this altitude was cool, at least in the shade of the multitude of surrounding pines. I sat in a comfortable spot and watched the peaceful village of Independence far below me go about its business.

In contrast, Greg followed the trail further to take a long look at the pass he would conquer a year later. Shepherd Pass is extremely steep and requires several switchbacks over an intervening *cordillera* in which the trail continuously reaches higher altitudes, and then lower ones than even where you began. Frustrating. But, according to him after later successfully reaching the top, it was worth the effort, especially for the view down the other side.

To give readers a sense of this area, Shepherd Pass is the first pass north of Mount Whitney, the highest peak in the contiguous United States. Supposedly its name derives from sheepherders attempting to take their flocks to greener pastures on the west side of the Sierras.

Two years later, I once again took Greg to the eastern Sierras of California. This time, to park his car near Whitney Portal below Mount Whitney for him to rejoin when he completed the John Muir Trail down from Yosemite. This two hundred and ten mile path duplicates part of the PCT or Pacific Crest Trail that crosses the US from Mexico to Canada.

When we arrived at Yosemite, Greg prepared his packs and we checked his various permissions to make the journey. Both he and I were getting a little anxious over what would be a nearly three-week journey into unknown territory. No motels or even campsites. With the exception of a couple of stops near camps where he could pick up his previously packed large cans of supplies, he had to fish or collect—not hunt—his meals, and rely on other hikers for any emergencies that might occur.

While he wouldn't actually cross Shepherd Pass, he would come close to the spot he'd previously reached from there a year before. Other than that, the trip was pretty much *terra incognita*. With sudden storms providing lightning, flooding, hail, and occasional snow flurries as well as relatively hot afternoons and views of bears and other beasts that seemed relatively harmless until you actually laid your eyes on them.

With no cell phone service, no radio, and only a backpack and a makeshift cane to help him along, the trip provided relatively few frills. Mostly above ten thousand feet and with many passes well above that altitude, this was a combination of love of wilderness and dreams come true for him.

I remember my return trip to the car that had brought Greg and me to the beginning of his hike. With mixed emotions. First, of my desire to accompany him, and second feeling that my youngest son could face many dangers with his Dad unable to help in any way. In fact, for the most part, *anyone* to help in any way.

Almost three weeks later, his parents were grateful to hear his voice again from his apartment in Pasadena where he then attended Cal Tech. With many pictures taken and stories to tell, he'd made it without too much effort, and dangers had passed swiftly and without dire consequences.

As he later told us of his conquest, I imagined what it would have been like had he taken the trip the year before. Of having 9/11 occur while he was up there. And of his noticing, as surely he would, that no planes flew overhead and that few hikers passed him by. And of those hikers who actually had taken the trail the year before, and of their imaginings of a world without airplanes and God only knew without what else.

On th*e* other side

folloWEd this coNviction

of fam**e**.

a fellow of infinite je**S**t,

of most exce**L**lent f**A**nc**Y**.

the right way **O**f spea**K** ing

to a mous**E**

and this other bo**d**y.

107

The Accident

to me, *H*ow*E*ver, the question of the

ti*me*S resolve**D** *it*self **I**n**T**o a

practi**cal** qu**E** stio**n** **o**f t*h*e con*d*uct *o*f

life whethe**R** the motion did *b*elong to

the globe*s* *o*r to the bodies.

2001

As an administrator, I seem to attract unique situations that those who came before or after me don't. Maybe I just react to normalcy with an intensity others do not. No matter, however, these situations—many of which I've described elsewhere in these volumes—are not imagined. And often they conflict me in ways I could have never imagined.

Smith Dobson was a man of many talents. The one I knew most about was his ability to play jazz piano. There was a certain sincerity about his performances that few could equal. Possibly more important to me personally, though, was his angelic personality. I have met few equal to his ability to see the positive side in almost everything. I take that back. Everything.

Then one day, or rather night, it all came to an end. On a freeway between Santa Clara and San Jose on his way home from a gig on the peninsula, he apparently fell asleep and his car plummeted off road and into a caisson holding up an overpass and died.

I received the news as department chair the next afternoon, a Saturday, and spent the rest of my weekend in a dire emotional strait. I simply could not imagine what fate, what God, what universe, could impose such a monstrous end for such a kind man.

On the following Monday morning, I attended each of Smith's classes as the department chair to inform the mostly freshman students that their teacher would no longer be their teacher.

As I expected, the students loved this man as much as I had, so the news did not come easily. Lots of tears, hysteria, and even some physical illness. Luckily, I came with a professional councilor prepared to deal with trauma of this sort. So my tendency to empathize with the mood of the students did not force me to make myself a poor excuse as a not-so-willing bearer of bad tidings. In other words, I waited until I got back to my office before I, too, cried. Yet again.

Interestingly, when I attempted to inaugurate the room in which he taught The Smith Dobson Memorial Room, I was met with absolute rejection by the university administration. It seemed that rooms and buildings could only be named for benefactors who'd given large amounts of money for such naming and, since Smith did not have large amounts of money, nor did anyone who knew him, I was thwarted.

But not for long. It seems we could post signs, as long as they did not contain words like Memorial or Dedication, and so on. So we devised a simple but effective phrase that broke no rules but, we hoped, had the same affect. This phrase said, "In honor of Smith Dobson," and was placed near the door.

he felt the wiry stra**n**ds of rope from our achie**V**ements th**O**ugh pe**R**formd at height and the light it re**CE**ives from the sun.

108

Chime

*a*nd i**t** would s*e*EM

th**A**t th*i*s t*o*o

is th**e** be*li*ef of the minds

u**P** on m*a***R** s

a*n*d r**O** me

*tha*t i**s** a**L** l wr*o*n**G** .

2001

On the evening of the last day I served as department chair
at UCSC in 2001, I stopped at a local store and picked up
something I'd seen there before, wanted, but had not bought.
This day I made the decision. I bought it.

When I arrived home and before doing anything else, I
attached it to the ceiling of my wind-chime collection along
with the hundreds of others I'd collected over the years.
Unlike the rest of the chimes of my collection, however, this
one was not that different from the others. At least in sound.
What made it different was that the upper non-sounding part

was built in the form of a wire cage with, believe it or not, a swinging door.

When I hung it from the ceiling, I carefully opened the door to the cage. It was a symbol of my freedom. While I would serve in various other capacities such as chair of committees and the like, I would never allow myself to become a part of the administration again.

When my wife searched for me that evening, she opened the door to the room and rang those, and only those, chimes as she did. I'd hung them in a place that made this likely. A musical signal to remind me that I was free and to never get trapped again.

and as pa**R**ts of revolving wholes

ende**A**vour to recede

fro**M** the axis

of their **M**otlo**N**s

ma**G**gots, he cried,
with a loud voice

sa**y**ing to a**ll**

we have been ridic**u**led

and ordered to re**m**ain silent.

109

Tom's Place

we beg y**O**u**R** kind a*C*ceptance
<u>O</u>f t**hi**s elegan**t** thimble

Wh***en*** we w**o**uld b*R*i**n**g

him *O*n to **S**ome <u>**C**</u>onfession.
*W*e men, the creatures
who inhabit this earth,
and the man *LE*ft more than
the secrets of water.

2002

The last time I camped in the campground above the small village of Tom's Place on Highway 395 in eastern California, my youngest son Greg and I witnessed something so obsessive and strange that I don't believe I'll spend another night there. Greg was preparing for a long solo hike on John Muir Trail, and I was going to visit Yosemite for the umpteenth time in my life where he was heading out.

Our usual camping spot, No. 1 on the map at the head of the grounds, had not been taken, and thus we had it all to ourselves. From there we could see maybe fifty miles to the north end of the White Mountains across the Owens Valley, where minerals mystically changed colors along a vertically straight line at a place called, enigmatically, The Jumpoff. Closer in, we could see parts of Crowley Lake, and even the remaining lava flows where the Owens' River crevasse cuts through them. It's a beautiful spot and the best campsite in the entire grounds.

The only thing marring our view were the local burnt trees from a fairly recent forest fire, one result of a continuing drought in the area.

We set up camp, lit a small campfire, cooked supper, played a game of chess while listening to late night radio at seventy-two hundred feet, and called it a night. After all, Greg had a busy day set for tomorrow, and I had a lot of driving to do.

Sometime during that night, most likely after one o'clock in the morning, I woke to the sounds of insistent drums beating and light flickering on the trees around me. Greg was already up and watching.

In campsite number 3, two down from us and maybe fifty feet away, a large group of what looked like stoned teenagers all dressed in white, were parading around with lit limbs of trees burning above their heads. A pagan ritual of some kind, no doubt. They were chanting something unrecognizable as they walked, and I wondered immediately if I was dreaming or if it were real. I checked with Greg. It was real. We were witnessing something very odd to say the least.

Greg asked if we should try to stop it. I counted the number of people I could see; more than twenty. Younger than both he and me yes, but their number was critical to the equation. I didn't know if we should attempt to stop them, and if that worked, if stopping them might make things worse. With the forest so tinder dry, it seemed like moving flames might be better than flames standing still. I wasn't awake enough to parse it out.

And so we watched. And watched some more. Waiting I suppose for some indication of when this madness would end, and whether the forest would suddenly jump to life in a full-scale maelstrom.

We could have driven away then. After all, nothing we had on the ground was worth dying for. But we didn't. We couldn't leave these people to die in their self-made nightmare.

Eventually the fires on their torches died as the fuel spent itself. With the fires gone, so, apparently, went the energy of whatever drugs had consumed them. After that, the yelling and sex began in earnest. And that in the dark.

With our immediate worries quelled, Greg and I eventually fell back to sleep. In the light of morning, our visitors had already left. The forest was un-torched, and, for the most part, the campground un-littered.

Life was good.

I could only imagine what our visitors felt like.

Had it been worth it?

and steamin*g* w*or*K

of ele**C**t**R**icit*Y*,

th**E** ductility of m**E**tals,

the chariot awaitin*g* you

on which on*e* can act

on the great earth with our sic**K**le.

110

Muddy Waters

n**o**t o**n**ly u**p**on an**i**mals

HAve no**t** been **a**C*cur*a**t**e

in **R**egard t**o** the **Z**on**e**.

and anothe**r** ange*L*

*As***C**ended f**RO**m th*E* east.

2004

Sometime in the late twentieth or early twenty-first centuries, I was asked to present my work in algorithmic music composition at Harvey Mudd College in Claremont, California, just northeast of Pomona. My resulting visit lasted less than twenty-four hours, and included a discussion and dinner at the President's home, a lecture, questions and answers, a night in a local hotel, and an early morning tour of the campus.

The discussion at the President's home seemed pleasantly innocuous, with the usual questions about the reactions I'd received over the years from my program Experiments in Musical Intelligence's—Emmy's—output.

The dinner was a somewhat different story, at least during the serving of the first course. As I received my salad, I became hopelessly confused as to the etiquette of which fork to use for which parts of the meal. There were so many of these utensils, that my complete lack of propriety in such situations became obvious. So, I turned to my left and found a gentleman dressed formally and using a small fork with his little finger extended as he did. Obviously, this man was well aware of the formalities of eating multi-course dinners and being exposed to the litany of ways to eat each course.

So I asked him, "I hope you won't be disturbed by my asking or be embarrassed by my question, but could you point out which fork I'm to use for eating my salad?"

He looked at me, at his own fork, and then said, "You're not embarrassing me at all. That one." And he pointed out the correct fork to me.

Of course, the minute the evening's soup was served, I asked him the same question. But for spoons. Along with my apologies for embarrassing him again.

He told me he was not embarrassed, to which I responded, "well there's still plenty of time for that."

He looked at me for a second, to see if I was serious or pulling his leg, determined the latter, and politely ignored me for the rest of the meal.

Luckily, sitting to my right was a younger man, dressed more or less informally as I was, who had as little experience in eating such formal dinners as I had. And, to top it off, he was the local electronic music composer and engineer. We got along famously, eating our dinners with whatever knife, fork, or spoon that suited us.

Following dinner that evening, my guide, a woman who had sponsored both my visit and an entire series of computer scientists doing what she felt was cutting-edge work, helped me set up my computer, projections, and sound playback.

Sometime during our preparations, I asked her who else had been in the series thus far. She told me about the last one, who'd apparently decided at the last minute to 'phone in' his presentation rather than actually show up.

I was then going to tell her that I hoped my presentation would go over well, but I didn't need to do that. After all, I'd shown up.

And the lecture I gave went swimmingly, or so I thought. Lots of energetic questions at the end from an enthusiastic crowd.

When the presentation concluded, I was driven to a local hotel and left for the night to my own devices. For me, that meant attempting to sleep which, for the most part, my insomnia prevented as usual.

The next morning, after dressing, brushing my teeth, and the rest of the usual ablutions were I thought complete, my guide, the woman who I mentioned previously, picked me up and took me out to breakfast. Having all the difficult work behind me, I was enjoying my freedom. I hadn't been in this area of greater Los Angeles in many, many years, and was interested to see how it had changed.

Sometime during breakfast, however, I realized that I had subconsciously continued my lack of propriety for, as men are wont to do occasionally, I checked the zipper on my pants and found I'd forgotten to zip it in my hurry that morning.

I was, of course, mortified. For here I was having breakfast in a strange city far away from my home and wife in an up-scale restaurant with my fly unzipped.

Worse yet, the table was arranged such that it literally prevented me from zipping it without incredibly acrobatic motions that I was not prepared to attempt at the moment.

My only choice was to turn to my right, somewhat exposing the aforementioned area, and rectify my uncomfortable situation in full view of anyone walking by and most likely my host for the morning as well.

What to do?

Just mention it, ask her to turn around, and fix the thing? Ignore the situation until a more appropriate time afforded me access to a restroom to do it? Or simply zip it as quickly as possible, and hope it went unnoticed.

For some reason, I chose the latter. After waiting until my host had gotten busy with her pancakes, I made the attempt. And succeeded. At least I thought so. I mention this part, for as soon as I'd fixed my problem, my host began talking about the wonderful marriage she had.

This struck me as an odd coincidence. For I had no intention of trying to lure her away from her husband. Even if I had, it would not be by the crudest way imaginable, that of exposing myself in public. After all, I was a university professor of repute and happily married.

As I flew back to San Jose that afternoon, I wondered about what had happened to me over the less than twenty-four hour period I'd stayed in Claremont and the time I'd spent at Harvey Mudd College. Everything had gone well, I thought, except for the strange bookends that had surrounded my visit. First, the dinner, then my *faux pas* with my pants. I decided to forget the whole thing.

Until now, that is.

and you yourse**l**f

                            sha**l**l k**e**ep the key of *M*en

rising *O*ut of the **g**rou*N*d

                        pr**e**occupied wi*T*h a thought

that rules them

                  and di***V***id***E***d them into parties,

readil***Y*** ar***M***ed.

                this q***U***antity hereafter is pi***DD***ling.

111

E-Mail

from
the white
mou*n*tain, and

all it**S** different

Parts, m*o*st exact**L**y.

As if from a *ve*r**Y**

Hi*g*h p*l*ace. and

that it i*s* **Si**l*l*y

t**O** le**aR**n,

Said **T** he

mou**S**e,

Turning

t**O** alice

Sighing.

2005

Like so many people in the twenty-first century, I rely more and more on electronic forms of communication. Not so much telephones anymore, but on e-mail, Facebook, and so on. It was thus a pleasure to hear from a number of my students in my year-long music theory course I taught at Prairie View A and M College in Texas in 1969-1970. Via e-mail. They were not likely to have found me by any other pre-Internet form of communication because of my numerous moves since then.

I replied immediately, and since then I have continued to be impressed by these students' successes in the world of music. Composing, performing, conducting, and so on. I quickly realized that I should not have forgotten the wonders of that class. How simultaneously we could work our tails off while still maintaining a sense of humor and good grace.

We are now scattered, yet held together by a means that will eventually hold the world together. Not as one being, but as one culture consisting of many, many smaller cultures, with none complaining for fear the whole will immediately find the culprit, and discover a way to prevent its bad temper from continuing.

fo**R**

on what has **b**een sa**i**d

d**E** pend**S** the who**l**e

d**O**ctrine of what **W**as

exceed**ing**

the wicked.

112

Concerts Too

and it vio*L*ently squ*I*rted

out o**F** the **pla**net.

2005

In *Tinman Too* I included a chapter titled simply, "Concerts." In that chapter, I listed a number of reasons why I do not like to attend live concerts. A number of friends that read that chapter asked me why I did not include my usual number of reasons—one hundred—and I've fended them off with comments like, 'not enough space,' 'no one except you would read them,' and so on. However, I now realize I should have included the complete list, and hereby do so.

100 things I hate about concerts

David Cope

1. having to dress appropriately
2. having to adjust my schedule to attend my schedule to get there on time
3. having to find a parking space a parking space

4. having to pay a parking fee a parking fee
5. having to find the hall the hall
6. having to wait in line to get tickets wait in line for tickets
7. having to pay to get in to get in
8. having to ask someone to help me find my seat
9. having to negotiate my way to my seat
10. having to sit in a seat four sizes too small for me
11. having to smell my neighbors
12. having to look around the hat on the woman in front of me
13. having to avoid the snot from local sneezes
14. having to listen to idiotic pre-concert conversations
15. having to discover gum wherever I put my hands or feet
16. having to wonder what diseases have been left on my seat
17. having to listen to neighbors opening their gum wrappers
18. having to figure out how I can make my way past 700 people in my row to get to the toilets
19. having to elbow wrestle both my neighbors for who's going to get the arm rest spaces on both sides
20. having to figure out where to put my feet under the seat in front of me
21. having to avoid getting leg cramps
22. having to watch the performers wander onto the stage as if they didn't give a damn
23. having to read the program notes with insufficient light
24. having to remember what they said
25. having to keep my patience knowing I can't stand most of the concert's music

26. having to look around to see who I might know who's also at the concert

27. having to figure out ways to avoid them during intermission

28. having to listen to the performers warming up

29. having to watch the performers warming up

30. having to guess from their expressions who the ringers are by the looks on their faces

31. having to pretend not to hear the large trucks outside the hall passing by and where they're going this time of night

32. having to sweat my clothes into wet dishtowels

33. having to try and not cough

34. having to watch the tuning process, which I've seen at every concert I've ever attended

35. having to listen to the tuning process

36. having to realize that after they've finished, one player is hopelessly still out of tune

37. having to wait for the conductor to arrive and applauding him before he's done anything except show up

38. having to watch the conductor smile and bow

39. having to watch the conductor turn his back on us and stay that way throughout the show

40. having to hope the conductor doesn't fall off the podium during the concert

41. having to hope the conductor does fall off the podium during the concert

42. having to forgive the conductor for taking the piece I love so much too fast (slow)

43. having to watch the performers prepare to play

44. having to watch them pretend they want to be here

45. having to realize that I'm stuck for the duration watching these people saw and blow their way through the pieces with one performer completely out of tune

46. having to wait for wrong notes

47. having to suffer through wrong notes knowing that I could be home listening to a recording with right notes in it

48. having to watch somebody stressing out not to make a mistake

49. having to watch somebody not giving a damn whether they make a mistake

50. having to listen to the audience cough the minute the music begins

51. having to attempt to reread my program notes in complete darkness

52. having to listen to my intestines growl in counterpoint to the music

53. having to wonder if the first cellist's hair is real or a wig

54. having to wonder how many of the performers on stage would give their right arms to pick some booger out of their nose at the moment

55. having to watch the conductor's gyrations resembling a symmetrical set of wings flapping

56. having to watch the conductor cue someone two measures early and then pretend he was just getting their attention

57. having to watch the conductor find his place in the score after turning two pages instead of one

58. having to watch the performers not watch the conductor anyway

59. having to look up and see the dark lights in the ceiling hung from wires connected to heavy metal bars and wondering if an earthquake would send them down to strike me on the head

60. having to forgive the lady sitting to my left who's busy drumming the snare drum part from Bolero with her fingernails in counterpoint to a work that's not Bolero

61. having to want to tell my neighbor to my right to wake up

62. having to wonder if the guy on my left two rows down who's 200 pounds overweight is going to fall through his seat

63. having to hope the piece we're listening to will soon be over

64. having to withstand the audience clapping like seals in heat

65. having to listen to those applauding between movements

66. having to watch the string players rip the broken polyester hairs from their bows without being seen

67. having to watch the spit drip from the brass players instruments during rests

68. having to watch the tuba player lose count of the thousands of empty measures between his two entrances and two notes played in the current movement

69. having to pray for deliverance from this nightmare

70. having to watch the percussionist's mallets only since my seat is so far in front I can't see who's holding them

71. having to listen to the guy behind me growling in an effort to quench a cough

72. having to watch a woman two seats down in front of me listing to the right and left trying not to fall asleep in her drunken stupor

73. having to realize there's still a half hour left before intermission

74. having to wonder if I can get away during intermission without being seen

75. having to check the time and discover that my watch has been stolen

76. having to realize that the smell I've been smelling is mine not from other people

77. having to find my cell phone that's ringing because I forgot to turn it off

78. having to get to the restroom before the intermission is over

79. having to beg my bladder to relax and failing when I finally arrive at the urinal

80. having to not watch my neighbors not watch me peeing

81. having to listen to a friend talk himself hoarse and giving me no time to respond

82. having to try and find a seat closer to the aisle, sitting, and then apologizing for taking someone else's seat, only to find that my seat has been taken by someone else

83. having to survive the second half of the concert while standing

84. having to stare at the large snail slowly crawling up the conductors trousers

85. having to listen to one of the most idiotic words ever invented: Bravo!

86. having to listen to the second (or maybe first) idiotic words ever invented: Encore!

87. having to listen to people guess what the performer(s) going to play for an encore

88. having to listen to the performer play hoping beyond hope that the audience won't do the bravo/encore thing again when finished

89. having to wonder when the opera stage will collapse sending half the singers into the pit

90. having to wonder what the composers of these pieces would do if they had a choice to attend or not attend their own works being performed this night

91. having to embarrass myself by not listening when asked if I enjoyed the concert

92. having to try and get to my car without hearing people discuss how good or bad the concert was and not knowing what the hell they're talking about

93. having to find my car in the parking lot when dark

94. having to explain why I'm trying to get in someone else's car to its rightful owner

95. having to wait in line behind hundreds if not thousands of other cars

96. having to listen to whomever I've come to the concert with explain their reactions to each piece as if it were God's honest truth and getting mad when I have a different opinion

97. having to discuss who has the raciest gown or the sexiest eyes on the stage

98. having to drive up my driveway and seeing that my house has been burgled

99. having to call the police

100. having to try and not shoot myself for attending this concert in the first place

and *F*or that r*E*ason

the **p**erson who g*I*ves

*L*i*M*it*S* to qu**a**ntities

in **r**ela**ti**on to th**e** principle of e**s**sence

the**y** can, in fact,

mimic the action**S** of
a human computer very closely.

113

Pescadero

i have *ma*de up my mind about it, and
the*r*e wa**S** found no p**lAC**e f**O**r them
with the mo*s*t **AB**u**N**dant and abst**R**use
propos**I**tions of p**L**atonic p*h*i**LO**sop**H**y
to go.

2005

There is a small town north of Santa Cruz and just a couple
of miles east of the Pacific called Pescadero. While it may be
large in square miles, one can drive from one end of town
to the other in less than a minute. No stop lights, no police
or fire departments I can see, and no gas stations. There is a
market, however, a few antiques stores, a couple of art studios,
and a restaurant of some renown, its specialty being artichoke
soup and bread. It also supports an event that takes place
there most Sunday nights.

This event requires the presence of two particular
individuals who just happen to be married. They sit in
roughly the same spots each time they appear, no doubt
reserved for them.

When we first ate in this restaurant on a Sunday night, we sat in the same room and near the table of this couple. And what a night it was. Before we even took a breath, they were at it. First one and then the other would angrily site numerous offenses that the other apparently had committed. They made these complaints loud and without the slightest bit of remorse. This was, obviously, a couple that thrived on fighting one another.

I'd never heard anything like this before. While my first inclination was to ask them to at least quiet their disagreements so the rest of us could eat, I didn't. This was far too intimidating. At least when the question of whether one of them might then beat the other senseless with a dinner plate.

Swear words were not *verboten* either. This was an all out battle with no victors. At least in the sense of the war. The arguments were fought with no rules and, as senseless as they were, verbal brutality was without peer.

The waitress came by, recognized us from a previous non-Sunday night visit, and apologized. She told us this couple were regulars and had been married for centuries. And I believed her. I also told her that she needn't bother with apologies. This battle was special. As entertaining and completely unpredictable as any between husband and wife I could remember witnessing.

While most of the rest of the customers in our room pretended the argument didn't exist and quietly, for no conversation beyond the fighting couple were possible, ate their dinners, I sipped my artichoke soup and ate my artichoke bread while staring in amazement at the pair to my right, blasting away at one another.

What was remarkable was that neither one of the couple looked toward the other as the fight progressed. They simply flapped their gums to an apparently memorized script of agonizing comments on the other's worthlessness. As if their partner could have gone to the bathroom and not be missed by the one yelling obscenities.

What a night.

Gone w**I**th the sto**R**m, th**E**ir world is far **GO**ne. its coolin**G** could not wit**H** all thei**R** quant**I**ty **O**f lo<u>ve</u>. **W**here there w**A**s nothing external with which the globes could be compared to **Y**ou.

114

Got To Have Hart

an*d r*ea*p*, for t*h*e t*i*me is come
for thee to reap the harvest of the
earth, so they sto*l*e into shadows
and waited. they have a*l*L b*e*en
Inv**E**nted over and over fifty
time*s*.

2006

During my many years of teaching an undergraduate course
in film music, I found that having at least five or more guests
actually in the business really helped cement certain ideas
in my students' minds. Or maybe it was just the break from
having me lecture. Whatever the case, I found—both to my
amazement and, to some degree, dismay—that Grateful Dead
drummer Mickey Hart made a big impact. On the benefit
side of the ledger, he brought with him much professional
experience, especially stories about when he worked on
Apocalypse Now. He'd beautifully describe his duties as sound
designer for that film, with very clear images of his having
speakers in every room in his home playing sounds from the

instruments he'd created to make the soundtrack heard in the film. On the debit side of the ledger, he'd also go into the various drugs and alcoholic beverages he consumed during their recording. It's not that I'm a prude, but that he would mark these drugs as a part of the creative process he used to make the film the success it was, was disconcerting. As if the only way my class could produce such success was by being stoned.

My film music classes usually filled the four-hundred seat recital hall on campus. And, because I made it almost impossible for anyone to be absent by giving a quiz at the beginning of each class, most of the time the entire class would show up. For Mickey, however, a line formed outside and many of my students couldn't even get in the room. This caused further problems that eventually forced me to video one of Hart's classes, and then show that video to future classes rather than have him visit. Even that caused some to miss class due to overcrowding.

Popular culture is an amazing phenomenon. Nothing about it rings true to me. Of course, I'm ancient, so it probably works that way. At the same time, the popular icon of my time, Elvis, was not my thing either. For some reason, I don't find it useful or even interesting to make personal decisions based on what other people think. On the other hand, what other people think, as you might imagine, still greatly affects what I do as in my film music class. You'd think, therefore, I'd want to be a part of it. I don't. Of course, the reality is somewhere in between. I wouldn't mind if popular culture wanted to join me. It wouldn't change my views. Unfortunately, that won't happen anytime soon. If ever. Thus, I continue as many of my colleagues do, following my own muses toward whatever end awaits me.

*t*hey have scr**U**tinised and studied positions properly, but have no quantity, nor do they so much as say we will have no

more marria**G**es than those

th**A**t have **BE**en ma**RR**ied already. with all this being

ri**g**ht, and with **S**een **M**en

ANd women **C**all**I**ng **A**ll.

115

Needles

and now,

for *T*He g**A**rden

is c*O*nfu**S**ed by the
babbling of the lewd but
heard by nobody.

e**V**ery c**A**la**mit**y

i**S** a s*P***U**r, and valuable

hints to where his very endeav*O*rs

do not yet fully avail. they tell tenden*C*y.

2007

One year, my wife and I decided to drive to Santa Fe from
Santa Cruz, with a stop in Phoenix to see my mother, sister,
and brother in law. We stayed our first night in Barstow, of
Harry Partch fame, and began our second day on Interstate
40. About fifty miles east of Barstow, amidst traffic moving
in the upper seventies, we were suddenly passed by a vehicle
making us seem like we were standing still. My best guess
told me that what looked like a van packed with many people
was going near one hundred miles an hour. A nearby semi

honked his horn as they passed, either in recognition of the van's right of way, or to caution it to slow down. And we kept on moving. After another fifty or so miles, traffic ground to a halt. A dead halt. Nothing moving on the road in either direction. Our side of the Interstate packed with bumper-to-bumper traffic, the other side completely empty.

Under ordinary circumstances, we'd just sit in our vehicles and wait, cooled from the August mid-day heat with our air conditioner. On this particular day, however, the sky was mildly overcast and, from the size of the puddles on the road, the desert had been drenched over night. Thus, the air outside was a pleasant seventy or less degrees. So my wife and I did as others did, cut the engine and stood outside to stretch and take a breather from driving.

The minutes then dragged on into hours. As they did, conversations between people unknown to one another until now began springing up. I was lucky or unlucky enough to find a truck driver who had a radio that included police bands. We began talking, mostly about the detritus along the side of the road, but eventually to the reasons we were standing out here in the first place. He, having his police band in full gear, told us the story.

'Remember the van that passed us a while back?' he asked. I did. 'Going really fast?' I did. 'Well it was full of two families including wives and kids, and, going as fast as it was, it hit an unexpected bump in the road ahead and splattered (his word) them all over the freeway.'

As if to verify his story, I saw medical helicopters flying in from the south and landing a couple of miles ahead.

He then continued his gruesome story. 'The cops think they've all bought the farm. Bodies everywhere. Car a total wreck. Found it upside down maybe a quarter mile from where they first applied the brakes.'

Talk about a sobering conversation.

And we continued to wait.

Sometime around three, the cars around us began to pull off our side of the Interstate going east, across the median divider, and then heading in the opposite direction. Not just a few cars, mind you, but every one of them. Directed by a highway patrolman I now saw. So my wife and I got back in our car and followed suit.

We drove several miles, and then took an off-ramp going south, then west, then north, then east again, and finally back to the Interstate several miles further than the approximate site of the accident. This detour took about forty minutes by itself. All the while driving, of course, our minds imagined the carnage that had caused this mess. Of the families involved. Of the needless deaths caused by a need for speed. Never getting where they were going because of some kind of desperate desire to get there a few minutes early.

The sky underneath which we drove got darker and darker from cloud buildup, an accompaniment to our moods. The first part of our detour, I realized, had been on old Route 66, the famed but now destitute highway that had stood so long as the only way to get to the east coast without facing an empty tank of gas along the way. Not that this mattered, really, just a thought to keep my mind off what we hadn't directly witnessed, but imagined had occurred that day.

We arrived in Phoenix much later than expected, called in our apologies from our hotel room, and tried to sleep. Under the circumstances, the best we could do.

and to every nation and *K*indred
and tongue and people that
the skull had a tongue
in it, and could sing
once the knave
knew it was
possible
that
under the

*m*icr*o*scope

has t*h*e s*a*me and

mo*v*ed *i*t to a more barren spot.

116

Dog

in neithe**r** aught

or in **e**xtrem**i**ty

but in **O**ur manner

of conceivin**g** it,

the o**L**d beautiful land

wa**s** g**O**ne. and it

nece**s**s**ar**ily

follows

th**a**t

it is

not o**n**ly

more **di**st**A**nt from

tim**e**s beginning, but nearer
its end.

and you

insu**l**t me by

ta**L**king such nonsense.

408

2007

My wife Mary Jane and I own a condo in Santa Fe, where we often spend our Augusts seeing operas, attending chamber music concerts, shopping, and visiting the extraordinary areas in and around the city. One day, we drove northwest to, I believe, San Ildefonso Pueblo. When we left our condo, the weather was sunny and bright, but as is often the case in the high deserts of the southwest, we almost immediately encountered various thunderstorms, each lasting but a few minutes before the sun appeared again.

As with most of the Pueblos in this area, we had to pay a modest fee to walk around and visit the various shops that for much of the town were actual homes laid out so that the living rooms became galleries with pottery display areas for tourists. From our first moment paying our fees, we picked up a mangy dog whose tongue languidly sloshed out of its mouth as he panted. While he sauntered, I told my wife he seemed to know where he was going. So we followed him.

Wonderfully, he'd lead us to a home, wait on the porch as we shopped inside, and then, when we exited, join us again to take us to the next place of business. As we followed, I realized we were taking the grand tour of the village with a dog as our guide. Graciously, whenever a shower suddenly burst from the afternoon clouds, he would find a covered porch where the three of us waited until it passed. Occasionally, he'd introduce us to people along the way by first finding them, then sitting and wagging his tail briskly through the dust or mud as we spoke.

Eventually, of course, we found ourselves right back at our car, parked in front of the fee station as we'd left it an hour or so previously. For a second or two, I thought of going inside and asking the personnel there if this were a standard tour, or if the dog had made it a special day just for us. But I decided not to. I did, however, find a treat in our rental car and passed it along to our guide. He took it in his mouth and wandered off into the bushes.

A thoroughly delightful afternoon.

i *d*idn t m*eA*n it, *Pl*eaded *p*oor alice,

for t*h*e devil is c*OM*e d*O*w*n* *U*nto you,

for w*E* *BeL*ieve that it i*S* n*O*t *O*nly true that

being regulated by law*S* of behaviour implies being some sort of machine.

117

Suit

no T by nu**m**be**rs**

and not by *Al***G**ebr**A**

but on**L**Y upon ani**ma**Ls.

2007

My second son, Stephen, has lived for over a decade with a wonderful woman who has two boys by a previous marriage. These kids are extraordinarily congenial and bright. We see them as a family once or twice a year and it's a joy. Several years ago when I arrived home after surgery for prostate cancer, a story I recount in the first volume of *Tinman*, Stephen's wife challenged me to a game of Sticks and Stones, a board game I designed several years back. Wanting to take my mind off the day's activities, I accepted and we began. As we played, the youngest of her sons crowded around the table and proudly proclaimed that his mother was going to win. I asked him how he knew this, and explained that I had invented the game, played it often, and she—at least at that point—barely knew the rules.

As we continued, so certain was this young man—

411

probably in the sixth or seventh grade at the time—that his mom would win, he offered me a wager. Now, before progressing further, I must explain two things. First, I was still more than slightly high from the morphine the surgeons had given me prior to filling me with radiation pellets. Second, and this is more difficult to explain, this young man, the one making the wager, had, for some reason, taken to wearing complete suits to his classes. Including bowler hats and a black business briefcase. He did this everyday and, at that moment, was actually wearing his trademark getup. Thus, he told me that if I accepted the wager and lost, I would have to wear a similar suit to school for teaching for the next six months. Note, here, that the dress code at the University of California at Santa Cruz was more similar to those worn by surfers than by traditional academics. No professor wore a suit to class. In fact, even the chancellor was on a first name basis with students and faculty alike. One could say the campus was casual. Me in a monkey suit would stick out like a severally swollen thumb. But, I was loopy and I took the wager. So loopy, in fact, that I didn't even ask what he'd have to do for me if I won the game.

So his mother and I played Sticks and Stones, and, of course, I lost. Quickly and decisively. I blame it on the morphine, of course, but truth be known I often get so interested in my games and in attempting what I consider brilliant moves, that I have more than once lost to a lesser opponent. Many times 'more than once' actually.

And so I went about purchasing the necessary jackets, ties, and so on—I hadn't worn one in so long, the ones I had were threadbare—and, according to the wager, went to school the first day after the game in my go-to-meetings suit. And, of course, questions ensued. Over and over again I was asked if I'd lost a bet. More than once I responded that I had. By the time my first day had finished and I was walking out of the music-building door, I answered my last question of the day about my attire. Yes, I said, I had lost a bet. But, I added, it wasn't a problem for me. Even though I'd promised the young man I'd wear this obscene gear for six months, he lived out of state and would never know if I completed the task or not.

"Oh," this person to whom I was talking said. "You must wear that outfit for six months."

"Why?" I asked. "He'll never know if I don't."

"But, *you* will know if you don't," she replied.

O say ghost,

do not fo**rg***E*t this visitatio**N**

as if the unequal *R*adii on drawn lines

from the *C*entre *O* of an**y** wheel if the thread**s**

es**PE**cially when a soul that e**X**ists is quick and docile.

118

Apple

another important result of preparing our Just machine for its Best pArt in the imitatiOn game, is By a process of teacHiNg and learning that's that human falliBIliTy is real.

2008

It may seem like a dream to me now, but it was most certainly real at the time. I had just finished performing or attending a premiere of one or more of my works, and was now in that state of euphoria that accompanies perceived success. I had left the hall and followed the path someone there had directed me toward to find a bus station to ride to the airport for a flight home. It was still early but after dark, and I was carrying a suitcase. I remember it was cold. Very cold. So, a winter's night in New York City. And I was lost.

The buildings—not skyscrapers but tall—blocked out most of the sky, but it wouldn't have helped much since it was snowing lightly and most likely overcast. I had long since passed the bright lights of downtown Manhattan, and the theaters and department stores had disappeared, replaced by rundown apartment buildings. I remember looking into an alley and seeing a bonfire roaring, with many people huddled around it. Most of the streetlights were out, either by disrepair or being busted by rocks or the equivalent, and thus the darkness was overpowering. And, as I said before, it was cold.

Every once in a while, I'd step over a vent for the subway and feel the heat. I remember it seemed like a drink offered to an alcoholic. I wanted to sit down on that vent and stay there forever. But I couldn't. I had to find a bus station. Of course I was having trouble doing that since I had no idea where I was. I'd walked into the good night reliving whatever had transpired that evening, only to find myself in that bad night carrying a suitcase, ill-dressed for the cold, and wandering I knew not where.

Could I be on my way to a worse place than this? Would there be signs for a bus station in this neighborhood? Would I be able to see the signs in the dark if there were any? Was I an obvious target for thieves carrying a suitcase as I was?

I remember imagining myself as seen from a hidden camera from a silent helicopter high above me. A man alone walking down a dreary street after dark with a suitcase in the worst part of the Big Apple in the snow. Not an endearing thought. But maybe endearing for the many others that didn't, at least yet, know I was there.

No matter the heat from the occasional subway vent, I had to find a bus station and get to the airport to fly home. I used that as my mantra as I looked in every direction for any hint of where I was or was not going.

I could hear voices now and again, mostly from the rundown apartment house windows above me. Yelling.

Screaming. And occasionally the screeching of tires or the sound of a siren moaning in the distance. No cars on the street I walked. No taxis, busy or not.

Even then, so real was my trauma, that I couldn't remember what I'd done that evening. Only the wonderful feeling that whatever I'd done had gone well. Very well. I remember it seeming funny to me at the time that I couldn't remember. But not funny enough to change my fear to confidence, my anxiety to calmness.

I decided I should turn. Toward the light. It was a lot better than going straight, since the neighborhoods seemed to be getting worse not better. So, the first cross street that showed more light than the street I was on, I turned. I remember that very clearly. I also remember wondering where the homeless people were. On a night like this, why weren't they sitting over the vents in the sidewalk breathing in the warmth? But I was alone. Except for the sounds, the darkness, and the snow lightly falling around me. A composer wandering into the armpit of hell in the middle of the night.

And then I saw it. Small lettering and bad lighting. But I had good eyes in those days. A sign that had two things on it. One, an arrow pointing upward, no doubt indicting straight ahead, and a simple three letter word, "Bus."

I arrived at the well-lit lobby, bought a ticket for JFK, made my flight, and returned around midnight to the San Jose Airport. I then picked up my car and drove home to Santa Cruz.

It could have been any one of a number of concerts I played in the city in those days. I was never sure whether they were actually successes or that I was simply happy they were over.

and ano**T**h*er* *a*ngel came ou*t* of th*e* temple

fo*r* like a creature, the whole world i**S** in

the flux **O**f matter or poi**N**ts, where it

would **b**uild <u>r</u>em<u>**O**</u>ter planets from the sun

<u>a</u>n**<u>d</u>** not begin an academic undertaking or

take a**way** the form.

119

The Dark Ages

there w*a*s *no*t a cloud i*n* the sky.

the wise **f**eeling th**a**t there is

somethi**n**G̲.

but **t**hey **a**re the O̲nly men.

2008

Two million years from now, no one will have ever heard of either me or you. No matter how many books we write, compositions we compose, paintings we paint, discoveries we discover, it will eventually be for naught. The legacy we may think we deserve will not exist. No one will give a damn.

So why do we do anything other than live our lives, enjoy what we can, and die with smiles on our faces? Those who wish to delude themselves into believing things differently can wallow in their illusions if they want, but two million years is still two million years. Who gives a damn?

Yet we go on making and discovering things. Why? What's the purpose? To make others momentarily feel better, live apparently better lives, provide noble goals for them so they might convince themselves that what they do matters in the larger scheme of things? Is there a special place saved for those who create the symphonies or discover penicillin? A place of great passage, of immortality, of congratulations, of prizes and honor? That those who spend their lives laboring on the nuts and bolts of our machinations, our cars, televisions, Internet, and so on, without even knowing what they're doing except making a living so they can retire and watch their grandkids can make the same damn mistakes they did at that age?

No. There is no special place. No matter our achievements, they will be forgotten. Forever. No doubt about it. Unless, of course, this thing we call reality is nothing more than a fantasy, a dream, a cockamamie and idiot game being played. On us. By us. Who knows?

So why do it? More specifically, why do I do it? Why do I write these words? For what purpose? What use?

I'll tell you why. It's actually rather simple. I do it because making and discovering things is absolutely the most fun one can have while living. And long term fun at that. Not two million years of fun, surely, but fun in the sense that I can look back at what I've accomplished, good or bad, and marvel that I was at least able to do it. After all, the universe making no sense no matter how much we create or how much we discover is a pretty big load to carry. And, momentarily at least, this illusion is all we have. So I grab it. Hold it in my hands. Like Sisyphus, we can find our sanity in the insanity by creating and discovering the twists and turns of the rock with which we forever labor to reach the top of the mountain, only to see that rock roll down yet once again.

And I do it because I believe that our journey through time, while seemingly fluid, is also saved in solid stone, with each microsecond frozen forever. And that in two million years will still exist. Not as a legacy, mind you, or known to anyone, but as a microsecond in time forever remembered by the universe. For, as ephemeral as life may seem, it is as concrete drying in afternoon sun, ever present, and ever there. No matter what.

the**S**e states are su**F**ficientl**y** <u>D</u>ifferent

f**OR** th**E** possibility of confusion between
words. her foot slipped on them
and the length which is as large
as the breadth and would be found

fore**VER**.

120

Alena

he expRESsed almost ANy idE a

that inteLlIgenT life might haVE

develoPEd theRe.

far from this argumEnt

is veRY wEll expressed iN lisTed oratIons

from whiCh I quote such a greAt man as he.

2008

Alena, an acronym for Artificial Life Evolving from Natural
Affinities, is my most recent project involving algorithmic
techniques for creating music, visual art, and modest
narratives in language. These creations emerge from simple
rules producing complex results similar to the evolutionary
processes that formed life on earth. The difference being, as
some have called it, life in silica as opposed to life in vitro.
The processes involved in this program created most of the
haiku in *From the Fiery Night* a book of two thousand poems,
visual art as seen in the book *ars ingenero*, as well as music

called *Prescience* for chamber orchestra recorded on Centaur Records.

The rules Alena uses have taken many forms, most involving some type of mathematical formulae involving feedback from initially random starting conditions. When properly graphed, such rules produce highly chaotic output that occasionally settles into what are called attractors; interesting organized structures that often suggest crystal-like forms and even aspects of some types of viruses. I use what are called analog computers to produce these forms, since these types of computers—a much maligned former incarnation of digital computers—do not *model* reality, but *produce* reality in that their output exists in the form of continuous electric current rather than digital representations.

The basic idea behind Alena is that certain attractors that form over time with proper initial conditions, remain in place—something I call persistence of memory—even when the conditions are altered to values that do not produce them. These attractors then seem to move independently and can even spilt apart as if imitating reproduction. Thus it was that I began writing a book called *The Transcendent Machine* that describes the processes involved in more detail.

Unfortunately, while such research can produce incredibly interesting results, the experiments themselves cannot be reproduced because they depend too heavily on initial conditions that require infinite precision. Even when created by accident, drifts in values cause analog computers to lose such attractors after a brief time.

One night, while agonizing over the conflicting views of my research on artificial life, I found myself in my backyard hot tub staring at a beautiful night sky full of stars. The question I was pondering seemed important. Should I continue and maybe waste precious time—one thinks of such things at age 71—or give it up for more conservative aims that I no doubt could actually complete before I die? Just as I thought I'd made up my mind, a meteor flashed soundlessly across the black depths from Cappella to Vega roughly, and then shattered into several brightly lit pieces before disappearing. It took no more than a second or two. An incredible sight.

I lay back in the hot water and thought it through. A sign perhaps? It certainly had arrived at just the right moment, for the book I was writing—*The Transcendent Machine*—was either hair-brain or brilliant. But which? And what did the meteor, so perfectly timed, mean? If anything?

You may now know the answer to my question by checking your favorite Internet bookstore to see if such a book exists and is written by me. If so, you'll know that I chanced what time I had remaining on earth to follow through with my ideas. If not, well it's either lying in my laboratory someplace unpublished, or on the desk of a publisher who no doubt has or had the same conflicts about its sanity and my own as did I.

You can also check Google for a novel called *This Matter of Life and Death* that I wrote that covers much the same territory, but is less detailed and instructive. I may have published this novel because producing the irreproducible as I had, caused even me to believe it was more fictive than scientific.

Important to note, however, the art that my program created—the poems, visual art, and music I discussed earlier—emanated from these processes and is as real as it gets.

fo**ll**owed by his conviction of r**a**mee

may be a mos**t** significan**t** name.

and in that case i can go back by **ra**ilway.
and melt in my own fire.

and pro**C**laim no shame.

and **t**he gun-metal gray cl**O**uds gathe**r**ed thu**S**ly.

121

ALS

i say **W e** will <u>**HA**</u>ve no more m**A**rr**i**ages.**T**hose that are marr**i**ed already, all right. a**N**d then i heard another voice from heaven sayin**G**, and in **T**he right **O**r**D**er and tense, go as brave as the zod**i**ac in ag**E**.

2008

A friend of mind, here called Nameless, phoned me in 2008 to tell me he had been diagnosed with ALS. Amyotrophic lateral sclerosis, often called "Lou Gehrig's Disease," is a progressive degeneration of the motor neurons that eventually leads to paralysis and then death. While at the time many experimental techniques were in their testing stages, none had proven effective beyond an extra few months of life.

This was incredibly sad news, as Nameless was in the prime of his life, and just beginning his compositional career. He was also a gifted music theorist and teacher.

My mother-in-law died of ALS in the early 1970s, so I was particularly aware of the manner in which the disease progresses, and the strain it puts not only on victims, but on those around them.

As I write these words at almost thirty years his senior, I cannot imagine why I've been spared and he will soon die. It makes no sense. Nature can not only be cruel, but is most likely always cruel. Just in different ways to different people.

As one of the most talented and kindest persons I've ever known, Nameless will, I hope, through his music and the memories he has given us, be appreciated to the fullest by those of us who remain behind.

W e *p*ut out *a*nother sort of perspiration, go*u*t, fever, rheumatism, caprice, doubt, fretting, and avarice, that periodica*l*ly i*n*und*a*te our temperate zone, and that verything is ca*us*ed KINdly by the ne*x*t finite, infinite, o*r* Circumscrip*t*ion in r*e*lation to Good o**ptions**.

122

San Francisco Street

wh*O* a**RE**, you said, a voi**C**e from be**H**ind t**h**E window curt**A**ins, who w**a**s in *l*if**e** a foolish *PE*ati**n**g knave, who wa**S** to **R**ule all nat*i*on**S** with **A** *R*od of iron.

2009

My wife and I have spent many hundreds of hours in downtown Santa Fe, most of these in rehearsals, concerts, used bookstores, or shopping. Thus, we have a pretty good lay of the land, and especially where the restrooms are beyond those in restaurants.

One afternoon in August, I left my wife and a couple visiting us to find one of those restrooms, this one located in a multi-story building of shops on San Francisco Street that borders the south side of the town plaza.

As I came up the outside steps and began walking toward the rear of this building where the restrooms are located, I noticed a well dressed man sitting in a wooden chair available most likely for husbands waiting on their wives. As I passed this man he spoke to me, saying something like 'Good afternoon. Nice day isn't it?' I replied that indeed it was, and continued on toward the back of the little mall.

As I walked, I heard footsteps following me where I'd heard none previously. But I gave it no mind. After all, no one was really following me, just going in my direction.

Toward the back of the building, upstairs, and into the restroom the steps came, never varying in either speed or direction to my own. Curious, I thought.

Inside the restroom now, the man headed for the single stall at the rear while I took up residence at the single urinal near the hand basins. As I tried to pee—I have a shy bladder as it turns out—I heard nothing from the stall next to me.

Then, out of the blue, the man who'd come along behind me said, 'Good afternoon. Nice day isn't it?' Exactly the same words he'd originally spoken.

Strange, I thought.

I continued to attempt to pee.

Then, once again the man said, 'Good afternoon. Nice day isn't it?'

This was too much. I suddenly realized it was some sort of code. The man who I'd met near the entrance was there to meet someone. They'd agreed on these words and the ones I'd initially spoken apparently. In short, it was a rendezvous between a male prostitute and someone interested in such things. Not me. For sure.

I must have embarrassed myself at that point, for I zipped my pants on the way out, forgetting either to answer the man or wash my hands, and made my way quickly out the front of the building toward my waiting wife and her guests. And, before anyone else could speak, I told them the story.

'My goodness,' the woman of the two guests of my wife said, 'That must mean he thinks you're handsome.'

I was stunned.

'No,' I replied, 'it means he thinks I'm someone else, and that I'm going to pay him for certain services in this case not rendered.'

She blushed then, and I hurried us along for fear my acquaintance might still be looking for me and request some kind of payment for him just showing up.

I later told my wife that I was—as she already knew, but I was confirming it once again—supportive of gay marriage, gay rights, and so on. There's little enough love in the world as it is not to allow people to love whomever they want and give them the same rights that heterosexual couples have. But we weren't talking about love here. This was business. And I wanted no part of it.

She said she understood.

And not to worry about it.

*A*nd we **m**en, the **C**reatures who inha**b**it this **ea**rth, f**L**ow**S** equably without regard to anything external, and by another na**m**e are called d**u**ration without uncovering what doe**s** not concern us. th**i**s question, the dodo **c**ould not answer without a great deal of thought.

123

Generative Music

i **P**r**A**yed.
and t**H**erefore th**I**s
endeavour **L**et us **ge**t
to the shore. a**n**d th**e**n i **L**l
t**E**ll you my histo**r**y.

2009

Several years ago, a student asked me to define 'generative music.' I thought about it, and soon realized—aside from its obvious dictionary meaning—that I really had no idea. Wanting to make sure I didn't face that question again and feel so ignorant, I visited the web, and YouTube in particular, to discover what I'd been missing. Especially since it seemed to have a great deal to do with algorithmic composition.

What I found there mystified me. In a short video called, I believe, 'An Introduction to Generative Music,' I discovered, much to my chagrin, that I was one of the two pioneers of this field along with Brian Eno. Following one of my composition teacher's dictums, 'any publicity is good so long as they spell your name right,' I should have been delighted at my pioneering efforts. And, while I don't feel that Eno's music and mine are particularly similar, I do respect his work and felt complemented to be included with his pioneering efforts. Unfortunately, I was still confused.

So I continued on with discovering what I'd been missing all these years. A definition and examples of generative music, some of the latter belonging to me. The film, as I remember it, gave the definition of generative music as, 'using algorithms to create original pieces of music from a finite set of parameters.' That sounded a great deal like what I did, but I call it algorithmic music, typically defined as 'music derived from finite sets of rules and parameters.'

So, I was a pioneer of generative music. Or at least a pioneer as stated in the definition provided by the makers of this particular video of generative music.

However wonderful that sounded, though, I must still caution those willing to give me that accolade. The pioneer status more rightfully belongs to those who actually pioneered it. And for that, one must include the composers of the late Middle Ages such as Guillaume de Machaut, whose extraordinary isorhythmic motets will testify, the infamous *musikalisches würfelspiele* of Haydn, CPE Bach, Mozart, Kirnberger, and others, as well as Xenakis, Messiaen, and so on.

But, I guess I will take credit whenever offered.

let us **R**eturn for

a moment **t** to

lady lov**e**lac**e**s

*o*bject**i**on. when her

second husband le**t** *m*e

be accur**s**t wh**e**n *proc**l**u*s diadochus

had **P**ublish**E**d fou**R** books on euclid,

*t*his j*e*t of fi*r*e had become invi*s*ible
about a quarter past twelve.

124

Kluckhohn

fAte, then, is a name.

foR faCts nOt yet passed under the fIre of

thought for cauSes are unpenetrated,

and take the Little bOok which is opeN In the hAnd
of the angeL

not by numbers and not by algebra.

2010

Clyde Kluckhohn was a notable anthropologist studying
the Navajo Indian culture during the twentieth century. He
died in 1960 from a heart attack and is survived by his wife
and research colleague Florence who lives in Santa Fe, New
Mexico, as of this writing. I include this brief background
here to give readers a sense of the lifelong pursuit of the man
and his wife, working together to attempt to understand the
nature of the Navajo Nation, then known as the Navajo Rez.

A good friend of mine, an American Indian and a well-
known author, told me a story once that remains imbedded in

my mind to this day. This friend is a man of logic and comes from a very different Indian culture on the eastern side of North America. This too needs to be said before recounting the story.

Sometime before the turn of this century, long after Clyde Kluckhohn's death but while his wife still lived in Santa Fe, Florence invited my writer friend to stay at her home while he was waiting for transportation to return home himself. During this visit, Florence Kluckhohn let my friend sleep in a small room near the front door, a place usually set aside to store many of the artifacts that her husband had collected from the Navajos. Boxes and boxes of these aniquities were stacked in this room along with larger items taken from the Rez.

Now, to understand this story it's important for me to underscore what I've already mentioned. My friend does not believe in ghosts, magic, demons, and the like, even though he was fully aware of the importance placed on such beings in the culture and lore of various Indian cultures including the Navajo.

So being assigned the bed in this room with the artifacts did not pose any problem for him. In fact, to the contrary, it seemed a logical and even welcome place for him to stay.

However, as he tells it, the minute he entered the room that first night, he immediately felt a presence of some kind. At that point, not sinister, frightening, or problematic, but simply a presence. He took it for what he assumed it to be. He, too, knew the stories, and his imagination had reared its head and created an invisible creature for him to share his sleep with. Not unusual in these circumstances.

With that in mind, then, he lay down and promptly fell asleep.

Sometime during the night, he woke to a sound he couldn't identify. He looked around for the source and could fine none. The boxes of artifacts were still in place, the larger items intact, and the window closed. While the door was open a crack, he seemed to remember it being that way before he'd fallen asleep.

So he chalked it up to the wood in the floor settling, or some such thing, and once again fell asleep.

But again he was awakened by the sound, or maybe something else he couldn't identify. He looked around getting a bit nervous by now, and watched the door to his room slowly open, revealing a very tall being covered in various animal furs, feathers, and a large headdress with strange markings on it. The vision of this creature standing in the doorway along with his continuing sensation of a strange presence made him sit straight up and stare.

The visitor stood there stoically, ramrod straight, and without uttering a word.

My friend was acutely aware of the Navajo concept of *chindi*, the ghost left behind after a person has died, and of *skinwalkers*, high priests that take the form of animals who inflict pain and even death on people, particularly at night, and to those who have broken the laws of The People.

Since my friend had not broken any such laws, he immediately thought of the artifacts and other tokens stolen by Kluckhohn for his collection. He was surrounded by such illegal things.

My friend—even though strong of body and mind—was absolutely stunned by this appearance. So, when this being— well over six-and-a-half feet tall and unimaginably large even given it was covered in many animal skins and furs—growled and made other threatening sounds, my friend leapt to his feet and ran out the door. So quickly, as a matter of fact, that the being had no time to stop him.

Outside now, in front of the house and in the middle of the night, my friend stood and waited for this spirit to chase or at least follow him. And he waited for the rest of the night like that. Until the sun rose. No one followed him.

In the morning, and very cold as Santa Fe lies at seven thousand feet above sea level, my friend weighed the possibility of entering the house and telling Florence that her home was haunted by a *skinwalker*, and that she should return the artifacts to their rightful owners, the Navajo Nation. But, for the life of him, he could not enter the house again.

So, without a word to anyone, he departed from Florence's house, thankful he'd left his pants on when he'd gone to bed and still had his wallet, and traveled by bus instead of plane to get home.

As he told this story, his descriptions of the feelings he'd had and the look of the *skinwalker* that had confronted him that night were so real, that I won't attempt to replicate them here. Suffice it to say, this experience will live with my friend for the rest of his life. He even added that during his first few nights away from that house he still dreamed of the experience, and could feel the same presence with him.

How could Florence not know of this thing that shared her residence? So he called her and told her of the experience and why he'd disappeared that morning. She told him she never felt safer than when she was in that house and that he'd imagined the whole thing.

When he'd finished telling his story to me and looked up, I saw a strange look in his eyes that I'd never seen there before. A fear still alive in him? A sense of the being with whom he'd had contact?

Before I left him that evening, I asked him if Florence still lived in that house and, if so, could he talk to her and see if I could at least visit the room where he'd stayed that night and if I, too, could encounter this monster. This *skinwalker*.

He didn't respond immediately, but eventually conceded that he would see what he could do.

But why, he asked me, would I wish to be in that situation? Had his story not been vivid enough to warn me away?

I told him it had, but I liked danger and would very much welcome the opportunity to see and hear this *skinwalker* in action.

Since I don't live all year around in Santa Fe, we agreed to revisit this question at a later date when I returned.

By the time I did, however, he'd moved away and had not, before he'd left, been able to arrange my meeting with Florence or visit the special room.

we won t talk abo**u**t the **ZON**e **A**nymore,
    if youd rather not,

but do you consent to re**p**roduce the argument?

125

Bingham

that whi**C**h I will p**R**ove th**A**t the n**U**mber**S** and
d**IS**t**ANC**es **O**f the p**L**anets, **R**ighte**O***u*sness that
both judges **A**n**D** makes wa*r*, and slowly and s*u*rely draws
Thei**R** pl**A**ns against us.

2010

Between the years 1912 to 1915, Yale explorer Hiram Bingham excavated several thousand items from the site of Machu Picchu in Peru, and exported them to Yale University in New Haven, Connecticut, where they've remained for nearly one hundred years. This was not a hijacking, but a special decree by the Peruvian government at the time. More recently, Peru requested them returned to their rightful owners: The Peruvian people. Enter one David Cope, who had been invited to lecture at Yale in the fall of 1910, and then writing a novel about the Inca of Peru and curious about the situation. I then wrote,

Dear Richard,

My name is David Cope, Professor Emeritus at the

UC Santa Cruz. I've been invited to give a lecture in music and computer science at Yale next week (Wednesday evening and teach classes in both areas on Thurs.) I will have several open times during my visit and was asked by the groups bringing me if I had a desire to see anything while I was at Yale. I immediately thought of Bingham's collection of artifacts from Machu. I am a nascent archeologist (avocation) and have written a novel about the Inca called *The Thirteenth King* which is nearing time for my last chance for corrections. I've read everything by Bingham and Savoy and have several friends who specialize in the Chachapoya and Inca (e.g., Keith Muscutt and Vincent Lee).

I was wondering if there was any possibility for a short tour during either the early afternoon next wed. or late Thursday morning of next week (13 and 14 Oct.)? I realize that there is a suit from Peru that may or may not hinder such a tour, but I have no interest in that whatsoever, just intense interest and some knowledge in the Inca Empire.

Thank you very much for your consideration.

All best,

Dave Cope

While the title of my novel had changed—now *The Death of Karlin Mulrey*—the need for my visit to the Peabody collection at Yale was important and vital to the research I was conducting for the book.

I then received a reply and I include it within my own response to that reply below,

Dear Dave,

I would be glad to meet with you. Please let me know when you will be free. There are some Bingham materials on display that you can see. Best wishes.

Dear Richard,

You're wonderfully kind. How would Wednesday the 13th work around 1 pm for you? No chance of seeing remainder of the collection if only for a moment? Or is it stored elsewhere? I have no desire to touch anything. It's just that I've studied all of the examples in the Citadel book and some are so exquisite, to actually see some of them in color would be an enormous treat. Or, second best, to purchase a catalog from the exhibit of some years past. As you can probably tell, while I am definitely an amateur, I am a very dedicated one.

This was great news for me, as while I was interested as well in my presentations to Yale's music and computer science departments, I was even more interested in archeological findings of the sort I was trying to arrange. So I carved out time from my schedule and found myself more nervous about meeting Richard Burger and Lucy Salazar than I was in standing in front of several audiences to explain my work in music composition and computer programming.

Our meeting took place as scheduled, and Richard and Lucy answered all of my questions including those about Bingham's boxes of antiquities from Machu Picchu. Unfortunately, this last answer was not what I'd hoped for. Bingham's storehouse of artifacts was located several blocks away and underground in a special area kept at proper temperatures to avoid degradation. The boxes were labeled, but closed, and we were not to open them due to restrictions made by both Yale and the Peruvian government due to a suit leveled against Yale for return of such to South America. But, the two archeologists told me that I was missing nothing. That most of the artifacts in those boxes were parts of ceramics and other utilitarian items rather than anything worth seeing. We did get a tour of a special small exhibit in the Peabody Museum set aside for the better items.

Not very long after my visit to Yale, I discovered that a deal had been made for all of the items in Bingham's boxes to be returned to Peru. In fact, according to the calendar, the court's sessions and arguments were coincidentally being made on the same day as my visit to the Peabody. Now I would have to go to Peru to see the treasures. If, that is, there were any. For, as the transcriptions of the agreement between Yale and Peru attest, the really wonderful items still reside in the states rather than where some feel they really belong.

I'm of mixed mind about this. On one hand, such beautiful works of art and culture belong to the people of earth, and should be shared so we can appreciate and better understand them. On the other hand, they can create so much more impact when seen in their native lands.

Regardless of coincidences and my not seeing them on my visit to Yale, my novel did not suffer. Machu Picchu is not it's primary focus, and its main characters are in search of a much greater prize as any one who has read this book will attest.

there are other respe*CT* s and similar res*U*lts to *b*ury

Church **K**leene ro*S*ser *a*nd turing, why not thou s*A*yst

who the*R*e interpret those words for their *m*easured

quantities. *Y*ou add so much to it, and will *b*e *a*live.

126

Zukerman

e**V**ery ent**I**re motion is com*P*os*E*d of

t*H*e mot*I*o*N* of the **V**icious

bo**D**y out of its fi*R*st

p*La*c*E* to do this

necessit**a**tes a

short a**C**count

of t**h**e nature
and vivacious
properties of
co*M*puters.

2010

I met renowned violinist Pinchas Zukerman in Santa Fe
while he was performing in the Chamber Music Festival
there. He'd never heard of me—nor had I expected him to—
but I continued to try and convince him I was a composer
and interested in writing music for the violin. He was all
for that, but, since he was soon to give a presentation on

playing the instrument, he didn't have the time to discuss it further. Having expected this outcome, since it had happened to me many times before with others, I was not surprised. What I was surprised about, however, was his extraordinary politeness in brushing me off. I almost felt honored by the manner in which he'd done it.

During his presentation that I then attended, he discussed and answered questions regarding the manner in which he approached the violin. In the examples he played of particularly difficult passages, he made them all seem easy. Tossing them off as bits of fluff necessary to convince audiences they were hearing the real deal.

they took the**M** to the stre*A*m f**I** rs**T** .

t**H**ey exist i*N* the divine mind, and

the first beast was **l**ike a lion,

an**d** the second

l**i**ke a calf with
his head and
shoulder
turned.

127

Wang

how doth the little c**R**ocodile

improve hi**S** shinin *G*

t**A**il **a**nd **in**

*R*igh**t**eo**u**sness
doth he judge
*A*nd make

Wa**r**?

2010

At age twenty-two, Chinese born American pianist Yuja Wang—pronounced Wong—was a true phenom. She had already performed many if not most of the major concerti for her instrument, and had done so on the spur of the moment, filling in for performers taken ill. I had seen her perform before, but the second time I witnessed her play— the difficult Prokofiev sixth piano sonata—I had to meet her. As I watched her sign her newest CD for me, I looked her in the eyes and told her to never stop playing the piano.

She promised me she wouldn't stop, and went on to the next person in line.

As she had played, I was struck by her ability to cover the entire range of dynamics—unlike most other pianists I knew—and present the work with a grace and panache that usually accompanies someone many times her age and experience.

Later that afternoon while eating at a local Indian restaurant and taking advantage of their buffet, I encountered her again as we both grabbed for Tandoori chicken. She looked at me quizzically, as I no doubt did her. And we went our separate ways. My first thought—that she recognized me—quickly spread to horror when I realized she might have thought me a stalker or some other kind of bizarre fan. I'm certainly not a stalker, but I might be a bizarre fan. She performs with such extraordinary joy and oneness with the music, being so enveloped in the sound and what she calls the 'zone' in interviews I've heard, that my eagerness—once I'd heard her play—to hear her again almost defies description.

I can only hope she fulfills her promise.

*F*rom i**t** as sleep**i**ng **s**oldiers alarm
the quality o*F* the thought

di_f_fe_r_en**C**es t*H*e

egypti**an** and the

ro**MAN**,

the austr*I*a**N**

and the a*M*eri**C**AN

dr_I_fted **S**ilently acr**O**ss the sky.

i do not think mr pickwick would mind the **V** ivid
comparison.

128

Nambé Falls

and yet i wi**S**h i could show you our c**a**t
di**n**ah, and **t**he city lieth **F**ou**R**squ**a**re,
BUt then in wh**A**t remai**N**s, we
Find a **F**urther skin to be stri**p**ped off.

2011

My wife and I like to visit various locales in and around Santa Fe, New Mexico. Recently we drove to a pueblo there called Nambé, thirty or so miles northeast of Santa Fe. The Nambé Pueblo has a reservoir to its east, and below that a waterfall called Nambé Falls. The reservoir can be reached easily by car, but the falls require a fifteen-minute hike, mostly going up. When we reached the falls, a wonderful two-decker with plenty of spilling water, we both noticed that directly above it was perched a large cement portion of the otherwise earthen dam we'd already seen from lakeside. My wife voiced what we both then thought. Had the makers of the dam diverted the water to go over these falls, or did Mother Nature?

The answer to this question was not altogether clear. On both sides of the falls were plainly visible scars suggesting manmade sculpting. On the other hand, the falls themselves simply looked too natural to have been carved by explosives just for visitors. Thus, too close a call to decide one way or the other. Of course, what difference did it make? The falls were there, we could see them, and so what matter who or what caused them?

But somehow it did matter. If these falls had been created naturally from the rock, they were somehow quite breathtaking. On the other hand, if they resulted from the hands of the Army Corps of Engineers or some other governmental agency, they were somehow shallow and meaningless. A sideshow. Like seeing a beautiful rock formation in the desert and being told someone had carved it and not the wind and rain.

This situation struck me then, as it does now, as ironic. For it is this very situation that I have found myself in for several decades now, only in reverse. People are disappointed to discover that the music they've heard and liked by my programs has not been composed by me or by the composer whose music the program has attempted to emulate. While I suppose context is everything, it does seem strange that these two situations are so similar and yet so contrary. In one instance we demand that the beauty we perceive be natural, and in another instance demand that it be contrived.

Of course, both of these notions are wrong. For thousands of years humans have been changing the weather and inadvertently the direction and location of waterfalls, and my programs are the result of Mother Nature, albeit round about. The simple black and white view so many hold regarding these two supposedly different sources is actually incredibly gray. The falls are there, we can see them, and so what did it matter who or what caused them? It doesn't. And Emmy's and Emily Howell's compositions do exist, so what does it matter who or what caused them?

*A*nd so one b*u*ys out th*e* *L*aw, *b*ut

tis n*OT* so above were entire*l*y

swept *o*ut of existen*C*e in a wa*r* of

extermination. t*H*e inside sheets of my bed were wet with sweat

UNDER the same prin*CI*ple

that al*S*o pervades all existence *U*nder

the *Z*one.

129

Bokator

As **AN**
endeavou**R** and
propensity of the

whole towards a **C**entre,

as in the exa**M**ple

d**OI**n**G**

2011

Writing novels, at least for me, requires serious research into areas I know little about. I find this aspect of the writing process fascinating.

One particular example of this is my character Will Francis, survivor of five novels and wielder of as much or more pain than he receives. For Will, I had to find an arcane or rare martial art that one would not ordinarily associate with a professor of computer science. By accident or fate, I found the Cambodian art of war called Bokator, rare now because the Khmer Rouge regime murdered almost all the masters teaching the art because they felt if the population had these skills, they might defeat the army defending the cruel dictatorship. If nothing else, that attracted me to Bokator, and thus my character Will.

Of course, having your hero know something like Bokator requires that I, the author, have some idea what the art entails. So, I studied as much material as I could find— not that much since the offensive-more-than-defensive moves are no longer well practiced since few masters still exist.

What I did discover, I paraphrased in ways that made Bokator sound as lethal as possible. For example, the three basic facets involved: No fear. No rules. No prisoners. I believe these three principles would be approved by most skilled Bokator experts, though, of course, I have no idea if I'm right about that.

Having a few of the animal names for particular moves, I had a lot more than nothing, so I paralleled them wherever possible with Will's actions. Mostly, however, I used logic to get me where I wanted to go. Or, rather, to get Will where I wanted him to go. This research—into the human body and its weaknesses—led me to one particular move that has served Will extremely well.

This move, which I have not given an animal name since I can think of no animal other than humans that might use it, is nearly impossible to defend against and can put opponents out of a fight within a few seconds. Since I have accidentally used the move on myself several times over my life, I can attest to one thing; it works. It doesn't kill, but forces your opponent to stop fighting and then vulnerable to almost any other attack you might wish to make. I highly recommend that anyone fearful of physical assaults become aware of it. These physical assaults include weapons like knives and guns and, while nothing you can do will guarantee not being shot by a gun, this will likely give you a real chance of coming away unscathed.

I would be remiss if I didn't tell you what the move is. After all, this much writing about something you can't guess would be a terrible mistake. I could, of course, tease you with the fact that I figured it out on my own for my character, so it shouldn't be that difficult for you to figure it out as well. But I won't. Here are the advantages:

1. Cannot be defended against;
2. Isn't lethal, but will place your opponent in a position without counterattack;
3. Leaves your opponent open to other more problematic attacks.

And, I will add one further advantage: it can easily be used to make your opponent an invalid for the rest of his or her life.

Most importantly, this maneuver will give you immediate self-confidence, something that in itself can avoid physical conflicts in the future should they arise. True self-confidence is a great weapon in itself.

In short, knees are the most vulnerable parts of the human body. Imagine ways in which you can defend your knees. Sans crouching—which actually makes them more vulnerable—or lying down—which would make you extremely vulnerable—there's no good way to protect them. Without knees in good working order, it's impossible to carry on a useful fight.

Knees are also easily disabled. One swift kick to a kneecap or especially to the side of a knee and your opponent is down and most likely out of a fight. For the duration. Not being able to stand is, as you can imagine, a real disability against someone who can. Even crawling becomes unimaginable.

And you can disable knees while simultaneously defending yourself. The way to do this is to fall to one side. As you do, cock your legs slightly, aim them at your opponent's knees, and strike them as hard as possible—or less, if this is just a practice move.

Of course, it's a good idea to put out your hands to avoid disabling yourself when you hit the floor or ground. Bokator doesn't cover this aspect of fighting much. The first of the three principles—no fear—suggests you simply take your own well being out of the equation. Your job is to win, not defend yourself against losing. Bokator is more an offensive weapon for use in actual battles, not so much a defense weapon to avoid getting hurt.

I recently had occasion to visit someone skilled in many martial arts, big as an ox, and ready to inflict incredible damage to most anyone in his path that wishes to fight. I asked him what would happen if I did to him what I described to you above. He thought for a second, and then told me that he'd be down on the ground and vulnerable to nearly anything else I wanted to do to him. Of course, we didn't try it. I liked him.

I can also state that Will Francis has used it to great affect in his numerous battles. And he's never once lost.

ho**mE**wor**K**

ta*k*es up t*h*e **bO**die**S**.

such **a** sigh**t** as this up to

the ve**R**y end of the
nineteenth century
shall only look
upon the sky
saying, who

a*m* i th*e*n

neve*r*
found?

130

Successful Failures

she must *ha*ve aCcelerated itS cOOling to the teMpEraTure at *Whi*ch life cOuld begin.

2012

One day recently I visited the John Steinbeck Center in Salinas with a friend to remind myself of the contributions to the Monterrey Bay that Steinbeck made. Books like *East of Eden*, *Of Mice and Men*, and *Cannery Row* come easily to mind. This center, like most such centers, laid out Steinbeck's literary career and personal life in general terms, with occasional enlarged pages from various of his books and snatches of films of his books that provided wonderful memories for me. However, in looking back, my best recollection that day is of the story my friend told me while driving there, rather than nostalgia for Steinbeck's literary works.

It seems that my friend, one who I've mentioned more than a few times previously in these books, had visited a special site in the Peruvian Andes the previous year, one with a small long-ago deserted and overgrown village aside a river that had not yet been looted, and an apparently untouched memorial across the river high up a cliff. Not having climbing tools, boats to cross the river, or the time at that point in his journey to investigate, he returned to the US with plans to follow through on his next visit.

And he did.

After hiring an archeologist, two professional rock climbers, a dozen or so local guides, and others who'd provide assistance, my friend once again took the two weeks or so traveling on foot and by mules through the jungle to return to the site and, after building several bridges—a severe storm up river removed the bridges so they had to be rebuilt—crossed over to the cliff side of the waters and climbed to the very large cavern that housed the memorial. Unfortunately, he found it had been looted by *huaqueros* several years previous. Skulls and other artifacts not considered valuable had been scattered about and a further exploration of the site proved fruitless.

This story, of course, involved many other incidents, but this was the gist of it. Considering the effort and money involved in his research, the exploration seemed tragic. Maybe a year of planning, ten of thousands of dollars spent, and with little to show for it.

Having for years believed that all research, not only the successful type, is incredibly important, I asked my friend whether there was a publication or other vehicle in archeology for presenting failures as well as successes. He told me there was not. It seemed to me then, as it had for many years prior and since, that repeating experiments that have already been proven unsuccessful by others simply because those previous results were not available, was a silly way to conduct business. I even took a guess that maybe forty percent of all research was thus wasted due to duplication of already proven failures.

Why not create a repository of failed research with anonymous but clearly documented entries available for anyone interested to check, therefore avoiding repetitions of experiments that don't work? After having discussed this issue with dozens of scientists who agree with me, nothing has been done to even begin to correct this problem. Apparently these scientists would rather continue their own research rather than help others continue theirs more productively.

I therefore plan to make this happen.

Somehow.

Someway.

For it seems to me that without such a repository, we are destined to continue replicating senseless experiments that a simple solution could avoid.

it is a line Of arguMent we must cONsiDER cloSed. then there were voices and thunders

Zapping it fOur times, as the

descriptioN in temperaments bY the force of a given velocity.

131

Children's books

And we muSt

 at least lISten

to what has to be said

in this Connexion,

although tHe light and

heat

it receives frOm the sun,

and like Other reLations,

are altogether Destitute

of Any real effect.

2012

The holiday season of 2012 brought joys to me beyond reason. My three grandchildren and two step grandchildren all visited my wife and I at the same time. Ages less than one, three, four, fourteen, and nineteen if memory serves, and the most wonderful young people in the world. After being Granddad as long as they could stand it, I returned to my office upstairs and began writing and illustrating what turned out to be the first of ten children's books. Each of these books had, for some reason only known to the muses, exactly thirty three chapters, one page of writing to the left, and one to the right illustrating the writing in some way. To make things even more constrained, I limited my illustrations to whatever I could accomplish with the track pad of my laptop, and a free drawing program downloaded from the Internet.

The ten books covered ages from about four to nineteen, so my grandchildren had plenty of time to grow into them if necessary. From this age spread, I learned that children's books are damn difficult to write. Like haiku, every word counts. Especially in the case where each chapter must exactly fill a certain number of lines available on a single page of text.

One of these books, a personal favorite, covered the theme of magic. I wrote this for a later age because its final chapters covered such things as making the Statue of Liberty disappear and walking on water with people swimming beneath you. Most of the tricks, however, are dedicated to simpler types of magic. And with these I dedicated myself to learning and practicing each so I could demonstrate the processes to my grandchildren as we'd read the story.

As of now, I'm still on the first trick, making sure that before I move on to the next one, I have completely mastered it. This trick involves ripping a straw wrapper to shreds, rolling it up, and making it appear as whole again. While most readers can tell how I do this by imagining what they would do to make it work, it's not so easy when you perform it in front of people. Smoothly. Effortlessly. Completely without sign that it might not be working as well as you'd like.

I'm closing in on perfecting this one, even though my wife is sick and tired of me performing it for every person we eat with, talk with, laugh with, or whatever with. As long as two straws are around—a dead giveaway—and I have time to prepare before anyone knows the trick is coming, I can bring it off. Even if they make me show both my open palms after it's done. Or show my empty sleeves. Or ask me to do it again—whereas, I smile and say only once per customer.

If you still don't know how the trick works, it's time you buy my book called simply *Magic*.

No matter what your age may be.

no to**Y**s to **P**lay with

ar**E** the characteristics

of qua**N**tities of the

a**N**tagonism taking

hindu fa*b*led v*i*shnu.

and**Y**ou a**S** it **W**as w**ORTH** it.

132

Playwright

we m**a**y
come to the

k**no**w*l*edge **O**f

their cau*S*es a***n***d

effects, but

we w**i**ll
never

BE
able

2012

The idea of writing plays came to me late in life. I've never been much for attending them—as can be understood from my earlier comments in these pages on attending concerts. However, having been an almost obsessive lover and watcher of films, it seemed like a natural for me. Dialog has never been a problem in writing novels and short stories, where description and other narratives—simile, metaphor, and other forms of references—are difficult. And, while I know a good deal about screenplays, filming, and so on, my knowledge is detrimental to my even attempting one of those. Plays are it.

Once on my way, I found writing plays fun, interesting, and incredibly invigorating. Since I'm a speed typist, I can write a stage play in a couple of weeks or so, read it aloud, play all the characters, and love every second of my time spent. And re-writes are few. Even my copy-editing unproblematic.

Most important of all, I like the results. Whether others do or not, is another question. But, unlike most of the rest of my creative work, I'm undaunted by suggestions for betterment and criticism. I don't get angry, even for a second, but simply resist most attempts to improve my scripts. I wouldn't call this arrogance, only confidence. They work, and I know it. Simple as that. Those disagreeing with me can stuff it. I'm not concerned with their views or with their problems. I can feel the words in my gut and know they're right.

to *UN*d**E**rstand the

har*Mo***o**nic ratios.

we shall **FI**nd

wha**T** we flee

fro*M* fl*E*e<u>**S**</u>

f*R*om **u***S*

as *TO*

la*CK*

discre**t**ion.

133

Contest

b_u**T**   _w**H**_{ose}   _{ma}**nn**_e**R**   _{of}

_{op}**E**_{rat}_{ion} **C**_{annot}b**E** _{satisfa}_c_{torily}

_d**E**_{sc}**R**_{ibed,} **H**_a_{ving} _{grea}**T** _{wrath}

_{beca}**U**_{se} _{he} _k**N**_{oweth} _{that} _{he} _{hath}

_{but a short t}**I**_{me.}

2012

During my retirement year from university teaching at UCSC, I created a contest for graduates majoring in music composition. Every student enrolled in our graduate composition course would be eligible, but only the works performed in the class recital at the end of the term would be considered. This gave everyone an opportunity, since this class could be taken as many times as one wanted so long as it was taught by a different teacher (possible because we rotated faculty assignments).

465

This process worked fine for five years, during which I still taught a course each quarter by the department recalling me into active service.

At the end of the sixth year, my actual final year of teaching since I needed more time to compose and write books, I received an e-mail electronically signed by several members of the class involved with the contest. While the letter made many fine points about me and my reasons for offering the contest, this group argued, and I'm paraphrasing here, that contests produce only one winner but many losers, and thus does a disservice to the profession. Again, even this paraphrase was qualified with praise toward my intentions. In effect, though, the signatories to this e-mail announced they did not want to be considered for the prize. Period.

Now I should mention here that this problem had bothered me as well from the beginning. I do not enter my works into contests for much the same reasons they cited. That, and the fact that most such contests require entrance fees, and those offering the prize actually make money from the process. I was never thus assured that my desire to have a so-called Cope Prize in Composition was really the right thing to do. But I'd done it, and no one had argued against it before this. To avoid university bureaucracy, I even wrote the prize checks from my personal bank account. I mention this, since the money, though a relatively small amount, still took a chunk out of my available funds.

What made me angry, however, was that none of the students arguing their point in the note had thought to speak to me about this privately or as a group before the note arrived in my e-mail, and copied to several other faculty. I am very approachable and around campus more than a lot of faculty. I'd even seen many of the protestors immediately prior to receiving the note and no one had mentioned it.

And so, without hesitation, I replied by simply thanking them for their opinions and retiring my contest as well as myself. After all, how could I give an award limited to one of the very small group of students who had not signed the document?

The result of this was that I heard from the author of the letter herself that it was not the signees' intention to have me withdraw the prize, only to step aside for someone else to win. Another letter told me that he'd signed the document without reading it, and felt it did not express his views.

Neither of these two defenses changed my mind and, uncharacteristically, I did not reply to either of them.

As I learned during my time at UCSC, graduate studies, possibly unlike undergraduate ones, require that students take full responsibility for their actions.

And I had seen to that.

speaking with a great harshness an**D** a g**RE** at deman**D**, he was torn **F**rom the earth with the w**I**nd whipping over the desert. can they **C**orrect this inequ**A**li**T**y for th**E** more accurate deducing of the celestial motions?

134

Grandchildren

Thi*S* a**r**gumen*T*

                         is seldom ex***P****R*essed

quite s*O* o**pe**nly

                     as in t***H****e* f***O*r**m a*BO*ve.

2012

With the recent births of three new Cope grandchildren—Zoey, Tessa, and Gavin—I was reminded of the difficulty of naming children, particularly prior to their birth. Before you really know how they are going to turn out. American Indians have a much better approach to this, naming children a year or more *after* they're born. Names such as 'walks on ice,' and 'never gets wet' as in my case, make more sense, even though they take longer to say and sign.

    I toyed with the idea of taking advantage of the name Cope when our children—the ones that granted us grandchildren—were born. For example, since I am an amateur astronomer, 'Tele' seemed like a good name for our firstborn. Then came 'Horace,' though it wasn't spelled the same way. 'Micros' seemed a bit silly, but 'Kaleidos' worked wonderfully well. 'Spectro' worked fine, too.

My wife, however, had somewhat different ideas, and she won the debate rather handily I thought, Timothy, Stephen, Brian, and Gregory being the ones we finally used.

finally, i give **This** advice t**O** a**n**y pe**O**ple
who might be completely unfamiliar with the questions.

135

Fiery Night

anD i sAw anothEr mighty angel

cOme Down fRom heaVen
and yelled theIr orDers,

warnIngs, and sang

their sONgs.

2012

One of the most horrific experiences that never occurred to me happened to a friend of mine recently. One of his sons, his son's wife, and his son's two preteen children took off in a small private plane from a local airport. This son was licensed as a pilot, but inexperienced and apparently unaware of the dangers posed by incoming fog and the turbulence it can create. He lost control of the plane and plowed into a then vacant physician's portion of a local hospital, killing all on board. I couldn't then, nor can I now imagine the pain this accident caused for everyone associated with the extended family. Hearing of it, I was literally mortified beyond description, even though I barely knew the son and had not seen his father in a number of years.

How does one convey sympathy at a time such as this? What to say? I thought of composing a piece in memoriam to express my emotions, but that, it seemed to me, would only make things worse. Particularly if the work were as effective as I hoped it would be.

In the end, my wife and I sent a card expressing our great sympathy for their loss and were comforted by discovering that the service for the family was attended by many hundreds of well-wishers.

Sorrow, or for that matter any emotion supposedly expressed in art, is but an accompaniment to the experiences they supposedly represent. Maybe they're meant to enhance the emotions, but that seems cruel. In the end, the tragedy is but itself, and art a weak excuse for it at best.

b**u**t

crowded

only with

what they

re**g**ard as prop**h**esy,

and **t**he electi**on** lights

providing geometry in philosophical

terms on behalf of the geometry of things.

136

Art

*A*nd its *L*ight r*E*flected.

aNd if there wou**l**d *be* no use for life
in the investi**g**Ati**o**ns of **P**hysics,

g**R**een would be the veget**a**ti**o**n,
and **GR**ey the w**A**te**r**.

2012

Over the past few years, I have used many of my algorithmic
programs to create visual art. For the most part, the images
result from using nonlinear mathematical formulae—
nonlinear here referring to equations that do not produce
straight lines when graphed. As I mention elsewhere in
this volume in my chapter on Alena, this math has taken
many forms, usually involving repetitively feeding back the
outcome of initial conditions into the formula producing
new outcomes, and so forth. When properly graphed, such
functions can produce highly chaotic looking results that
sometimes settle into what are called attractors, interestingly
organized structures that often suggest crystal-like forms

and even viruses. When complete, the resultant images are algorithmically colored to show the intricacies of the fifteen thousand by fifteen thousand dpi. The image is then infused into an aluminum surface, not so much on it, and thus becoming part of the metal. Most typically these are three feet by three feet in size and hung without frames.

My living room walls are covered with these paintings—I call them that to emphasize their artistic qualities—as are other people's living room walls. A number of them also appear in my book *ars ingenero* available from Amazon.

I mention this aspect of my work to re-emphasize my desire to work across and with many different mediums rather than just one. Thus my novels, non-fiction books, short stories, plays, poetry, children's books, music, as well as my art must be considered integral parts of my work and not separate attempts at spreading myself too thin.

and he cr**i**ed wi**th** a lo**U**d voice

saying **t**o all the fowls that fl**y** in the **M**idst of heaven,

we **M**ust see that the world **I**s rough a**N**d surly.

that we find out the causes of this effect to be a centripetal force

that is by which bodies are drawn or i**m**pelled by **G**o**i**ng

ballisti**C**.

137

Skywalker

as she we**re** sayi**n** *G*,

lessons of the light

come to o**u***R* eyes
as we see, else not.

*A*nd i*F* truth come to our minds,
we suddenly expand to its dimensions.

2012

When a former student of mine from the early 1980s invited
me to visit him at Skywalker Ranch north of San Francisco, I
jumped at the chance. Not only had I vaguely known George
Lucas, director of the Star Wars saga and owner of the famous
ranch—named after his main character in the science fiction
trilogy—during my student years at USC, but his ranch,
coincidentally on Lucas Road, represents the state-of-the-
art in recording technology, most noted for the THX brand
of sound design. Leslie Ann Jones—daughter of the comic-
musician Spike Jones and former president of a branch of the
National Academy of Recording Arts and Sciences—had told
me the place was incredible and suggested I visit when I got
the time.

My friend Keith drove, and, with the exception of discovering and phoning 911 about a minor automobile accident en route, we arrived in good shape for our extraordinary tour of the facilities by my former student, four-time Oscar-nominated Ren Klyce. After several visits to high-tech mixing studios with in-progress sound editing, and experiencing several theaters with surround sound including ceiling mounted speakers, Ren took us to visit the main house, alongside the lake and aside the olive groves that occupy several of the over twenty-thousand acres on the property.

While Lucas himself does not live in the grand multi-story house, it's where he works most of the time. As we entered, I asked if it would be kosher to visit him and say hello. Ren said 'absolutely not.' Usually mild-mannered and incredibly gracious, I immediately thought I'd misheard him, and asked him what would happen if I tried anyway. He stated unequivocally that he would have to stop me from doing so. I then agreed to stop asking, and joined him for a visit to Lucas's library.

As we began our tour of George's book collection that, by the way, took up two stories of the house, arranged using the Dewey Decimal system, and having a full-time librarian to tend to questions and check out books, I noticed several glassed-in display cases. Ren provided a guided tour of these that included the chalice from Indiana Jones's third film, 'The Last Crusade,' and the whip that Harrison Ford used in those films. I also recognized numerous pieces of hardware from R2-D2 and C-3PO as well as the mask used by Yoda. For those of us dedicated to Lucas's films, I felt honored to have the opportunity to see them.

After returning home from the wonderful exposure to so much lore of recent filmic history, I discovered that George had not been in his house the afternoon we visited Skywalker Ranch after all. Instead, he'd been down south in Los Angeles that very day signing the final papers to sell his properties, rights to his films, and projected three last episodes of the Star Wars nonology to the Walt Disney Corporation for three-plus billion dollars.

i*F* we grew to worlds,

If *T*he mart*I*ans warred

in the same **k**ind of spirit.

for what do**e**s it matter

if the **K**ind of ta**l**l p**y**thagoreans

did attri**B**ute these f**IG**u**R**es f**O**r simpli**C**ity?
suppose that only digits are used as symbols,

then the sun of the bro**K** en **C**louds,

just for a f**e**w seconds may be progress.

138

YouTube

its **J**ust th**A**t no writer of those beasts **g**i*v*es
gl**O**ry and h**O**nour and thanks to h*i*m that
sits on the throne li**CK**in**g** her **PA**w**S**
an*d* washing h**e**r face.

2012

In August of 2012, I set about to create a new audience for
my music. Tired of concerts with twenty or so people in a
hall accommodating many times that number, I decided to go
where technology seemed to be taking the world and develop
new resources.

I decided my first goal would be to create three hundred
and sixty-five videos, one for each day of the year, each
containing my music paired with abstract moving images in
no way synced with that music. I even created one of these
per day for one year with the idea that if anyone wanted, they
could watch each day for that year and then begin again,
having forgotten the initial ones. The video portions were
created algorithmically so that, for me at least, they took less
than ten minutes on average to produce.

My second goal was to share these videos on Facebook and collect as many friends as I could, not stopping until I maxed out my account. My friends now number well over three thousand. Of course, I don't know all these people personally, but they would at least get to know me a little through my music and images.

After the first year, I had received several hundreds of thousands of listening/viewings of my works, and many people were subscribing to my YouTube channel. This process had obviously proved far more satisfying and real than having these same works performed live for a small audience. Not only is my music now available to many more people, but the members of my virtual audience may be anywhere in the world. The videos also serve as advertisements for complete recordings of my music and art, an important advantage over single performances.

Interestingly, I have spoken to many of my composer friends over this same year and, while granting my addiction to technology has its advantages, none of them have followed suit, apparently satisfied with the status quo.

and she is such a nice *so*ft thing t**O N**urse

her answers from. but it wi**l**l avail nothing,

as th**e** man can make similar remarks on
the alternate faces of the globes to diminish

their circular motions. necessit**Y** **P**l**A**nts
the rose of beauty on the brow of chaos, and

disc**L**oses the central intention of nature.

139

Jam

it **A**rgues

*h*at a *Ve*ry
just act hath three

bra*N*ches. i*T* is t**O** act

and to **P**erfo**r**m in i**t** as she states.

2013

As part of my duties as one of the founders of Recombinant Inc., I developed an application prototype for use on Apple iPhone and iPad hardware. My idea for this app was simple. In my youth I occasionally performed in Dixieland bands, and loved it. Given an established harmonic progression and a known melody, performers improvise within the confines of the former and on the ideas of the latter. Straightforward. So straightforward that even amateurs can usually begin creating interesting music within a few minutes. It seemed to me then that if this worked with traditional instruments, it could certainly work with electronic ones. Thus, the basis for JamBandit was created. All one needed to do was select a tune provided by the app and follow along by touching the screen. In its easy mode, the app allowed only correct notes to sound as you moved your finger(s). More difficult modes allowed more chromatic possibilities. By yourself, or with as many friends you wanted, users could then play along with a melody having no knowledge of exactly what they're doing except what their ear tells them is correct. In the process, these performers learn by osmosis—by simply making music—and therefore get better at doing rather than just listening.

Along with many others in our corporation capable of providing very real sounding virtual instruments, graphical user interfaces, and using songs from all manner of music literature, JamBandit was born in 2013. And is still going strong.

My three fundamental ideas—music speaks louder than words, teaching music by ear is better than by rote, and creating is more interesting than just passively listening—may actually mean something to a few people out there. All manner of variations on well-known melodies have arisen from people otherwise incapable of producing them. New works—produced by using only the harmonic progression and not the melody—have appeared. Everyone writes words, draws, and now those who have limited themselves to singing in the shower can create music without learning to read it.

A good thing?

Yes.

no **P**retensions to originate anything,
like somewhere in the city a door

b**LE**w o**pe**n in the wind,

and the clo**u**d thr*U*st i**n**

his sickl**e** on the ea*R*th

could not b*E* ignored.

and so a*C*celer*A*ted
its cooling the high

tem*P*erature

at wh*I*ch

it mus*T*

be

sm*AL*l

again.

140

Lasers

witness yes, *b*ut n*O*bo*d*y w*a*nts to be co*m*p*A*red to a winter*S* day. to th*e* *L*one b*A*rd tr*U*e witness ba*R*e. and he that sat *L*ooked *U*pon us like jasper and a sardine.

2013

I had the good fortune recently to make an acquaintance with the father of a former student of mine who happens to run a company involved with diagnosing finely tuned laser-producing machines. Since this field has occupied my attention for several years, our meeting was fortuitous. I had been searching for someone to discuss in detail the critical role that lasers play in the construction and use of quantum computers. This was a great opportunity for me to do just that.

For those unaware of quantum computers, they might best be summed up by stating that they begin by isolating electrons, firing laser pulses at incredible speeds with a pulse creating a spin in one direction representing 0, and a lack of pulse creating a spin in the opposite direction representing 1. Since computers use the basics of binary mathematics, this process mimics today's laptop computers, but at a fraction of the size and an incredible factor of speed. For example, lasers can blink at just a few femtoseconds which, to get a good idea of how fast that would be, think of one femtosecond compared to a second as one second compared to thirty-two million years. With many electrons working in parallel being flipped by an equal number of lasers, this speed increases exponentially.

Why, you might ask, would anyone be interested in such speeds? The answer is that there are many problems that cannot be solved without speeds approaching that of the speed of light. Some of these problems—many of them quite important—can only therefore be solved by quantum computing. And I am one of those people with such problems.

Therefore, whenever I am around those having something to do with lasers, superconducting, quantum mechanics, and so on, I encourage them to understand the critical need for these computers becoming available in less time than the current projection of forty years.

Readers may now be wondering how all this falderal got included here. My answer is simple: art, no matter how simple the results may seem, is a complicated business. So complicated, in fact, that to make it truly possible for computers to create sophisticated output requires the likes of quantum computers. Thus, I am using any spare time I can find to study and advance the cause of these computers so I might be able use one before my time on planet earth is up.

stone M<u>a</u>Y be co<u>N</u>s<u>I</u>dered both as resista**N**ce and imp**U**lse. i a**M** inclined to think that this may ha*v*e be *if* i might venture to ask the question as he sai*d* the lory of your mind will forestall its repair.

141

Motorcycles

aNd thE
wordS did not

Come the Same

As they used to do. this
insight throws us on the PArty,

aND intErest of the uniVerse

against all and sundry things.

against ourselves as
much as others.

2013

A friend of mine in Santa Fe told me a true story about a friend of his who lived in Los Angeles. This friend lived in a more or less quiet section of the city, but was woken up early each morning by the revving engine of a motorcycle. This sound not only woke him, but continued its assault for several minutes before finally motoring away with a scream of its tires and several more blasts from its muffler.

This occurred seven days a week and my friend's friend had finally had enough of it. Thus, one day he woke earlier than the motorcyclist did, got dressed, went outside, and stood in the middle of the street blocking the cycle from passing him without wheeling up a sidewalk or bashing into parked cars.

As predicted, the motorcyclist came out at precisely the same ungodly hour as he had previously, revved his motorcycle, and eventually backed into the street finding my friend's friend waiting for him with outstretched arms.

The two faced off for several minutes until the motorcyclist turned off his engine. My friend's friend was about to read the motorcyclist the riot act, when the cyclist flipped up the visor on his helmet and said "Good morning."

My friend's friend stood there staring at the cyclist, realizing as he did that the man who'd woken him so many times was the actor Steve McQueen.

That recognition changed the tenor of the predicted argument dramatically, and before they had finished conversing they'd become great friends.

From then on they cycled together, drank together, and God only knows what other kinds of trouble they may have gotten themselves into together.

we *n*eed no*t*
be troubled by this
objection, but must remember

what ruthlessly ha**P**py persons

have and that w**E** are not over-happy.
There, spinning in the sky,
was the midnight sun.
and there fell a great
star from heaven

in pe**BBLES**.

142

Memorial

tₕat no writ*E* r

in that ca*s*e

can **G**o back by rai**l**way

and **EX**ᵢ**T** ,

a**N**d tₕ**E**ₒ**R**ₑ**M**ₛ **IN**

numericₐ**l O**rder **A**s i did.

2013

In my youth I had seen numerous black and white films of burial sites containing the bodies of those murdered ruthlessly by the Hitler Regime during the Second World War. Therefore, I felt more prepared than my wife when we visited the Holocaust Memorial in Berlin in February of 2013. I was wrong. There is no way, at least for me, to ever prepare myself for the horrors depicted there.

Arriving at the Memorial gives little indication of what lies below ground. Up top, in and above the snow, are virtually hundreds of various-sized tall cement blocks with pathways between them for visitors to walk. Representing gravestones, I presumed. We wandered silently between these markers imagining what they represented. That scene alone should have prepared us for what was coming. It didn't.

The entrance to the center of the Memorial is a set of stairs leading underground, where we were required to pass through security by removing all materials from our pockets and place our belongings on a conveyor belt so they could be X-rayed. This alone, a reminder that there still exist people who would cause damage to that which commemorates those six or more millions of Jews and others who needlessly died, would sober anyone who felt the seventy-plus years since had somehow improved our world. That they had the will to resist being incredibly affected by what lies within the Memorial because of that distance of time.

Once inside, I felt almost buried by the chronologically presented history of how the unthinkable became thinkable. The brutality, inhumanity towards man, and impossible to fathom sorrow for the millions that died such horrible deaths confronts you in a way that cannot be described. The reaction of reading the last scribbled notes of victims before they were herded into gas chambers to die is impossible to recount. As I walked, I knew I had to compose a work in their honor and memory. I call it *Holocaust Memorial*, and know that it could not represent anything other than what one person feels about the events that took place in the 1930s and 40s in Europe. If the piece conveys but a fraction of the tragedy I felt about that period in world history, I am at least a little consoled. And I share the meaning of the words that many declare: Never again!

in *T* *h*e d*IO*pti<u>C</u>s

a**N**d <u>I</u>f the answers
were satisfactory

an<u>**D**</u> sustain<u>**E**</u>d
as in the above passage.

143

The Labyrinths of Santa Fe

we ought to abstraCt fRom our sEnses,

and consider Things as thEMselves.

it will be that provided by waiting for
the end of the century, And then doing the
experiment described.

2013

On Museum Hill above Santa Fe, New Mexico, stand two
interesting labyrinths. Facing east, the one on the right is
more or less a traditional labyrinth, sans hedges or other
view-obstructing separations between walkways. Since this
particular labyrinth is designed—according to the small sign
at the entrance—for meditating, the process for walking it
is to randomly pick an entrance, slowly take the path until
you reach the center or an end to that path. I, of course, took
the opposite approach, that of standing on the outside of the
labyrinth, plotting a successful route in my mind's eye, and
rushing through the process to victory.

The labyrinth to the left when facing east is quite different. Built no doubt to slow people like me down and confuse the issue, this one has no signs and might easily be misconstrued as a design rather than a labyrinth. Like the right one, it too has no view-obstructing separations. So, someone like me can stand beside it and plot out a winning strategy. The problem with this labyrinth, however, especially for someone like me, is that there *is* no winning strategy. None of the four entering pathways leads to the center. None of the paths leading from the center outward can successfully be traveled without encountering a dead end. Like Sisyphus, one can attempt what appears to be different approaches for an eternity without ever achieving victory.

One day, recently, I stood on the edge of this labyrinth and watched an ant, who surely could not see the entire puzzle at once, slowly make its way from a point near the center to my shoes, inch around my shoes, and disappear into the cracks between patio stones. Obviously oblivious to the rules of the game, this little guy had solved the puzzle in his own way. And I, apparently, having taken ten minutes of doing nothing but watch this ant, had achieved meditation without instruction.

but in the meantime, i wonder who wi*l*l

p*U*t on your *S*hoes, for i scarcely need
remind the reader that i saw a star fall from
heaven unto the earth, and its light reflected
her winks and nods as gestures yielding
*Ze*ro.

144

Berlin Musical Instrument Museum

is an*ot*h̲er *V* es*l* cle,
if after five hundred years

l*O*nd*O̲*n is the capita*L* of pa*rl̲* s.

2013

The Berlin Musical Instrument Museum houses many extraordinary musical instruments from the past, not the least of which is known as Bach's Cembalo, supposedly given by J. S. Bach to his son Wilhelm Friedemann Bach. This harpsichord of two manuals has an extraordinary sound. I know this because, contrary to all the signs surrounding the instrument, and guarded by at least three custodians, I played it myself. Risking, I thought, bodily harm as well as arrest. It just didn't seem fair to me that having come all that way I wouldn't be able to at least in spirit connect with Bach somehow, if only in my imagination.

Luckily, the powers that be protected me for that ten-second period of law breaking, and I was spared both violence and imprisonment. For the rest of my tour, however, I felt the many eyes of those in charge keeping me in my place, readying themselves to pounce on me the minute I came within a foot of any other seduction the instruments might pose.

it is **N**ot, <u>n</u>or it cannot come to good.

it i**S** natural that we **S**hould wish

to permit every **K**ind of **E**ngineering technique.

therefore, it will *b*e *fo*und

in th*e* point, and

an**Y**one who has

written a commentary on

BOARDS

will be thus.

145

Kaleidoscope

o*r* not at all. it is usually call*e*d an electronic
or di$\mathbf{G}$ita$\mathbf{L}$ computer.

2013

I love kaleidoscopes. I suppose because they represent the visual correlate to wind chimes. While not collecting them in quite the manic way I do chimes, kaleidoscopes are algorithmic in much the same way my chimes are. Some elements set in stone, others not.

Approximately two decades ago, I came across a kaleidoscope that was both unique and wonderful. A rare combination. This kaleidoscope was battery powered, and when you looked into it, all you saw initially was darkness. Then, at an arbitrary point in time, the thing lit up with fantastic images while simultaneously sounding loud thunder or the blast of fireworks, both frightening and thrilling simultaneously. And then, after a short period of time, the thing arbitrarily went dark again. Apparently these outbursts occurred whenever the kaleidoscope wished them to; sometimes dormant for minutes to hours, and then exploding into life.

I rushed to find my wife to let her see this kaleidoscope and agree to my purchasing it, but when we returned, the storeowner had sold it. He told me that his distributor had simply run out of them and had no way to get another. Sorry.

For years thereafter I have looked for another of this type of kaleidoscope without success.

Then one day, while shopping in Albuquerque, New Mexico, I found another kaleidoscope shop with examples incredible in size, shape, operation, and numbers.

I immediately asked the shop owner if she had the fireworks version I had seen so long ago but not since. She shook her head sorrowfully saying that she had once seen one of these too but it has not been available since. She'd never seen one again.

Her guess was that over the past few decades, Japan had become one of the world's greatest exporters of kaleidoscopes, they had produced this version, and it had not created the kind of experience for everyone as it had for her and me. She suggested I seek it there, as she would as well, and keep me informed.

To date, we've never found such a product available anywhere. Several 'fireworks' wands and sound products can be found on the Internet, but nothing like what I have described above.

How could this be? How could such an amazing combination of sound and sight in such a beautifully small package not be something everyone would want?

so they thin**k** **O**_f_ wh**A**t wa**S** ca_ll_ed the element**S** f**O**r health, **S**o that in that second genera*tion*, the sun ***B***rok***E*** th***E*** cloud***S*** for a f***E***w seconds, making quite a commotion in the pool as it went, and ***YE***t wa***S*** as mortal as his own.

146

Klingon

it **r**etain**S** it in its **O**rbit.

        an**d** because i was n**O**t able to overcome

my effort t**h**e obsc**ur**ity

                      of the subject m**a**tter

an**d** i cri**e**d,

        a ma**n** **b**uff**e**ts and **r**ewa**r**ds his mind.

2013

    While in Berlin recently, my wife and I attended what its creator calls a Klingon opera. Created by Marc Okrand and Floris Schonfeld with music by Eef van Breen, the opera, called simply *U*—with a glottal stop before and after—was billed as the first ever Klingon opera. And we didn't doubt it, while we also secretly suspected it to be the last Klingon opera ever as well. But, even though on arriving we found the lobby filled with people dressed in the famous Klingon, Federation, and Romulan costumes and began thinking we'd made the wrong choice, this was not the case. The opera was actually good to excellent, with the phrase "Heghlu 'meH QaQ jajvam" meaning 'today is a good day to die' being an especially notable example of the lyrics. In fact, there exists a complete dictionary of the language, and even a few people who speak it fluently.

My wife and I—mostly I—being Trekkies, we soon fell into the magic of an opera sung in a language used in many television series and several films as well.

The small core of singers and instrumentalists created an extraordinary ensemble that, given all the audience had was a rough translation of the words, produced a *Carmina Burana* Orff-like sound that fit perfectly, no matter that most of us couldn't follow much of anything going on.

I present this little review to indicate my general feeling that no matter how things may seem before you hear them, leaving room for divine intervention is not only a reasonable course to take, but one that can provide extraordinary rewards.

I'm told that several more such operas are in the works.

My intuition, though, tells me that one might be enough.

the hum**P** w**O**uld be seen

                                              if a woman has a seesaw

and hears voi**C**es.

                                              it will run into sentences

and his poem

                                        into the structure of his fable,

into his speculation,

                                                  into his charit**y**,

and as every man is hunted,

                                    and his feet li*K*e unto f*IN*e **K**iln

as if they burned in a furnace and *GON*e away.

147

Sleep

and behOld,

a throne **waS**
set in heaven and
one sat on the throne

to maKe it possible

for a sequnCe of
opeRatiOns
to be replaced
over and over
again.

2013

Every little random sound I hear at night wakes me, and I
immediately begin preparing to protect my family at any cost.
So, since my home is secure and anyone attempting to break
in would need to make enough noise to wake everyone in our
neighborhood, I long ago decided to use earplugs so that if by
chance I fell asleep and a non-emergency sound occurred, I
wouldn't be jarred from my sleep.

This meant using earplugs. Knowing that even when I began this habit that night is when human ears typically drain collected fluids, I guessed that using such plugs would prevent that and I would, every few months, need to visit a doctor to have my ear canals drained.

But so be it, I thought. Sleep's worth it, even the little amount I need to retain my sanity.

However, after twenty years of this earplug wearing—the type that swimmers use—I tried using an app for my iPhone I found that played sounds for those like me who couldn't otherwise sleep. It worked and I now have, of the incredible number of choices thought by the manufacturer to do the trick, settled on two. The first of these is my standard choice, the one that I begin and usually end my night's sojourn with. It's the sound of large raindrops hitting the top of a tent. The length of the loop the application no doubt uses, is precisely the length it needs to be to fool my addled brain into not being able to predict the sound of the next drop.

When things get out of hand, however, I turn to my hardcore sound, that of a 747 cruising at thirty-five thousand feet. From inside the cabin, lest anyone imagine the contrary. With this as my backup, I can resist the other fifty or so sounds available—which include but are not limited to wind chimes, various birds in heat, new-age piano, and frogs croaking.

until
some condition

is fulfilled. glass Wor**ks**,

he said soft*L*y, and again the

Wind carried it away for what

ha*S* been **S**aid depends the
whole doctrine of
mechanics.
variously
demonstrated by
different authors for
what does it matter if
you sit up and beg
for your dinner

for wa**X**.

148

Branson

un*t*il *a*t la**S**t,

the wh**O**le mena**G**erie,

the who**L**e chemical mass,

is mell**O**wed and **R**efined for

higher **U**se.

2013

Once every two or three years my wife Mary Jane and I visit what is called her cousin's reunion. This provides an opportunity for her to reacquaint herself with various cousins and their spouses. The locations are usually a timeshare condo somewhere in the US that we can all attend without driving or flying too far. This is problematic since these cousins generally live all over the Midwest and West. Nonetheless, these events get good crowds. We eat together, talk over old times, tell jokes, ride the boats, tour the sights, or see events of particularly regional interest. These reunions usually turn out to be fun, and the individuals quite interesting to talk with.

One year we held the reunion in Santa Cruz. That was the time during which we drove to Big Sur and I had the opportunity to ride with a rare visitor who spent the time talking incessantly, and whenver I got the chance to reciprocate, began whistling just as incessantly.

The reunion in Branson, Missouri, was an exception to the rule. Not that the players in our docudramas and comedies weren't as interesting and lovable, they were. Nor were the events lacking, though not particularly interesting to my wife and I since our tastes don't run towards country and western, bawdy and grand-old-opry comedy, and show-tunes. It was all about an event for which I was the star and only player.

We had, as a group of sixteen, eaten at a roll-tossing place—where rolls fresh from the oven are physically tossed to whoever wants one by them raising their hands and the waiters taking their best shots at tossing them there—and we'd gotten up to leave. As I watched her cousins and their respective spouses rise from their seats, I noticed that many of them demonstrated aches and pains visible by the lethargy in standing up while I simply felt great. How wonderful it was to be seventy-two years old and still have that umph that young men have. So, I took the opportunity to stretch my back in an inverted way—meaning that my stomach and lower back pushed forward while the rest of me remained in place. I did this to impress myself with my agile body and confidence that I'd somehow staved off the inevitable aches, pains, and canes that many of the others in our party sported.

That's when I heard it. A singular 'pop' in my right knee. Loud enough that I imagined people within a yard or so of me could hear it as well. Suddenly, I didn't feel so good. My knee not only hurt, but it was difficult to stand erect on both feet. Elsewhere in this volume I describe self-inflicted Bokator to my knees. This was one of those situations.

Since no one noticed my knee 'pop,' I tried to hide my limp as we walked to our transportation for the evening. There, my pain became even more pronounced and I could no longer hide my suddenly acquired malady.

Realizing my anguish, Carol, my wife's sister in law, kindly loaned me her cane and I was able to load myself into a car and get home for the evening.

The next day, a visit to the doctor proved that I seemed not to have broken anything, but he wrapped it anyway and for the next twenty-four hours I limped around with my borrowed cane just as many of my compatriots did.

I felt more like a true member of the group, then. But I'd lost something precious at the same time. No doubt, taken from me by my alter ego, which has been my worst enemy since birth.

it pleases us at a sufficie**N**t

per**S**p**E**c**T** ive whose end *b*oth
at first and now in this force is ever

proportiona*l* to th*e* bod**Y** whose fo*r*ce

is numer*o*us **Z**eros. the de**a**d asked who a*r*e you?

i as**K**ed, and the creature**S** who inhabit this *k*ind earth said.

149

Requiem for Emmy

wh$E$th$e$r by it$s$ own gr$a$vity or by the

blow of a **MAL**let, it Is Impelled

In the dire$C$tion of th$E$ Iine towards
both planes. whether they are random
elements or not.

2013

On a late evening in mid-September of 2013, the last usable
version of Experiments in Musical Intelligence died on the
machine that died with it. Being a program with a significant
amount of code required to run, and my not having kept it
up to date with new operating systems, hardware, and current
proprietary versions of Common Lisp, it quickly became
obvious that I couldn't keep using it while at the same time
maintaining my creative life.

Thus, with this last version no longer functioning, I
can no longer demonstrate the program nor use it myself.
Of course, I can still rewrite the code, but it would take a
Herculean effort to fit whatever new computers exist at the
time it's finished.

My comments in *Computer Models of Musical Creativity* about it still existing are thus no longer correct. I had hoped to continue composing using Emmy, but soon found, as I've just discussed, that the benefits far outweighed the problems.

However, the program lives on in my writings and various published code. Someone reading and skilled in programming should be able to rebuild Emmy, a recipe for such soon to appear in a reprint of my book *Experiments in Musical Intelligence*. Maybe those following that recipe will make as good or better version than my own.

I, of course, knew this was coming. At the same time, like losing a loved one after an extended illness, no amount of preparation can actually fortify one for the moment when the time finally arrives.

So, Emmy is dead. Long live Emmy.

for a similar effect can be produced

b**y** suc**h** devices by making

ch**O**ices. and they all cro**W**d**e**d round it panting, and asking why the

windows of his eyes were not ab**l**e to overcome the obscurity of

a**l**l subjects by righteousness.

150

Glass

j u*S*t then,

if by bein*g* th*a*t person,
with the most abundant propositions

of p*l*atoni*c* philosoph*y* the*n* filled with water.

a*n*d then it stared li*k* e *a* gui*l* ty one toward the sky.

2013

It never occurred to me while I pulled melted glass from an oven, turned it through the colored glass on a metal table, re-heated it, turned it, spread it, clipped it, and so on, why glass blowing was considered a craft instead of an art. When I finished, however, the thought came rushing back in a torrent. I was drenched in sweat—the ovens typically soar to 2700 degrees Fahrenheit, and then curing involves putting my art away for eighteen hours in a freezer. A vase and a bowl. And, of course, that was my answer. Art is useless except for its appreciation. Crafts, on the other hand, have very definite uses. Utilitarian. To drink from, store candy in, look through, stick your flowers inside of, eat from, and on and on.

Yet the Taos Pueblo native who watched me with an eagle eye to keep me from hurting myself had told me of his four hundred pound glass sculpture hanging from someone's ceiling somewhere. No function other than to appreciate. Now that must be art. And what about the smaller pieces that adorn the mantles of fireplaces around the world? Not art? After all, it has no use. Therefore, it must be art.

Eighteen hours later, or the next day, whichever you prefer, I looked at my accomplishments and said to no one in particular, "If this ain't art, than the bastards don't know what art is." My best guess at that moment was that those who make such decisions have been too invested in their smugness to give glass blowing a try. Fearful of the impossible heat, the incredible risks, the dangers, and the high prospects of failure that arts such as glass blowing present. They'd rather sit in their towers of mindlessness away from the tactile feel of it and invent their definitions on the basis of syntactic and semantic comparisons to other words, rather than actually participating in the acts they themselves judge.

glassw**O**rks, he said softly,
and again the wind *Carri**E**d* it away.
so fa*R* as a man thinks he is f*R*ee, and though noth*I*ng
is more than the **C**r**O**wing abou**T** *L*iber**T**y of *L*avender.

as m*OS*t men are fli**ρ**pantly mistaking some paper preamble

for fr**e**edom, like a declaration of independence so mighty.

\